International's Series in

MARKETING

Consulting Editor

RALPH L. DAY

Professor of Business Administration
Graduate School of Business
Indiana University

Business Research:
Concept and Practice

Business Research:
Concept and Practice

ROBERT G. MURDICK

Professor of Management
Florida Atlantic University

INTERNATIONAL TEXTBOOK COMPANY
Scranton, Pennsylvania

Standard Book Number 7002 2232 4

Library of Congress Catalog Card Number: 73-76401

Preface

The basic objective of this book is to develop the meaning of business research in relation to both the theory and practice of business. This objective is sought by relating research to science and business, exploring concepts in research, attempting to identify investigative projects which qualify as research, and developing practical systematic approaches to the principal phases of a research project.

There are numerous books available which deal with business research from the viewpoint of techniques and tools. As a result many students and researchers end up by believing that fact-grubbing and mechanical techniques define research. In contrast, this book was written to stimulate the student's thinking about the nature and objectives of research in relation to science and practice. Many questions to which definitive answers are not available are intentionally raised in this book in order to make the student aware of the crudities, limitations, and falterings of current business research. The motive throughout is to induce in the student the curiosity, skepticism, and thoroughness of the scientist without relieving him of the practicality of the business practicioner.

This book depends heavily upon concepts developed by many scholars over a long period of time. I wish to express my deep appreciation to these people and to their publishers for so kindly allowing me to draw upon their work. I am grateful to Mr. Robert B. Chatterton of the State University of New York at Albany Library for his review and helpful suggestions in Chapter 9. Dr Albert C. Mossin provided me with both encouragement and facilities for this project. And finally, I wish to acknowledge with many thanks the contribution to Miss Dian Chartrand, whose careful typing, editorial assistance, and handling of the many detailed tasks required to prepare a manuscript for a publisher made this project far easier.

ROBERT G. MURDICK

Boca Raton, Florida
April, 1969

Contents

Contents

PART II   THE PRACTICE OF BUSINESS RESEARCH

List of Exhibits

part I

BASIC CONCEPTS

chapter 1

Science and Knowledge

INTRODUCTION

Research as a means of developing better plans and better decisions has been wholeheartedly accepted by American industry. An examination of organization charts of large well-managed companies will show organizational components such as Economic Research, Marketing Research, Personnel Research, and Management Research. In smaller companies, individuals are usually assigned such duties even though the title of the position may not make this evident. Such evidence indicates that business research is not just an added cost but rather an activity contributing to profit and even survival.

Much has been written in recent years about the how-to-do-it aspect of business research; little has been said about what it is. As a result, students taking research (project) courses conclude that fact-grubbing and mechanical techniques are synonymous with research. This book has been written, therefore, to stimulate the student's thinking about the nature and objectives of research. The short-range and long-range types of research are both considered in proper perspective, the former in relation to operational decision making and the latter as a means of developing scientific generalizations.

As stated in the Preface, many questions will be raised in this book to which definitive answers are not yet available in order to make the student aware of the crudities, the limitations, the lack of consensus, and the falterings of current business research. The purpose, which will bear repeating here, is to leave the student with the curiosity, skepticism, and thoroughness of the scientist without relieving him of the practicality of the business man.

At first glance the business practitioner or student might think that a discussion of science and knowledge is rather far afield from business research. The relationship among science, research, and effective business management is, however, surprisingly close in modern times. Although in the past businessmen could make adequate decisions on the basis of experience and hunch, the rapidly changing world of today makes this type of decision making obsolete. Businessmen must base decisions on understanding, on knowledge of *how* business variables interact, and on *why* they do so. Only through such knowledge can managers recognize changes in conditions which call for new patterns of behavior.

Only through such knowledge can managers predict the outcomes of their decisions with justified confidence.

An explanation of the full value of science and research as the foundation of modern business management requires an elaboration on the nature of science and on the function of research in linking science and business practice. Such an elaboration should in itself be scientific. It should make clear that the manager of today must start by being a social and economic philosopher with regard to entrepreneurial objectives and must continue to be a philosopher of another kind—an epistemologist—with regard to methods of operation if he is to achieve his objectives.

"DEFINITIONS" OF SCIENCE

Attempts have been made to define science in terms of (a) its structure, (b) its purpose or goals, and (c) its method as well as its distinction from other methods of adding to knowledge. Because all of these can contribute to a description of the nature of science, all are discussed briefly here.

Structure

From the viewpoint of structure, science has been defined as knowledge which has been tested and set in order. A science (in a specified area of interest) is a set of internally consistent propositions, principles, laws and theories describing some significant portion of man's knowledge. The theories or beliefs of science are never indefensibly true and infallible guarantees of truth. In the early development of a science propositions may be dispersed over a wide area of knowledge and not be connected by research. In such a case it is not always possible to show internal consistency among principles.

The structure of science consists of:

1. Observations (empirical data).

2. Concepts and constructs which are abstractions of phenomena or of other higher-level concepts.

3. Hypotheses which express possible explanations of causes of effects.

4. Principles or laws which consist of hypotheses that have been subjected to some form of experimental verification.

5. Theories or derived propositions which relate data, hypotheses, and laws in a general and consistent structure.

The economist Samuelson defends at length his view of the structure of science in terms which encompass the above four ideas:

> There has been no successful demolition of my view that science consists of descriptions of empirical regularities; nor of my insistence that what is called explanation in science can always be regarded as a description at a different level—usually a superior description in that it successfully fits a wide range of empirical regularities.[1]

[1] Paul A. Samuelson, "Professor Samuelson on Theory and Realism: Reply," *American Economic Review* (December 1965), p. 1171.

Besides considering the structure of science from the viewpoint of its building blocks, science may be analyzed and viewed in terms of its component disciplines. Thus science may be considered to be composed of the following:

1. Abstract formal science (logic, mathematics)
2. Empirical science
    (a) Natural science
        (i) Physical science (such as physics, chemistry, astronomy)
        (ii) Life science (such as biology, zoology, botany)
    (b) Behavioral science (dealing with the observable behavior of men in *societies,* generally distinguished by the central focus on human sign behavior)
    (c) Applied science (such as economics/business, medicine, law, engineering)

Objectives

Science is often identified by its purpose. Beliefs as to the goals of science have changed over the times. For example, Morgenbesser writes:

> The once popular thesis that science describes but does not explain has few adherents today. This is also true for the extreme pragmatic thesis that science, or at any rate, physics, is a collection of theories which are not true or fake statements or bodies of statements, but instruments for the solution of problems, intellectual or otherwise.
>
> With the demise of these and other theories, e.g., that science is distinguished by its method, and not by its content, an abhorred vacuum was created. To fill it many philosophers of science adopted the view that science is *explanatory and predictive,* or its kin that science aims at *explanation and prediction.*[2]

The goals of science as explanation and prediction tend to emphasize the pure search for knowledge of the world about mankind. A broader meaning of science would include the solution of problems which man faces as well as the general inquiry into nature. This meaning has been expressed as follows:

> Science is also characterized by the goals of self-perpetuation and self-improvement. It is an ongoing institution which pursues an ideal: to increase without limit our knowledge and our ability to answer questions and solve problems.[3]

Albert Einstein proposed two goals of science. The first goal is for man to make as complete as possible his comprehension of the connection between his sense experiences in their totality. The second goal of science is to achieve the first goal by the use of a minimum of primary concepts and relations. Primary

---

[2] S. Morgenbesser, "The Explanatory-Predictive Approach to Science," in Bernard Baumrin, (ed.), *Philosophy of Science, The Delaware Seminar*, Vol. 1, 1961–62 (New York: John Wiley & Sons, Inc., 1963), p. 41.

[3] Russell L. Ackoff *et al., Scientific Method, Optimizing Applied Research Decisions* (New York: John Wiley & Sons, Inc., 1962), pp. 3–4.

concepts are those directly connected with sense experience and are presumably reduced in number by developing logically derived concepts which require primary concepts to deduce all others.[4]

Carl Hempel has formulated objectives for empirical science, of which business and economics form a part, as follows:

> Empirical science has two major objectives: to describe particular phenomena in the world of our experience and to establish general principles by means of which they can be explained and predicted. The explanatory and predictive principles of a scientific discipline are stated in its hypothetical generalizations and its theories; they characterize general patters or regularities to which individual phenomena conform and by virtue of which their occurrence can be systematically anticipated.[5]

A possible distinction between two goals has led to the idea of two types of sciences, *positive science* and *normative science*. Positive science is a systematized body of knowledge about what is, including a description and explanation of existing relationships. As such it is useful in predicting on the basis of derived propositions. For example, many economists claim that economics as a *science* cannot include solutions to economic welfare problems.

Economics as a positive science must (1) be concerned with *what is,* not what *should be,* (2) stop with description, analysis, and explanation, (3) deal with cause and effect, (4) be concerned with means of attainment of ends, not with what the ends should be or whether the ends are good or bad, desirable or undesirable, and (5) start with relevant hypotheses and utilize valid reasoning to reach conclusions capable of being verified.

Normative science is concerned with what ought to be. This may be further subdivided for clarity. If criteria are accepted as given, normative science is concerned with answering how to achieve the goals established from the criteria, and in the most efficient manner. Much of normative science, however, is concerned with the development of criteria which involve value judgments. It is questionable in this latter case whether the activity is truly science.

Simple examples which demonstrate the meaning of these concepts of science to the business world may show their significance.

1. In an oligopolistic market (few sellers, identical products), if one firm lowers its price for its products, the other firms will follow suit. (Positive science)

2. To achieve rapid communications from top to bottom within a company, the company should try to organize with as few levels of management consistent with the conflicting needs for supervisory control. (Normative, Type I)

---

[4] Albert Einstein, "The Method of Science," *The Structure of Scientific Thought,* edited by Edward H. Madden (Boston: Houghton Mifflin Co., 1960), p. 83.

[5] Carl G. Hempel, *Fundamentals of Concept Formation in Empirical Science* (Chicago: University of Chicago Press, 1952), p. 1.

3. The business firm should limit its return on investment in order to permit its employees and customers to share the increases in productivity. (Normative, Type II)

Distinction of Method

Science may not be identified by its method, but it is distinguished and united by its method. Scientific method is first of all controlled method. Considerable effort has been devoted to scientific methodology or the study of improvement of procedures and criteria for scientific research. Various approaches have been developed to obtain knowledge under both controlled and not well-controlled circumstances. The standards set for scientific method provide a basis for evaluating the work of researchers. At the same time, all applications of scientific method do not represent science. For example, scientific method may be employed to analyze handwriting, yet handwriting analysis is not considered to be a science. This suggests that arbitrary definitions of the field of inquiry have led to definitions of branches of knowledge which are considered to be sciences.

Finally, the methods of science are *systematic, cumulative,* and require that results of research be widely and freely *communicated.* "Systematic" means that scientific method is orderly, not random; that other scientists can, and would be apt to, follow similar steps in approaching similar problems; and that classification and evaluation of apparently relevant variables is a part of the process. "Cumulative" means that the results of knowledge are not discarded upon discovery or use in immediate application. Rather, new knowledge is built upon old knowledge to form the body of science. This is the ultimate essence of semanticist Alfred Korzybski's statement that man is distinguished from all other forms of life because of "time binding." Man is bound together through the generations by knowledge passed on from one generation to the other.

The requirement that results of research be freely communicated is necessary for orderly and efficient advance of knowledge. Such communication provides the basis for knowledge to be built upon knowledge and for reducing the number of starts up blind alleys. Conflicting results are uncovered through broad communication of research so that further investigation may be directed toward uncovering the true state of nature.

THE BUILDING BLOCKS OF SCIENCE

The building blocks of science have been identified (with some overlapping and fuzziness) as:

1. Facts, observations, experiences, data
2. Concepts, constructs
3. Hypotheses
4. Principles, laws
5. Theory

These are tied together by the process of research which adds to man's knowledge. An understanding of these basic terms is necessary for the understanding of the research process. This process of research is the major concern of this book.

Facts, Observations, Experiences

A fact is that which exists; it is a situation, state of affairs, or phenomenon which is true. It is a true proposition—that is, a generally accepted proposition. "Facts" arise from observation or other sensory experiences and are often equated with them. Yet it is extremely doubtful if any observation or experience is entirely free from interpretation. Facts are thus conceded to be those phenomena which can be generally agreed upon by all who observe them. An interesting illustration of the difficulty in determining facts is the modern phenomena of unidentified flying objects (UFO). Despite observations of many skilled and unskilled observers which indicate the existence of real objects not known to scientists of this planet, governmental sources have investigated these claims and adamantly deny the existence of such outer-space objects.

"Data" is the term used for a collection of facts. Data may refer to original observations or recorded items. Data in the latter form may suffer from various deficiencies which may be recognized, and yet the data may be used in applied business research simply because nothing better is available.

Facts or data may be collected in the business research process by:

1. Direct observation or sensing of natural phenomena or of experimental results.
2. Direct inference from other data which are directly observed
3. Original documents.
4. Reports and publications of fact-gathering agencies and researchers.
5. Questioning of individuals.

Excluding direct observation, sources of data are classified as *primary* sources and *secondary* sources. Primary sources are original documents or official files or records. Secondary sources are publications of data gathered by other investigators. Secondary sources thus are subject to all the errors of initial observation plus errors in selection, transcription, printing, explanation, and completeness. Primary sources themselves are not necessarily free of error, and thus the competency of the primary investigator as well as the publisher is at issue in the utilization of secondary sources.

Another classification of data which is particularly significant for applied research carried out by a business firm is *internal* and *external*. Internal data is that generated by the company. In a broader sense it may be defined as that generated or *stored* by the company for use when needed. External data refers, of course, to events and things external to the company.

In gathering data firsthand or from other sources, the scientist must recognize the distinction between facts on the one hand and beliefs about facts, opinions, and attitudes. This is even more confusing at times in socioeconomic research where the attitudes and opinions of interviewees *are the facts* of the research.

Some sources of errors in facts used in the structure of science are:
1. Sensory errors due to illusions or lack of discriminatory ability.
2. Psychological interpretations.
3. Constant error due to lack of precision of the instruments used.
4. Bias due to miscalibration of instruments.
5. Errors in recording data.
6. Errors in manipulating data.
7. Errors due to bias or prejudice of the investigator.
8. Lack of recognition and control of relevant influencing factors.

Concepts and Constructs

Concepts are essential to the development of science in that they are the point of departure for experimentation and testing. Concepts represent new ideas, new meanings, and new creations of explanations. The formation of a concept is a necessary early step in scientific problem solving and often is itself a major problem.

Concepts are abstract representations, and abstractions, of reality. Concepts are created from sense impressions or experiences, but the assumption often made that concepts exist as phenomena leads to many errors. In simple terms abstractions (concepts) are not identical to reality (empirical events or phenomena). The differentiation between signs and meaning which arises in explaining the nature of concepts is pointed out by Felix Kaufmann.

> In what follows, we shall, in accordance with prevailing usage, understand by "term" and "sentence" linguistic signs for meaning, by "concept" and "proposition," meanings regardless of the type of linguistic signs by which they are represented. Accordingly, we may say that terms and sentences *have* meanings, whereas concepts and propositions *are* meanings.[6]

Paul Rigby brings out the abstract nature of concepts in relation to science and research, in particular, when he says:

> Concepts are inventions of the human mind to provide a means for organizing and understanding observations. They are not discoveries. The concepts of price, credit, debit, and employee were not discovered any more than were such things as automobiles, accounting techniques, or assembly-line balancing methods. We may discover items in the environment to which we attach concepts, but we do not perceive the concepts. We invent them.[7]

[6]Felix Kaufmann, *Methodology of the Social Sciences* (New York: Oxford University Press, 1944), p. 18.
[7]Paul H. Rigby, *Conceptual Foundations of Business Research* (New York: John Wiley & Sons, Inc., 1965), p. 15.

Since concepts start with observation of phenomena, new concepts are formed by an inductive process. Starting with a group of objects or events, the scientist observes similarities, differences, and irregularities. It is the formation of categories of these characteristics and the distinguishing between groups which represents the birth of concepts. This flexibility of choices in classification of abstractions provides the opportunity for creating new patterns of thought.

From concepts representing first level abstractions directly related sensory perceptions, higher level concepts may be formed. These are not distinct levels of concepts in a hierarchical structure since concepts may be formed from other concepts at all lower levels and even encompass some empirical data directly. The term *construct* is used to denote concepts derived from other lower level concepts or concepts which are intangible in nature. Thus *personality, attitude,* and *group cohesion* are constructs whereas *organization* is a concept rooted in tangible phenomena.

Formalized concepts developed by scientists and applied researchers are now generally known as *models.* Such explicitly stated concepts as models permit considerable manipulation of variables in the department of a theory or in applied science. The relationships among variables are usually quantitatively stated so that interactions are easily seen. A discussion of models at a later point in this book will indicate the versatility of these concepts in organizing and clarifying natural phenomena.

Hypotheses

A hypothesis is a proposition or conjecture which has not yet been tested. It is a provisional explanation of a phenomena or tentative solution of a problem. It provides the structure for research in its final stages. Thus a hypothesis which has been tested becomes a part of the body of knowledge making up science or a solution to an applied problem.

A hypothesis is a concept by the previous definition of concept. The hypothesis, however, is a type of specific concept or a narrow portion of a complex concept. The hypothesis is a proposition which has so been stated that it can be tested by the rules of logic and comparison with empirical data. The broader "concept" may need to be broken down into propositions or reformulated before testing is possible. It is also important to note that while all hypotheses are concepts, all concepts are not transferrable or convertible to hypotheses. Primary concepts such as "color" or "space" are analogous to "facts" such as "number of purchasers" or "physical assets of a company" in the development of science.

The usefulness of the hypothesis is that it makes a statement which can be tested and subjected to retesting and checking by any researcher who wishes to challenge it. The hypothesis narrows down the research, and the argument, to a clear specific statement. The hypothesis may be subject to varying degrees of confirmation, and in the business world the statement of the hypothesis and relatively fragmentary evidence may often prove to be a very useful solution to a problem.

Hypotheses appear in the form of assertions such as

1. If event A occurs, it is necessary for event B to occur, and vice versa. This does not imply that A is the cause of B, but only that they are related in some system so that A and B appear together. Thus both buyers and nonbuyers are present in a department store. If one group is not there, it is not likely the other group is there. Yet the presence of one group is not the cause of the presence of the other group.

2. A particular person, object, or event or situation has a certain characteristic. For example, "Shopping centers appear as clusters of specialty stores grouped around a department store, chain variety store and supermarket." Another example might be: "Consumer innovators (first to try new products) are socially mobile and venturesome people concerned with status."

3. A is the cause of B. This "causal hypothesis" is different from (1) above which merely states that A and B are related. The casual relationship, if such can be determined, is very useful for prediction purposes.

4. "The probability that specified interest rates fall between 4 and 6 percent at any given period of time is .95." Another example of such a probabilistic assertion is: "If the price of a product is lowered the probability that unit sales will increase is .80." This contrasts with deterministic relations between variables which give unique values of dependent variables. (See the discussion of "weak" and "strong" laws in the following section.) Many hypotheses today are stated in probabilistic terms and are tested by the logic of probability and statistical methods. All of the above hypotheses in (1) through (3) could be reformulated as probabilistic assertions.

Laws and Principles

Both the scientist and the businessman would like to have statements about their field of interest which describe invariable relationships. These would be in the form of hypotheses which have been tested. Some of the most confusing and contradictory discussions about the elementary building blocks of science are those dealing with definitions of laws and principles. Consistent explanations of these terms are developed here which are both useful to the researcher and practitioner as well as substantiated by many other writers.

A law is considered to be a well-verified hypothesis and asserts an invariable association among variables. This association may be of a deterministic or probabilistic nature. "Weak laws" are often found in economics and business. Two ways of stating weak laws are:

1. Under *perfect competition* firms *tend* to adjust their size in the long run to minimize their long-run average cost.

2. If prices are lowered more people will purchase a specified product, *except* certain prestige or status products.

In economics and business, the environment is generally not subject to control and human behavior exhibits many inconsistencies so that laws are often qualified or exceptions are understood to exist.

Laws have been classified as empirical (experimental) laws and theoretical laws. The empirical law is derived from actual observation of phenomena in nature or in a controlled experiment. The theoretical law is a statement of relationships based upon other laws, premises, or assumptions.

A *principle* is a fundamental, primary, or basic law which offers direction for action to be taken. Thus

> A principle can be defined as a fundamental statement or general truth providing a guide to thought or action. The fundamental statement applies to a series of phenomena under consideration and signifies what results to expect when the principle is applied.[8]

In summary then, laws represent advances in knowledge which are useful primarily in the development of "pure" or "basic" science and secondarily in application of the underlying principles. Principles are those laws or restatements of laws which are useful to practitioners such as businessmen The term *principle* has occasionally been tinged with disrepute when been used to denote an unsubstantiated (by scientific method) rule of thumb.

Theory

Facts do not speak for themselves, and therefore laws and facts combined into a consistent system of explanation is necessary. The system of explanation is called a *theory*. A theory may also encompass hypotheses as well as the better established laws, but theory is supported by facts and laws. Theory has the erroneous connotation in the minds of many people as unproved product of the imagination. While theories are generally of a high-order conceptual nature, they are supported by the facts and laws which they incorporate. Theories, like laws, are susceptible to testing, modification and rejection at all times. They may become outmoded by the formation of a new concept or discovery of a new law which leads to a better or more universal explanation.

> Theory . . . in the scientific sense, consists in a logically integrated set of propositions about the relations of variables, that is, abstract conceptual entities, in terms of which many statements of fact can be systematically related to each other and their meanings for the solution of empirical problems interpreted. Beside the all important empirical relevance, the principal criteria of good theory are conceptual clarity and precision and logical integration in the sense not only of the logical compatibility of the various propositions included in a theoretical scheme, but of their mutual support, so that inference from one part of the scheme to other parts becomes possible.[9]

[8]Reprinted by permission from George R. Terry, *Principles of Management,* (3d ed.; Homewood, Ill.: Richard D. Irwin, Inc., 1960), p. 6.

[9]Talcott Parsons, "Comment" on "Preface to a Metatheoretical Framework for Sociology," *American Journal of Sociology* (September 1961), p. 137.

SCIENCE AND BUSINESS MANAGEMENT

Much knowledge of the socioeconomic environment and internal aspects of the management of business enterprises has been gained in recent years. Many laws, principles, and theories that were once considered to be useful only for the development of further theory have found direct application in the business world. If not much has been explained by science in business research, much of what needs to be explained has at least been uncovered.

Besides the tremendous complexity of social systems and extreme difficulty if not impracticability for performing controlled experiments, a basic concern of social scientists is what constitutes scientific explanation in social science. As Nagel brings out:

> In particular, there is a long-standing divergence in professed scientific aims between those who view the explanatory systems and logical methods of the natural sciences as models to be emulated in social research and those who think it is fundamentally inappropriate for the social sciences to seek explanatory theories that employ "abstract" distinctions remote from familiar experience and that require publicly accessible (or "intersubjectively" valid) supporting evidence.[10]

It may perhaps be profitable to redefine "science" for the purposes of the social sciences in the light of objectives and criteria for explanation which serve the purposes of inquiry in these fields. With the development of better techniques for quantitative analysis, new experimental approaches, and results of voluminous research to work with, social sciences and associated research should be able to achieve a reputable standing among philosophers of science.

For the business manager, the above philosophical argument has two important implications. First, he will be able to understand a lot more about his business (what things will happen and why they will happen) because knowledge will be added very rapidly to the storehouse of management science. Second, the explanations and predictions supplied by the application of management science will be increasingly more reliable.

SUMMARY

1. Science and research are becoming increasingly important in the management of business enterprises.

2. It is important for the business researcher to have a good understanding of the nature of science.

3. Science may be examined by analyzing its structure, goals, and methods.

4. Briefly, the purpose of science is explain and predict, to answer "why" and "how" and thus increase man's knowledge. Formal systematic methods are employed to test conjectures and establish laws.

---

[10]Ernest Nagel, *The Structure of Science* (New York: Harcourt, Brace & World, 1961), pp. 448–449.

5. Concepts are abstractions which are useful in suggesting and guiding research.

6. Theory represents the logically integrated relationships among facts, hypotheses and laws. Theories are based on much that has been tested by formal research so that a high degree of reliance may be placed on explanations and applications derived from them.

7. The basic building blocks of science consist of empirical data, concepts, hypotheses, laws and theories.

8. The meaning of "science" for the social sciences and the natural sciences may well be different. This has implications for the rapidity of development of management science and the increasing rate at which businessmen will need to utilize research and science to remain competitive.

QUESTIONS AND TOPICS FOR DISCUSSION

1. Do small local businesses conduct business research or utilize the results of business research carried out by trade associations?

2. Is data gathering generally considered to be research? If not, how is it different from research?

3. What is the relationship of research to science? Can there be science without research?

4. Does modern business management have a foundation in science?

5. What is science?

6. Five "building blocks" of science have been listed in this chapter. Evaluate this list or construct one that appears to be better.

7. What is a "fact?" Are facts interpersonal—that is, does a fact mean the same thing to all people?

8. Do observations and experience make a good foundation for the construction of a science?

9. How are concepts and constructs useful to the business manager?

10. Would all research have to start with a hypothesis?

11. What are some "laws" or "principles" of management? Are there any? Will it be likely that there will eventually be a large body of laws?

12. Do business managers use hypotheses regularly in the process of managing?

13. Should theory be defined as a completely unsubstantiated speculation or as a consistent system of explanation based upon at least some evidence?

14. Do you believe that the "science" of social and business research must have methods of explanation completely different from those of the physical sciences. Explain why you take the position you do.

15. "The purpose of science is explanation and prediction. Therefore any means which advances man's ability to explain and predict is justifiable." Discuss.

16. "Business management will always be predominately an art because predictions of the future and of the behavior of people in the organization will never be solved by research and science." Discuss.

chapter 2

Scientific Method and Business Research

RESEARCH AND SCIENCE

One purpose of research is to fulfill the goals of self-perpetuation and self-improvement of science. Another purpose of research is to identify needs, develop alternatives for satisfying these needs, and evaluate these alternatives in terms of given criteria. Research is thus the process, the vehicle, the generating power for the advancement and utilization of science wherever it exists. Research is an intrinsic aspect of science, and science is the outcome of research.

Research seeks to answer the questions of science and major affairs of life by means of careful, formal, systematic inquiry, investigation, and study. Intuition, creativity, and speculation often play a large part in suggesting or directing research, but they do not by themselves constitute research. Research has often been mistaken for data collection. Research is *not* simply gathering and classifying facts; it is *not* an exercise in application of a technique or tool; it is *not* the study in which no conclusions are drawn.

One definition of research requires that the investigation satisfy the final four criteria below. The latter two are said to be desirable:

1. That it be an orderly investigation of a defined problem.
2. That appropriate scientific methods be used.
3. That adequate and representative evidence be gathered.
4. That logical reasoning, uncolored by bias, be employed in drawing conclusions on the basis of the evidence.
5. That the researcher be able to demonstrate or "prove" the validity of his conclusions.
6. That the cumulative results of research in a given area yield general principles or laws that may be applied with confidence under similar conditions in the future.[1]

Research is characterized by its objectives, the methods, and the relationship to science. Its objectives are to uncover truths and universalities on the one

---

[1] David J. Luck, Hugh G. Wales, and Donald A. Taylor, *Marketing Research*, 2d ed. (Englewood Cliffs, N.J.: Prentice-Hall, Inc., 1961), p. 5.

15

hand and to seek solutions to man's problems on the other. Its methods are its own, the result of continuous studies on ways to separate objective inquiry from subjective conclusions. Research represents an objective, universally acceptable, reliable, and repeatable search for answers to questions. Research is an intrinsic aspect of science and interacts with the basic building blocks of science. Research is an institutionalized procedure for advancing science or solving significant problems.

While the one measure of the quality of research is the degree to which the researcher has been able to quantify his concepts and conclusions, good research may be of an entirely qualitative nature. Darwin's work on the theory of evolution is the classical case.

A small qualitative research project conducted by the author dealt with the process of product engineering design. The purpose of the project was to elaborate upon the conceptualization, analysis, synthesis, search, and decisions involved in product engineering design in order to determine the potential for substitution of computers for engineers. For example, one company enters cus-

SUMMARY TABLE

I. Research Activity	Social Scientist	Applied Scientist	Consultant	Practitioner
Function	Producing general knowledge	Producing generalized applied knowledge	Applying knowledge to practice	Implementing knowledge in particular context
Research Production	Basic research	Applied research	Developmental research	Decision
Deductive Consumption		Basic research	Applied research	Developmental research
Inductive Consumption	Applied research	Developmental research	Decision research	
II. Training Program				
Training in Social Sciences	Advanced specialization in one of the social sciences	Partial specialization in one or more of the social sciences	General background and selected knowledge	Selected knowledge
Training in Skills of Administration	Little or none	Intensive in conceptual skills	Intensive in conceptual skills, less intensive in human and technical skills	Intensive in conceptual human and technical skills
Training in Statistics	Advanced technical	Advanced technical	Intermediate technical, advanced interpretive	Elementary technical, intermediate interpretive
Internship	Apprenticeship to social scientist	Apprenticeship to applied scientist	Apprenticeship to consultant	Apprenticeship to practitioner
Training in Research Methods	Theoretical-experimental	Theoretical-experimental	Empirical-experimental survey	Research procedures applied to decision-making, survey
Thesis Requirements	Basic research	Applied research	Developmental research	Decision research

Source: John H.M. Andrews, "Differentiated Research Training for Students of Administration," Jack A. Culbertson and Stephen P. Hencley (eds.), *Educational Research: New Perspectives* (Danville, Ill: Interstate Publishers, 1963), p. 361.

Fig. 2-1. Differentiated research training.

ing Theory by Michael Halbert (McGraw-Hill, 1965). The content of this book was developed under the auspices of the Marketing Science Institute. Generally, the marketing theory and applied marketing problems deal with the same topics. An outline of such topics follows.

1. Marketing Policy

Pricing	Inventory
Advertising	Salesmen's compensation
Service	Customer relations
Channels of distribution	International operations

2. Product Research

New-product ideas	Product standardization and variety control
Improvements and new uses for present products	Brand names and trade marks
Packaging	Company and product image
Customer preferences	

3. Market Research

Economic forecasts	Market and sales potential by product, customer, area, salesman
Industry forecasts	Competition
Sales forecasts	Technology forecasts

4. Sales Management and Methods

Type of organization	Effectiveness and efficiency of the sales organization
Quantity, quality, and type of personnel	Customer service
Compensation	Sales operation control
Long-range organization planning	

5. Channels of Distribution

Evaluation of alternative channels of distribution	Inventory control
	Logistics

6. Advertising and Sales Promotion Research

Consumer-motivation studies	TV-commercial measurements
Media selection	Trade-show participation
Advertising appeals	Point-of-purchase advertising
Copy testing	Premiums, deals, and special promotions
Readership studies	

Some specific applied research topics which have been investigated are:

1. Market Facts, Inc., reported that a manufacturer of a cake mix sought a product modification which would win greater consumer acceptance. A preliminary research project uncovered the main product effects and consumer terms as taste, texture, and cake size. A second research project, by means of scaling techniques and comparisons, attempted to measure the qualities as most consumers preferred them.

2. A graduate student sought to develop and test a model which related sales response to advertising for industrial products. He surveyed the literature, obtained data from a large manufacturer of chemical products, and developed a model which seemed theoretically justified and appeared to represent data for the single manufacturer.

3. A company hired a marketing research agency to appraise company sales compensation practices in relation to the industry.

Production Research

Production research has tended to focus on materials and equipment rather than on the human aspects. Research on the behavior of people in organizations has developed primarily in the field of organization theory and administration. Since the worker has been treated primarily as a unit of labor, considerable quantification has been possible in construction principles of production management. Thus much of so-called management-science research and operations research treats production problems. The principal topics of research have fallen under the following general headings.

1. Capital Budgets
   Site and facility planning and principles
   Equipment purchase and replacement
2. Plant Layout
   Arrangement and work flow
   Materials handling
   Work environment
3. Wage Administration
   Work methods
   Work measurement
   Wage payment plans
4. Procurement
5. Inventory Control
6. Quality Control
7. Production Control
   Control systems
   Scheduling
8. Cost Control

Examples of specific research topics are:

1. What are capital equipment replacement practices in manufacturing companies? Who recommends replacement? How are decisions made? What quantitative approaches are used?

2. Scheduling independent tasks on parallel processors. (M. H. Rothkopf, *Management Science,* January 1966).

3. How can a classification system be developed which will provide the lowest-cost process for making a metal part? Size range, tolerance, surface finish, total quantity in a run, and pieces per hour are parameters. Tooling, labor, material waste and cost are the dependent variables and the process is the independent variable. (See H. L. G. Leslie, "Design Guide to Value," *Product Engineering,* October 28, 1963.)

Financial Research

Financial research has not attained the distinction which it deserves, and much research in this area has been carried out by researchers from other fields. Capital equipment replacement research, for example, has been conducted by economists and industrial engineers. An outline of major topics follows:

1. Financial Analysis
   Capital structure
   Ratio analysis
   Valuation of companies
   Acquisitions, mergers, reorganization, liquidation
2. Rationing Resources
   Sources of funds and cost of capital
   Opportunities for profit
   Liquidity constraints
3. Management of Funds (short-, intermediate-, and long-term)
4. Management of Assets

Examples of specific topics in finance which might be researched are:

1. Evaluation of the price-earnings ratio as an analytical tool.
2. Potentialities and use of the computer for credit analysis.
3. "Least-Cost vs. Opportunity Cost in Make-or-Buy Decisions," Robert W. Rosen, *Financial Executive* (January 1966).
4. Use of probability in cost control.

Personnel Research

Research in the functional area of personnel management may range from very simple problems to highly complex problems of all types. Because personnel management is concerned primarily with the human aspects of the business firm, the amount of research and reporting on personnel problems has been exceedingly large. Much more basic research in this field would be valuable. Broad areas for research are outlined here.

1. Personnel Policies
2. Personnel Organization Structure
3. Job and Manpower Requirements
4. Recruiting, Selecting, Hiring, and Placement of Employees
5. Training and Development of Employees
6. Promotion and Transfer
7. Morale and Attitudes
8. Communications
9. Wage and Salary Administration
10. Health, Safety, and Working Conditions
11. Fringe Benefits

Some examples of specific research topics are:

1. What is the work background, education, salary, and status in the organization of industrial personnel managers in a specified metropolitan region?

2. What types and mix of training and development programs are most suitable for a certain company?

3. The repetitive job versus job enlargement.

4. The impact of automation and the computer on organization structure.

5. What are effective and what are harmful methods of employee appraisal?

Organization and Management Research

The arrangement of people and their relationships for the purpose of accomplishing tasks in the concern of organization theory. In our business culture, responsibility for organizing falls to managers who themselves are part of the organization. Research may be directed toward:

1. What types of organizations are most effective for setting and accomplishing business goals?

2. If we start with the assumption that a hierarchical organization is in effect, what should be the functions of managers?

3. What principles can be developed to guide managers?

4. How do people behave in organizational situations and how can their behavior be modified favorably?

An accepted general theory of management is lacking at this time, although much recent research has contributed to our understanding of business organizations. Researchers from the social science disciplines have found this to be a fertile field. For most graduate students, research into what exists, or in the development of concepts, is apt to be more appropriate than the difficult investigation of human behavior.

Economic Research

Economics, like finance, covers a wide variety of business activities. Unlike finance, it has achieved considerable veneration and attention by research scholars. One of the common definitions of economics is that economics is the science which studies the principles governing the allocation of scarce means among competing ends in order to optimize the benefits from these ends. Much economic research has been devoted to

1. The theory of the firm—pricing of goods and factors of production.
2. Economic forecasting.
3. Macroeconomics—the study of economic systems and their manipulation.

An outline of topics under which research papers were classified in the May 1966 issue of *American Economic Review* (AER) is given below.

1. Allocation and Distribution Theory: Technological Innovation and Progress
2. Capital Theory: Technical Progress and Capital Structure
3. Economic Developments: Advanced Technology for Poor Countries
4. The Economics of Science Policy
5. The Production and Use of Economic Knowledge
6. Labor Economics: Effects of More Knowledge

Some specific research titles from other AER issues are:
1. "A Survey of Investment Management and Working Behavior Among High-Income Individuals" (James Morgan, Robin Barlow, and Harvey Braer, May 1965).
2. "Firm Size, Market Structure, Opportunity, and the Output of Patented Inventions" (F. M. Scherer, December 1965).
3. "An International Comparison of the Trend of Professional Earnings" (Tibor Scitovsky, March 1966).

SCIENTIFIC METHOD

"Method" is a procedure which applies a systematic pattern or ordering to man's activities. Scientific method is the set of norms which govern the development of science. It is a set of rules by which researchers are guided. To a great extent the scientific method is an attitude rather than a unique procedure. Certain basic rules such as confirmation of prediction as a necessary step remain constant. Other rules may be developed and justified as required for the particular science and type of research.

Characteristics of the Scientific Method

The "scientific method" is derived from methods used in the natural sciences which have been found to be most generally useful in advancing these sciences. Some alternatives to the scientific method are tradition, intuition, authoritarianism, judgment, and revelation. The scientific method is not limited to the natural sciences but is adaptable to any of the empirical sciences. The scientific method is a way of "making sure" by attempting to consider all possibilities without prejudice. The neophyte researcher too often starts with strongly pre-conceived notions and searches only for evidence which supports his ideas.

Scientific method must therefore be critical and analytical in nature. In the descriptive (positive) sciences, the scientific method starts with the premise of rationality of nature. This leads to the belief that phenomena have a cause. Further, if phenomena do have a cause or complexity of causes, the scientific method will lead to the underlying mechanism relating the causes to the phenomena. Arguments have been advanced that cause and effect cannot be connected; rather functional or probabilistic relationships can be established. While it is unlikely that the scientist will ever achieve knowledge of the complete and true relationships, he knows that he will be able to learn enough to either advance the science further or make application of knowledge in the real world.

Scientific methods make use of concepts and structuring theories as opposed to the less systematic direction on nonscientific methods. Thus scientific method makes greater use of accumulated knowledge for its direction. It also makes greater use of existing knowledge in the form of facts or data which are available.

The scientific method uses more careful and uniform definitions of terms than do nonscientific methods. Whenever possible, quantitative definitions are used and ordering, counting, and numerical measuring techniques are sought.

The scientific method is more rational than nonscientific methods. It seeks to uncover all possible causes of phenomena and investigates each before reaching a conclusion. It continually criticizes and reevaluates assumptions, methods, and conclusions in the light of empirical evidence.

The scientific method is characterized by more objective procedures than nonscientific methods. This means that the methods are such that an independent investigator is able to follow exactly the steps of another and achieve the same results.

Some researchers believe that there is no *one* scientific method, but rather there is a systematic method of inquiry characteristic of each field. Whether it is easily possible for a trained researcher to adapt his research skills easily to another field has been debated. Louis Pasteur's transference of his skills from pasteurization studies to silkworm diseases is a single example which shows the possibility.

Steps in the Scientific Method

In basic research, the general steps in the scientific method of research are:

1. Observation *or* perception through a searching process. Knowledge about the world must start with observation. Often experience or memory of events is the starting point.

2. Definition of the research problem. This means determining in specific terms the purposes or objectives of the research. It must state *why* the research is being done, *what* it is supposed to accomplish. Often in basic research the

objective is to test a hypothesis of cause and effect (relationship between two events separated in time). In applied research, the objective is to determine (1) *why* a cause-and-effect relationship exists, (2) *how* a certain task may be performed (or a goal accomplished), or (3) *what* alternative courses of action are available and which one *should* be pursued.

3. Formulation of a research plan. This consists of a detailed plan for valid explanation. It may consist of testing a hypothesis or concept of evaluating evidence of a relationship.

4. Gathering data and facts and testing the hypothesis or evaluating the relationship or concept.

5. Formulation of new hypotheses, decision rules, or generalizations in the form of conclusions.

6. Documenting the research project.

Observation or searching leads to identification of a problem. A problem is indicated by a variation from the expected or by observation of something new to the experience of the observer. If it is new or different in terms of all that is included in man's knowledge of the field, then it constitutes a subject for basic research. In business applied research, operation problems are identified when:

1. Current performance is not meeting current goals.

2. Current methods or performance will not be adequate to meet established future goals.

3. Planned action is not adequate to meet future desired goals.

Identification or definition of a problem is first usually represented by only a crude general expression. The researcher needs to rework his formulation, perhaps several times, in order to eliminate ambiguous and irrelevant ideas and terms. The final formulation may require that the problem be described as a series of problems because of its complexity. It may also be desirable to break it down into such subproblems in order that manageable research projects may be selected.

Formulation of the research plan consists of

1. Selection of a strategy

2. Selection of techniques and tools

3. Detailed steps for implementation of (1) and (2)

4. Schedule for conducting research

The strategy is the general approach taken to solve the research problem. The techniques and tools are the common, more or less standardized, procedures such as specific forms of sampling, statistical experiments, laboratory measurements, library techniques and forms of comparison, evaluation, and analysis.

Empirical data or "facts" are next gathered in order to compare them with the prediction derived from the hypothesis. If the research is an evaluative investigation, the facts are used as a basis for analysis and comparison.

The results of the entire research process leads to new knowledge expressed as the conclusions of the research. The results are new relationships, new knowledge regarding different systems or alternatives, or new methods, processes, or concepts.

The above procedure is quite general and is suitable for both natural and social sciences and both basic and applied research.

Special problems of methodology are often attributed to the application of the scientific method to the social sciences and not to the natural sciences. As pointed out by Ernest Nagel, these problems are not insurmountable for the social sciences and exist to a greater degree than usually admitted in the natural sciences.[2] The difficulties in business research are:

1. *The difficulty of controlled inquiry.* It is difficult in business research to study relationships when the investigator cannot control the variable of interest and hold other variables constant. Further, a controlled experiment is understood to be one that may be repeated over and over. In the business world the controlled experiment has sometimes been claimed by some as impossible to achieve. The use of certain statistical experimental designs and the development of laboratory experiments have, however, weakened the claim that controlled inquiry is not possible in some cases.

2. *Difficulty of generalization because of cultural differences.* Social phenomena are said to be culturally or historically conditioned. Thus research in one society may not be applicable to another. Even within the U. S., regional differences exist in culture, and research results between regions must be extrapolated with caution. On the other hand, differentiation among regions or societies does not preclude the existence of universal principles.

3. *Knowledge of predictions as an influence on events.* In economics and business, research which results in published predictions may influence the course of events. Thus if a forecast of inflation is published, people will rush to buy early and the prediction will be borne out. Or if a recession is predicted, businessmen may reduce inventories and take other preventive action to reduce the effects of such a recession, thereby counteracting the recession. To prevent such predictions from being invalid in the social sciences, alternative predictions must state the alternative assumptions of human behavior. This difficulty of the investigator affecting the occurrence of events in natural sciences is not unknown, since often the measuring instrument represents a perturbing factor in an experiment in the natural sciences.

4. *Subjective nature of much of business systems.* The psychological and value aspects of business activities make identification, comparison, and measurement basic methodological problems in business research. Operational definitions of subjective ideas are not possible. Behaviorist investigators can, however, accept introspective reports by experimental subjects as *observable responses* rather than statements *about* psychological states.

[2] Ernest Nagel, *The Structure of Science* (New York: Harcourt, Brace & World, 1961). See Chap. 13, "Methodological Problems in the Social Sciences."

5. *Value-bias of investigators.* In the natural sciences, values do not represent a part of the subject matter. In business research, it may be argued that value-neutrality does not hold, since each researcher has his own distinct set of values. These values may enter into choice of problems, methods of investigation, or assessment of facts. In the sense that value judgments relate to *estimates of measurement* rather than approval or disapproval, social research may be concluded to minimize value influences.

Systematic Approaches to Applied Research (Operational Decision) Problems in Business

The scientific method in applied business research finds its expression in the major phase of Operations Research (OR). The steps in the solution of OR problems run parallel to the steps in the generalized approach:

1. Formulate the problem.
   (a) Analyze the system and its components.
   (b) Formulate the business problem.
   (c) Formulate the research problem.
2. Construct a model to represent the system of interest.
3. Obtain a solution from the model.
   (a) Select input data.
   (b) Manipulate the parameters of the model to find the most suitable values.
   (c) Compute output data to give predictions based upon the model.
4. Test the model by comparing predictions with empirical data obtained from operations of the business.
5. Establish controls over the solution to signal changes in methods or the environment which require modification of the model.
6. Put the solution to work by utilizing it to assist the decision maker.

When there are many qualitative factors and value judgments involved in decision making, the research process consists in gathering and evaluating evidence for alternative solutions to the problem. The steps are:

1. Identify the real problem as distinguished from problem symptoms.
2. Formulate a "reasonable" number of alternative solutions. A "solution" consists of a course of action and the predicted outcome. Rationality cannot be complete, since it is not possible to identify *all* possible solutions. Several alternatives are apt to lead to a better solution than just one alternative, however.
3. Develop a set of criteria for evaluating the alternative solutions.
4. Gather evidence that shows the advantages and disadvantages of each alternative as measured against the desired criteria.

Another approach to problem solving in the business environment is shown in Fig. 2-2. This offers a systematic approach to minimizing effort in handling

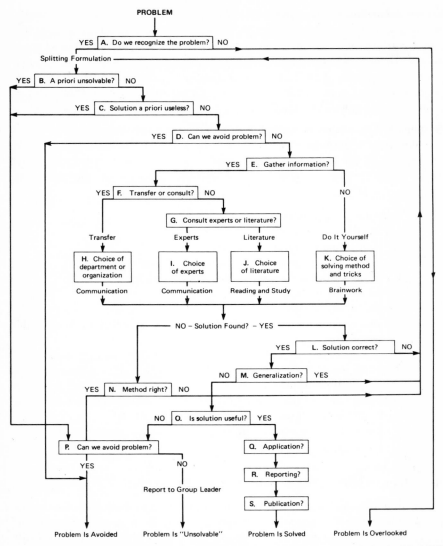

PROBLEM

YES | A. Do we recognize the problem? | NO

Splitting Formulation

YES | B. A priori unsolvable? | NO

YES | C. Solution a priori useless? | NO

YES | D. Can we avoid problem? | NO

YES | E. Gather information? | NO

YES | F. Transfer or consult? | NO

G. Consult experts or literature?

Transfer   Experts   Literature   Do It Yourself

H. Choice of department or organization | I. Choice of experts | J. Choice of literature | K. Choice of solving method and tricks

Communication   Communication   Reading and Study   Brainwork

NO – Solution Found? – YES

YES | L. Solution correct? | NO

NO | M. Generalization? | YES

YES | N. Method right? | NO

NO | O. Is solution useful? | YES

P. Can we avoid problem?

YES   NO

Q. Application?

R. Reporting?

Report to Group Leader

S. Publication?

Problem Is Avoided   Problem Is "Unsolvable"   Problem Is Solved   Problem Is Overlooked

Source: Ir. A. H. Boedijk, "Step-by-Step Guide to Problem-Solving Decisions," reprinted from *Product Engineering*, Feb. 4, 1963. Copyright 1963 by McGraw-Hill Publishing Company.

Fig. 2-2. Decision paths for problem solving.

operational problems. The investigator checks sequentially various sources of knowledge which require increasing levels of effort. At one end of the spectrum the problem is avoided. At the other end the investigator is required to conduct a complete research project.

Economics of Business Research

Research provides the supply of knowledge in response to the demand for knowledge by business.[3] There is always an inherent risk in research that the results will be of limited value. In advance of conducting research, the research has an "expected value." In fact, if research is considered to be made up of a sequence of possible research projects designed to provide additional information, the value of going beyond each research project may be estimated.[4,5] If a deterministic viewpoint is taken as in most economics problems, the value of the marginal units of information decline as the supply of information increases. At the same time, the marginal cost of research directed toward refinement of the increasing knowledge available tends to increase. This may be represented by Fig. 2-3.

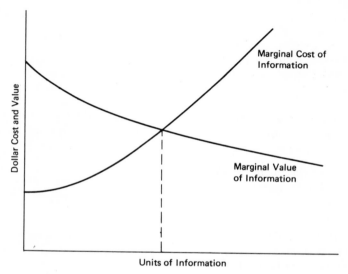

Fig. 2-3. Marginal cost and marginal value of information.

It should be the responsibility of the academic researcher, therefore, to use his judgment to select problems that are worth solving in terms of his time and resources. In business, an attempt should be made to utilize the most rational approach possible to determine how much information to gather in problem solving.

[3] See Adrian M. McDonough, *Information Economics and Management Systems* (New York: McGraw-Hill Book Company, Inc., 1963).

[4] See, for example, Wroe Alderson and Paul E. Green, "The Fundamentals of Bayesian Decision Making," Chap. 5, *Planning and Problem Solving in Marketing* (Homewood, Ill.: Richard O. Irwin, Inc., 1964).

[5] See also Frank Bass, "Marketing Research Expenditures: A Decision Model," *Journal of Business*, Vol. XXXVI, No. 1 (January 1963), pp. 77–90.

Creativity in Business Research

Much of the research on business problems is conducted in a routine way using well-known methods. Too few researchers deliberately seek other imaginative approaches. Everyone has creative ability; it is only in degree that differences exist. Creative thinking in research may lead to

1. New and better selection of problems
2. Ingenious methods for studying difficult problems
3. Unthought-of explanations of phenomena

The distinction between the creative and noncreative processes in problem solving and research are:

Creative	Noncreative
Formulation of the problem	Observation
Intensive concentration *with critical judgment suspended*	Remembering or storing information
Intermission periods—creative solutions cannot be forced, but require an incubation period	Reasoning
Illumination or inspiration	Judgment

The researcher must develop an independence and feeling of confidence that by his careful study, his creative ideas will prove out in the long run. Barriers to creativity are caused by

1. Fear of ridicule by associates
2. Desire for security
3. Fear of dreaming and a desire to be "practical"
4. Lack of faith in one's self
5. Self-satisfaction
6. Biases
7. Resistance to change and new ideas
8. Unwillingness to seek help from others in related specialties
9. Preference for the logical over the intuitive approach in early stages of research
10. Desire for quick results

To develop his creativity and its application, the researcher should observe, question, associate, and practice predicting and checking his predictions.

QUESTIONS AND TOPICS FOR DISCUSSION

1. What purposes does research serve?
2. What is the difference between research and simply gathering and presenting data in coherent form?
3. What are some examples of *qualitative* business research?

4. What kind of training or development program do you think would develop good researchers?

5. "Common-sense" approaches to business problems obviously require some organization and data. How does research differ from the common-sense approach?

6. Can you think of any other features than those in the text which distinguish common-sense methods from scientific methods?

7. Is there a general theory of marketing to guide the business researcher seeking a solution to his company's market problems? What is the status of marketing theory?

8. What areas of production in addition to those given in the text, can you think of which might require research in a business firm?

9. What are some specific topics in finance that might be investigated?

10. What obstacles appear to stand in the way of developing a general theory of organization and management? What specific areas seem to require highest priority research?

11. Is there any overlapping between economic research and personnel research?

12. "All business research falls under the heading of economic research." Discuss.

13. "Scientific method in the social sciences must be completely different from scientific method in the natural sciences." Discuss.

14. With your own ideas, describe what you think the scientific method *should* be, particularly as it applies to business research.

15. How do you recognize a problem?

16. Make a list of problems in applying a scientific method to business research.

17. Does Fig. 2-1 represent a scientific method?

18. "In Fig. 2-1, the step which suggests that we try to avoid the problem is equally applicable to basic research." Discuss.

19. Make up a flow chart for basic research in business analogous to that of Fig. 2-1.

20. Do you agree with the approach shown in Fig. 2-2?

21. Are experience and knowledge assets or handicaps to the researcher seeking new basic concepts?

chapter 3

Concepts Used in Research

IMPORTANCE OF CLARIFYING CONCEPTS USED IN RESEARCH

There are a number of concepts which are used repeatedly in research. Often these are used implicitly without the researcher's concerning himself with explanation. For example, a market researcher may report on research of brand switching by detergent consumers. If his report is a complete one, he will specify how he determined that brand switching occurred. From this point on, the percentage of brand switchers is taken either as a "fact" or an assumption without explicit clarification.

It may well be impossible to distinguish assumptions from facts or previously tested propositions from reading a report. Not a bit atypical is the following statement introducing a study of a particular company:

Salary administration is a growing problem in research management regardless of the size and character of the establishment.[1]

This is a broad generalization. Is it a fairly well established fact that salary administration is a *growing* problem in this area? Is it growing relatively or absolutely? Is it growing in intensity? What is the basis for saying that *all* firms face this problem regardless of size? Is this salary administration problem distinguishable from the salary administration problem for the entire company? These questions suggest that researchers should understand the concepts of assumptions, premises, facts, and other basic terms. The need for explicit use of such terms and concepts has been reinforced by the current popularity of mathematical models which require explicitness of concepts.

If business research is to be objective, in the sense of the repeatable investigation and common body of knowledge and theory, the concepts characteristic of all investigation and knowledge in the field of business research must be established. Clear exposition of these concepts is necessary for researchers to communicate descriptions of their studies to others. The researchers themselves

---

[1] See *Research Management* (September 1963), p. 355.

cannot understand the process of research without an understanding of the concepts involved in research methodology. It is bad enough that so much effort has been spent on constructing business research propositions employing vague, ambiguous, or multiple-meaning terms without such looseness appearing in the methodology itself.

Unfortunately, much work remains to be done with respect to clarifying methodological terms. Therefore, definitive descriptions of all concepts of interest are not now possible. Yet a discussion of the nature of the problem and the issues in each case will perhaps make the researcher more cautious and more skilled in communicating his work.

FACTS AND DATA

Facts and data have been discussed in Chapter 1 in connection with the building blocks of science. A closer look at the meaning of "fact" seems advisable. F. S. C. Northrup states that

> The second stage of inquiry begins with immediately apprehended fact and ends with described fact. Fact in these two senses must not be confused. Only fact in the former sense is independent of all concepts and theory.[2]

The next question which arises is, What is "immediately apprehended" fact? Since all facts which are immediately apprehended must reach us through the senses, these facts are either interpreted in some way based upon experience and psychological factors, or else they are extremely limited in nature. For example, if a person stands five feet in front of a mirror, he sees his image apparently ten feet away. Yet he "knows" that the image is actually at the surface of the mirror.

A more common example occurs whenever a three-dimensional object is observed. The observer sees three sides of a book, say, and assumes as a fact that a solid object of a certain color is present. Actually, the "book" may be simply a three-sided shell or, if it is solid, the other sides may be of a different color. If the observer lifts the book, he may conclude that it is heavy. However, if someone else lifts the book, he may state as a fact that the book is light.

Two ideas relating to psychological interpretation of facts thus seem to be present. In the first instance, determination of a fact may require several sensory perceptions and observations. Simply observing the back of a person without seeing his face and listening to his words is unlikely to indicate what he is actually doing. In the second instance, it appears that a desirable characteristic of a fact is that it is interpersonal. Although when each of two individuals lift the book, they feel the same downward force, they describe this effect differently. It is the attempt to *verbalize* the sensory perceptions which results in

---

[2]F. S. C. Northrup, *The Logic of the Sciences and Humanities* (Cleveland: The World Publishing Co., copyrighted by Macmillan, New York, 1947), p. 35.

variances. By use of a scale to measure the weight, the variance may be *reduced* to the magnitude of observational error involved in reading the scale. Appropriately designed measuring devices may greatly reduce the variance in observed physical phenonema.[3]

If the researcher is using secondary data, these data become assumed "facts" for his investigation. They are eventually interpersonal, since discrepancies among observations of the secondary data may in general be eliminated. Such facts are similar to Northrup's "described facts" in that they are taken as the "given" or the empirical basis for the following steps in research. Since Northrup means by described facts propositions developed from immediately apprehended facts and theory, described facts are subject to attack in terms of the development of theory, but they are accepted as working facts until they are negated.

DEFINITIONS

The field of business is notorious for its lack of definitions of even the most commonly used terms. Within the business firm itself this results in communication breakdowns, confusion, and a flood of memoranda. The situation is little better among researchers and theorists. An analytically minded person who attends management symposiums will observe again and again discussions in which participants are using identical words to mean completely different things.

Some examples of terms which are used so loosely as to be practically meaningless are: long-range plan, program, manager, professional, organization, cost, marketing, image, ethical behavior, system, small business firm, and operations research. It might be expected that technical terms employed in basic or applied research would receive better treatment. Yet in the highly developed science of economics, terms such as wealth, income, value, and market, among others, are listed by Rollo Handy and Paul Kurtz under the heading of "Problems in Terminology."[4] While the greater emphasis on mathematical models forces careful definition of terms, these definitions are often simply identities with symbols, and empirical application, meaning, or interpretation is still not clear.

Even in the highly developed process of sample survey design, applied researchers employing statistical methods do not invariably define terms carefully. Too often the definitions of "population" or "sampling elements" are not specified. Thus a loose definition of the population as, "This survey covers the metropolitan area of _____," may be stated in which neither the geographic area is defined precisely nor are the elementary units (such as "male headsof households") specified. In fact, the research is not infrequently reported in such

---

[3] For a further discussion of invariant elements, see "Knowledge and Reality," Chap. 1, Felix Kaufmann, *Methodology of the Social Sciences* (New York: Oxford University Press, 1944).

[4] Rollo Handy and Paul Kurtz, *A Current Appraisal of the Behavioral Sciences* (Great Barrington, Mass.: Behavioral Research Council, 1963), Sec. 3, p. 53.

a manner that it implies it is a probability sample survey when this attribute has been lost by some step in implementation of the method.

While developing better definitions is a continuing process in developing the scientific features of business knowledge, as precise definitions as possible are desirable at all times. Clearly defined terms are required at the very start of business research in the formulation and reformulation of the problem. Usually the methodology employed in the research, including criteria and units of measurement, also requires the introduction of technical definitions. Construction of explanations in theory development may necessitate the specification of the meaning of new terms which must be coined by the investigator or old terms which must be defined more sharply.

There are considerable difficulties in establishing a set of fundamental definitions. A survey of the nature and problems of definitions will assist the researcher in several ways. First, it will make the researcher aware of the importance of striving for meaningful and useful definitions in the development of his research. Second, it will assist him in achieving better definitions.

Types of definitions have been described by Henry S. Leonard as five pairs of contrasting nature. They are as follows:

1. Nominal versus real
2. Informative versus hortatory
3. Complete versus incomplete
4. Linguistic versus conceptual
5. Extensional versus intensional[5]

Of considerable importance to the researcher is the basic nature of definition. Is the definition an equivalence of expressions or is it an attempt to circumscribe the qualities of a real thing to distinguish it from all other things? The convention which simply introduces an alternative—usually an abbreviation or shorthand form—is called a *nominal definition*. Hempel states,

> A *nominal definition* may be characterized as a stipulation to the effect that a specified expression, the *definiendum*, is to be synonymous with a certain other expression, the *definiens*, whose meaning is already determined. A nominal definition may be put into the form
> Let the expression E_2 be synonymous with the expression E_1.[6]

An example of a nominal definition is:

> Let the word "bias" be synonymous with "difference between the expected value of the estimate and the true value being estimated."

---

[5] Henry S. Leonard, *Principles of Right Reason* (New York: Henry Holt and Co., Inc., 1957), p. 311.

[6] Carl G. Hempel, "Fundamentals of Concept Formation in Empirical Science," *International Encyclopedia of Unified Science*, Vol. II, No. 7 (Chicago: University of Chicago Press, 1952, pp. 2–3.

All nominal definitions are of the form

$$\underline{\qquad} = D_f \underline{\qquad}$$

where $= D_f$ means "equals by definition."

A nominal definition thus singles out a concept such as a property, a class, a relation, a function, or a group of these and lays down a special name for it.

According to Leonard, a nominal definition is the meaning which the author himself attaches to a term. For example, "leadership" has been defined in many ways by many people. A researcher using this term would want to clarify exactly how he is using it. In contrast, the researcher might wish to examine the use of "leadership" in other research. He would then want to give the "real" definition, the meaning of the term as *others* use it.

The nominal definition may thus on occasion be the same as or different from the real definition. In either case, the purpose of the definition is to *inform* the reader how to interpret these words in the future, and thus these definitions are informatory definitions. *Hortatory* definitions are recommendations to potential *users* of a word to use it as the researcher recommends. The American Standards Association (ASA) is an unofficial association of business and government representatives which attempts to obtain a concensus on definitions as well as equipment and design and manufacturing procedures. The ASA definitions are hortatory since the ASA can only *recommend*.

Generally, complete definitions are desirable in research, and incomplete definitions are suitable mainly for social discourse. Complete definitions are those used to explain or determine a concept, word, or phrase uniquely. Incomplete definitions point out only one or a few attributes of that being defined. Incomplete definitions do have a place in business research when they are used to remove ambiguities or are used as part of an already specified context. In the first instance, a market survey may have specified the elementary units as heads of households. An incomplete definition of the elementary units as "male respondents" would serve to eliminate the ambiguity as to whether female heads of households were being considered.

The meaningful use of an incomplete definition is the following: "A business is a collection of problems to be solved."[7] This by itself certainly does not distinguish a business from many other types of goal-oriented organizations. However, in the context of a book devoted to management-information systems, it serves the purpose of the author in identifying that characteristic of business firm which is the focus of systems analysis.

Linguistic definitions are used to convey information about the language; they explain the use of an expression to indicate a thing already familiar to the receiver. A conceptual definition has great importance in theory development

---

[7]Adrian M. McDonough, *Information Economics and Management Systems* (New York: McGraw-Hill Book Company, Inc., 1963), p. 144.

and will be discussed further on. A conceptual definition conveys information *about* the entity being defined.

The extension of a term is the class of those things which have a specified attribute in common. An extensional definition is one which refers to each thing which belongs in a class. For example, "The 500 largest firms in the U.S." means "firms like AT&T, General Motors, etc.," is an incomplete extensional definition. An extensional definition attempts to explain by indicating those things which belong in the extension without indicating the essential (if and only if) characteristics. The intensional definition specifies those characteristics which determine whether an object belongs in the extension of the term. "The 500 largest firms in the U.S." means "in a ranking by value of assets of all profit-making organizations in the U.S. engaged in the production of goods and services, the firms corresponding to 500 highest ranking of assets" is an intensional definition.

Extensional definitions are usually incomplete, yet they provide knowledge which cannot be provided by intensional definitions. Often the receiver is familiar with the extensions of a term so that a complete listing is not desirable nor required. The advantage of the intensional definition is that it calls attention to characteristics of objects and may lead to generalization and development of extensional definitions.

A universal problem in setting up a science is establishing the basic definitions. These are sometimes called *fundamental* or *primitive* definitions. Definitions may be based upon observable things or may relate to abstractions. Such words as *personality, judgment, motivation,* and *attitude* are examples. These expressions do not refer to things, properties, relations, or processes which may be observed directly. As principles and theories are developed, higher levels of abstraction lead to definitions which depend upon other definitions which depend alternately upon primitive definitions. *Behavior space, semiotic,* and *social system* are illustrations of such terms. In an empirical science where every statement and prediction should be able to be tested in the real world, it would seem that it should be required that all definitions ought to be subject to reduction to observable entities. Such entities if they do not exist at a particular desired time and place might be "actualized." Thus "small group decision making" as a process may be actualized by setting up a group of five people, assigning them a problem, and observing the decision-making process.

The importance of defining terms in a manner which serves the purpose of the researcher is illustrated by Russell Ackoff. Dr. Ackoff was asked to determine the precision of the results of a survey designed to determine the number of rooms in dwelling units. "Room" had not been explicitly defined, and Dr. Ackoff asked what definition the survey designers had implicitly used. The conversation went approximately as follows:

 " 'A room is a space enclosed by four walls, a floor, and a ceiling."
 The author asked, "Can't a room be triangular?"

"Sure. It can have three or four walls."
"What about a circular room?"
"Well, it can have one or more walls."
"What about a paper carton?"
"A room has to be large enough for human occupancy."
"What about a closet?"
"It must be used for normal living purposes."
"What are 'normal living purposes?' "
"Look, we don't have to go through this nonsense; our results are good enough for our purposes."
"What were your purposes?"
"To get an index of living conditions by finding the number of persons per room in dwelling units."
"Doesn't the size of the room matter?"
"Yes, we probably should have used 'square feet' of floor space, but that would have been too hard to get."
"Doesn't the height of the room matter?"
"I guess so. Ideally, we should have used volume."
"Would a room with ten square feet of floor area and sixty feet high be the same as one with sixty square feet of floor area and ten feet high?"
"Look, the index is good enough for the people who use it."
"What do they use it for?"
"I'm not sure, but we've had no complaints.' "[8]

The reaction against purely conceptual definitions which do not relate directly to experience or experiment reached its ultimate in P. W. Bridgman's operationalism.[9] The operational definition tells the observer what to do in order to observe the meaning of a term. "A statement can be said to have meaning, according to operationalism only if it can be translated into physical operations to assertain its truth or falsity."[10] The scientist defines his terms by telling how to proceed and what to observe. For example, to define "retail firm," examine a firm's sales, and if over 50 percent of sales are to ultimate consumers, it is a retail firm.

Another approach to definitions which is best applied to basic definitions is the contextual approach. The term is defined by defining expressions containing it. A discussion is given which covers various aspects of the term. An illustration of the contextual definition follows.

A business enterprise or firm—the two terms will be used interchangeably—is an independent private organization that (1) mobilizes

[8]Russell L. Ackoff, *Scientific Method, Optimizing Applied Research Decisions* (New York: John Wiley & Sons, Inc., 1962), pp. 147–148.
[9]P. W. Bridgman, *The Logic of Modern Physics* (New York: The Macmillan Company, 1927).
[10]S. I. Hayakawa, "Semantics, General Semantics and Related Disciplines," in S. I. Hayakawa (ed.), *Language Meaning and Maturity* (New York: Harper and Row, 1954), p. 22.

economic resources (land, labor, and capital), (2) produces goods or services for sale in a market, and (3) relies primarily on the proceeds from the sale of its product to meet its costs. The characterization of the firm as an "organization" implies that it is a unified group of interacting participants. Among the participants in the firm are owners, managers, employees, and also, in some respects, customers and suppliers.

Embraced by this definition are enterprises in all industries including agriculture, enterprises of all sizes from self-employed persons to giant companies, and enterprises of all legal forms from individual partnerships to cooperatives and corporations.[11]

As a final remark on definitional problems, attention is called to Ernest Nagel's statement that there is no conclusive proof available (and perhaps none is possible) to show that the theoretical notions employed in current science cannot be explicitly defined in terms of experimental ideas. However, he observes, no one has yet constructed such definitions.[12]

MEASUREMENT

Measurement is closely related to definition. Whereas definitions are concerned with the nature of objects or concepts, measurement is directed at the representation of properties or *attributes* of these. Measurement "is a way of obtaining symbols to represent the properties of objects, events or states, which symbols have the same relevant relationship to each other as do the things which are represented."[13] Campbell defines measurement "as the assignment of numbers to represent properties." It is important to understand that by assignment of numbers is meant the numerals, not the concept of number and associated arithmetic. In the general sense of measurement, symbols such as letters could be used such as B for blue and R for red in the measurement of color. More commonly, research in science is concerned with the restricted meaning of measurement by means of numbering, counting, ranking, and arithmetic and geometric definitions.[14]

Business research is concerned with these broad areas of measurement:

1. Objects and systems of a physical nature
2. Performance characteristics of people at work

[11] Howard R. Bowen, *The Business Enterprise as a Subject for Research* (New York: Social Science Research Council, 1955), pp. 2–3.

[12] Ernest Nagel, *The Structure of Science* (New York: Harcourt, Brace & World, 1961), p. 98.

[13] Ackoff, *op. cit.*, p. 179.

[14] A large part of modern measurement in social science is based on the writings of N. R. Campbell such as *What is Science?* (New York: Dover Publications, Inc., 1952) and *An Account of the Principles of Measurement and Calculation* (New York: Longmans, Green & Company, Inc., 1928). See Aaron V. Cicourel, *Method and Measurement in Sociology* (New York: The Free Press, 1964), particularly pp. 10–38, for a concise discussion of the problems of measurement.

3. Psychological concepts

4. Social and cultural attributes (as, for example, reference groups, role-playing, ethical values)

The first type of measurement is well known from everyday use and the natural sciences. Businessmen are concerned with measurements in terms of store area, volume of packages, shipping weight, and movement of goods.

The problems of measuring such things as time required to perform tasks, ability to perform mechanical operations, ability to manage, intelligence, attitudes, and degrees of preference—to name a few—are more difficult. As for the fourth area mentioned above, it may be impossible to measure such attributes in terms of what we now define as measurements.

In order to measure things, a standard of measurement must be established. Such standards are called *scales,* and there are scales of differing qualities.

Four types of scales have been summarized by S. S. Stevens:

1. Nominal
2. Ordinal (ranking)
3. Interval
4. Ratio[15]

Nominal measurement is simply classifying like items together. Thus a single number or letter could be assigned to each male in a group and another numeral or letter could be assigned to each female. On the basis of the numeral, the individual would be assigned to one class or the other.

Ordinal scales are those which provide an ordering of some attribute. Thus one element has "more of" or "less of" something than another. In symbols, x is related to y is shown by $xRy,$ and in an ordered system $yR'x$, where R' is the complement of R. As an example, the relationship R could be "darker red" so that R' would be "lighter red." Note that there is no measure of *how much* darker red one object is than the other. There are various types of ordering from weak to strong. The relationship could represent "greater than," or, in a weaker ordering, the relationship would be stated as "greater than or equal to."

The interval scale provides units of measurement and is more useful in science than the nominal and ordinal scales. Fahrenheit temperature is such a scale. It is possible to measure in equal intervals (degrees F), but it is not possible to say that 60°F is twice as warm as 30°F. The origin and unit of measurement for such scales are selected arbitrarily and ratios of measurements have no meaning.

The ratio scale has an advantage over the interval scale in that any value on the ratio scale may be expressed as a multiple of another. The weight scale allows the representation of 10 lb of potatoes as twice the weight of 5 lb of

[15] S. S. Stevens, "Measurement, Psychophysics, and Utility," in C. W. Churchman and P. Ratoosh (eds.), *Measurement: Definitions and Theories* (New York: John Wiley & Sons, Inc., 1959), p. 25.

potatoes. Regardless of whether the units are pounds, ounces, or kilograms, this ratio holds. Other examples of interval scales are length, velocity, time, and absolute temperature.

Warren S. Torgerson proposes four types of scales: ordinal, ordinal with natural origin, interval, and interval with natural origin. The relationship among these is shown in the table.[16]

	No Natural Origin	Natural Origin
No distance	Ordinal scale	Ordinal scale with natural origin
Distance	Interval scale	Ratio scale

Although multidimensional scales are possible, the above one-dimensional scales are most significant in business research. Torgerson discusses three approaches to the measurement problem of scaling. The first is the subject-centered approach in which the reactions of subjects to stimuli are attributed to individual differences in the subjects. The purpose is to scale the subjects, as in mental testing.

The second approach is the stimulus-centered or judgment approach. The objective here is to scale the stimuli as is done in the *construction* of attitude scales. Three problems which arise are developing scales with equal intervals for measuring attitudes, accounting for intensity of feeling, and determination of error. The third approach, typefied by the Güttman technique, is the response approach in which variability of reactions is ascribed to variation in both the subjects and the stimuli.

In developing scales or measuring attributes, it is extremely important to define the attribute being measured and to use the proper dimensional scale. It is not reasonable, for example, to say that color can't be measured because one of two things is neither redder nor less red than the other and yet they are not equal in color. In this case, proper definition of color into hue, value, and intensity permits measurement of any single dimension. The same holds for attitide scales. The researcher must make sure that he is scaling a one-dimensional question; otherwise the replies will be meaningless. An illustration from a questionnaire actually used posed the question:

> If you knew the cost, and it was proven to be inexpensive, would you send out the heavy part of your laundry, such as sheets?

Since the respondent might send out heavy laundry regardless of whether it was inexpensive, a simple "yes" or "no" cannot provide an answer to this two-dimensional question.

In addition to considering the type of scale to employ, the researcher should consider the formal properties of the scale. These properties determine what

[16]Warren S. Torgerson, *Theory and Methods of Scaling* (New York: John Wiley & Sons, Inc., 1958), p. 16.

mathematical and statistical operations may be performed with the measurements.[17] Other properties such as accuracy, precision, and validity are discussed in following sections. Properties of measures of individuals must fulfill other conditions. Paul Horst states that measures of attributes of individuals must be considered in relation to the particular group being measured. These measures must satisfy the following conditions:

1. *Average level of performance.* The test of a function should not be too easy or too difficult relative to the level of performance expected of the individuals. If the function is to be performed on a job, then people who will perform well on the job should not be making scores on the test.

2. *Variation in scores.* The test instrument should be able to discriminate among individuals.

3. *Homogeneity.* This applies to measures considered to be made up of replications. The items within the test should be of the same type in that they require the same sort of response function.

4. *Objectiveness.* The method of arriving at the numerical index should lead to essential aggrement among different observers.

5. *Stability.* The measure of an individual should be consistent over a period of time.

6. *Specificity.* The attributes being measured should be independent of each other.

7. *Validity.* There must be correlation between a predictor measure and a criterion measure.[18]

In applied business research, the development of interval and ratio scales is often limited by time, cost, or complexity of relationships among attributes. General Electric, in an attempt to measure the success of each of its businesses, established key result areas:

1. Profitability
2. Market position
3. Productivity
4. Product leadership
5. Personnel development
6. Employer attitudes
7. Public responsibility
8. Balance between short-range and long range goals

It is easy to see that scales for profitability, market position, and indexes of productivity may be developed. The difficulty of developing indexes for product leadership, public responsibility, and balance between short-range and long-range

[17]Ackoff, *op. cit.* For a concise and excellent treatment, see his Chapter 6, "Measurement."

[18]Paul Horst, "The Logic of Personnel Selection and Classification," in Robert M. Gagne *et al, Psychological Principles in System Development* (New York: Holt, Rinehart and Winston, 1962), pp. 256–258.

goals is equally evident. It would be possible to define specific narrow objectives in these areas and perhaps obtain some crude kind of measure of the extent to which they are achieved. Lengthy research to develop scales in each instance for each business, scales which may constantly be subject to change, is probably not worthwhile. The "measurement" which is of most significance in this case is based on the establishment of criteria (identification of attributes) with the use of judgmental evaluation of extent to which the business performs in terms of these criteria.

Certainly such methods of measurement in business problems are useful, even if they do not fulfill the mathematical criteria established for measurement systems in the natural sciences. As with definitions, the closely related concept of measurement should serve the purpose of the investigator. Andrew L. Comrey expresses it thus:

> If numerical methods of description can be applied that aid in describing and predicting human behavior, then it is absurd to object to their use on the basis of failure to satisfy a set of conditions designed for *different context*. A practical purpose which methods are to serve must be considered. A blind struggle to satisfy a set of logical criteria may not be successful or may prove to be disappointing.[19]

RELIABILITY, PRECISION, ACCURACY, BIAS, AND VALIDITY

The business researcher, when he comes upon the terms reliability, precision, accuracy, and validity should be aware of the application and exactness of meaning which is involved. Even more important, he should understand enough about these terms and their limitations in application so that he can use them correctly. These words are used loosely or incorrectly in some instances and with very specific technical meanings in others by various authors.

Reliability and Precision

Reliability is used to describe an attribute of secondary data, of statistical experiments, of criterion data, and of models or experiments in general. Reliability as used to describe secondary data means, loosely, untrustworthiness. This is likely to be based upon some previous experience that the researcher has had with the data or knowledge about either the source of data or the medium of communication. No measure of "unreliability" is attached to this common language usage.

Reliability as used in statistics has, on the other hand, a very exact meaning. It means the ability of a technique to yield the same result if repeated under the same conditions. It is measured by the probability that data or estimates of

[19] Andrew L. Comrey, "An Operational Approach to Some Problems in Psychological Measurement," *Psychological Review* (July 1950). See also Charles E. Lee, "Measurement and the Development of Science and Marketing," *Journal of Marketing Research* (February 1965).

statistical parameters will fall within a specified range. Thus if a sample is drawn from a normal population and the mean of the sample is used to estimate the mean of the population, the means of all possible samples will fall within two standard deviations of the population mean 95.5 percent of the time. The reliability is 95.5 percent and the *precision* is the range of ± (two standard deviations) about the sample mean. If less precision is desired, then the reliability of the estimate will be higher, since it is more likely that the estimate will fall within the broader range specified. Reliability and precision are thus inversely related.

Reliability is also used with regard to the operation of systems. Such systems could vary from complicated electronic systems to management-information systems. Reliability is defined in such cases as "the probability of a successful operation of the device in the manner and under the conditions of intended customer use."[20]

The application of reliability measurement to criterion data shows four causes of failure of such data:

1. Instability inherent in the criterion performance. The performance cannot be predicted because the performance itself is erratic.
2. Disagreement among judges.
3. Entries of data by clerical personnel who perform some operation in it.
4. Inadequate sample of performance.[21]

Accuracy and Bias

Accuracy is a term applied to either a measurement or a statistical estimate based upon a sample. If measurement is taken to be a single reading or datum, then the accuracy is the difference between the reading and the "true" value being measured. The true value is rarely known and the only way it can be estimated is by averaging many measurements. Errors resulting from a single measurement may be due to:

1. Personal observation
2. Instruments which are used
3. Environment or ambient conditions
4. Method of measurement (direct or indirect)
5. Incorrect reporting and processing of data

When a sample of measurements is taken of a single attribute, there will be variability of observations. The accuracy of the sample estimate of the true value is measured by the difference between the sample estimate and the true value. Two types of errors appear in probability samples:

1. Sampling error due to the fact that the sample contains only a fraction

[20]David K. Lloyd and Myron Lipow, *Reliability: Management, Methods, and Mathematics* (Englewood Cliffs, N.J.: Prentice-Hall, Inc., 1962), p. 20.

[21]John G. Jenkins, "Validity for What?" in W. Leslie Barnette, Jr. (ed.), *Readings in Psychological Tests and Measurements* (Homewood, Ill.: Dorsey Press, 1964), pp. 157–158.

of the entire population. This is a function of the sample design. This error can be determined.

2. Nonsampling errors due to the five causes cited above for a single measurement. These are of unknown magnitude, so that great effort should be expended to minimize the upper bounds of such errors.

If a number of probability samples of a specified size were taken, the mean of each sample is an estimate of the population mean of the attribute value. The "expected value," or average value, of all such estimates should be equal to the population mean. The amount that the expected value of the sample means differs from the population mean is termed the *bias*.

Both accuracy and bias are often used in a nonstatistical sense which leads to some confusion. A measurement such as 97.2 is said to be accurate to three significant figures. Thus the number of digits in a *properly rounded-off* number indicates the accuracy of the number. Accuracy is a term also applied to the result of manipulating or processing such numbers. If the processing is error-free, it is said to be accurate. If errors are made, it is said to be "approximately accurate" or "inaccurate." Obviously, descriptions of inaccuracy are vague.

The "bias" of the researcher or of participants in an experiment or survey often means preconceived attitudes or prejudices. The two instances can be quite different. Bias of the researcher can influence the results of the research improperly. In measuring attitudes or opinions, this so-called bias may be just what the researcher is attempting to check on.

Bias and accuracy are often confused when referring to measuring instruments. If the instrument requires calibration, it is sometimes said to be "inaccurate" when actually it provides a biased sample of readings.

Validity

In a very general sense, information is said to be valid if it represents what it is reported to represent. It is a statement which is "defensible" or "strong." Validity is a term applied to:

1. *Deduction.* In logic, a deduction or conclusion is said to be valid if a set of premises are accepted, then the conclusion drawn from these premises must be accepted. Under the rules of logic, there must be an internal consistency among assertions.

2. *Content, data, source, or observation.* Validity in such cases simply is a question of meaning of the face value of data. Do the words, data, or observations, as given, actually represent what they are stated or implied to represent?

3. *Measurement.* Often measurements are stated as representing one attribute, but actually include several. In measuring a consumer's preference for a product, the researcher may actually be measuring preference for the packaging or the manufacturer, or status associated with use of the product. Even in physical measurements, a somewhat similar situation may occur. A manufacturer may measure paper from his mills and sell it by the pound. If humidity is not carefully controlled or a correction made to his measurement of weight, he may

be selling a significant amount of water which is represented as the weight of paper. Validity of measurement must be concerned with both the validity of the measuring instrument and of the procedure employing the instrument.

4. *Construct.* A construct is an abstract attribute rather than a physical one, and therefore it is connected by definitions and propositions to real-world observable things. Intelligence, aspiration level, attitudes, and group cohesion are examples of constructs. A construct is said to be valid if measurements on the construct are related to measurements on other constructs and empirical events in a manner which yields logically consistent statements of relationships and/or useful predictions. Construct validity must be concerned with both the measuring instrument and the theory underlying the construct.

The question of what constitutes validity in measuring psychological and social constructs is not entirely clear. It is true, however, that companies and business researchers all over the country are busily mailing out questionnaires presuming to measure abstractions without too much thought concerning the validity of measurement or application. What Robert L. Ebel points out with regard to the validity of psychological tests can readily be extrapolated to many types of measurements commonly used in business research.[22] He brings together various definitions of experts as to what constitutes validity of mental tests which are incorporated in the following list:

1. The validity of a test is its correlation with some criterion. (A criterion of intelligence, for example, could be the judgments of a group of trained observers.)
2. Validity is the correlation between raw test scores and "true" or perfectly reliable test measures.
3. Validity is the accuracy with which a test measures what it is supposed to measure.
4. Pragmatic validity is the extent to which the device is useful for a given purpose. In other words, if a test works, it is valid. There are two applications of pragmatic validity as follows:
   (a) *Concurrent validity.* If a test measures the difference between two presently existing attributes, it has concurrent validity.
   (b) *Predictive validity.* This is applied to the capability of a test to distinguish among behavior of individuals in the future.
5. The more fully and confidently a test can be interpreted, the greater its validity.
6. *Face validity or empirical validity.* Measures which are applied directly to the phenomenon or behavior in which the researcher is interested are said to have face validity. As Claire Selltiz points out, two major questions must be considered: (1) Is the instrument really measuring the kind

[22] Robert L. Ebel, "Must All Tests be Valid?," in W. Leslie Barnette, Jr. (ed.), *Readings in Psychological Tests and Measurements* (Homewood, Ill.: Dorsey Press, 1964), p. 234.

of behavior that the investigator assumes it is, and (2) does it provide an adequate sample of that kind of behavior?[23]

It is apparent that the problem of establishing validity is a difficult one in much social science research and hence business research. Even a definition of validity which would encompass the various meanings given by experts would have to be so broad and general as to be useless. The concept of validity with respect to social and psychological attributes implies a belief in (1) the existence of quantifiable human characteristics which (2) have values which exist long enough to have practical significance. Further, criteria which are used to validate such measurements are usually based upon ratings obtained from direct observation. The criteria are less accurate than the measurements are presumed to be.

One controversial solution to the problem is to avoid the need for establishing validity of a measure. Instead of being concerned with defining a construct such as intelligence and devising means for measuring it, the researcher develops a test and defines intelligence as the score obtained on the test by the person tested. The criticism of this approach is that there is no basis for relating one construct to another in the development of a theory.

It is interesting to note that researchers in the natural sciences are not concerned over the validity of their measurements. They *are* concerned with validity of their hypotheses and models, however. John L. Finan suggests a distinction between basic research and applied research in physical science. Perhaps this idea could be extrapolated to the behavioral aspects of business research.

> The term *validity* refers to the degree of correspondence of a model to germane observations. To the extent to which it can be demonstrated to be homologous with observation, a model is valid for the purpose of establishing scientific laws. . . .
>
> To distinguish validity as a concept appropriately applied only to theoretical research from its counterpart in engineering, we have somewhat arbitrarily labeled the latter *fidelity*. The sufficient condition which defines fidelity is that a given variable permits us to forecast a second, critical variable to the extent required by the problem at hand.[24]

5. *Model.* A model is said to be valid if it truly represents the set of relationships or system for which it is designed.

6. *Experiment.* Validity of an experiment may be divided into two types: *internal* validity and *external* validity. The experiment is internally valid if it permits prediction in the situation in which it took place. This means that all

[23]Claire Selltiz *et al*, *Research Methods in Social Relations* (New York: Holt, Rinehart and Winston, 1962), p. 165.
[24]John L. Finan, "The System Concept as a Principle of Methodological Decision," in Robert M. Gagne (ed.), *Psychological Principles in System Development* (New York: Holt, Rinehart and Winston, 1962), p. 532.

relevant variables have been segregated into either controlled variables or randomized variables in the design of the experiment.

External validity means that the experimental results apply to some defined population or situation outside of the limited situation in which the experiment was conducted. If a population is defined and a sample drawn by accepted probability methods, the estimate obtained from the sample would have external validity, if nonsampling errors were controlled.

NORMS, STANDARDS, CRITERIA, AND OBJECTIVES

The terms *norm, standard, objective,* and *criterion* are sometimes misused because of confusion as to the distinctions among them. Some times, however, several of these may in practice designate the same thing. It is this coincidental overlapping that leads to the failure of researchers to recognize fundamental differences in the concepts.

Norms are those measurements of attributes which represent the average or typical group. Norms are not standards, goals, or objectives, but rather reference points indicating the typical performance for a specified group of people. If norms were used as standards or objectives, the result would be to encourage mediocrity or continuously declining performance. "Performance" has been used in two slightly different senses here. In one case, performance is attainment of scores on devices such as tests used to measure attributes of individuals. In this instance, performance relates to behavior of people in their everyday life. In each case, however, the norm means the typical behavior or "that which is the rule." Since the population changes constantly with time, it would be expected that there is no invariant norm.

Whereas standards and objectives state what "should be," norms state "what is" and only coincidentally do norms describe what should be in cases where individuals know the norms and use them to prescribe their own behavior. As Kaufmann explains it,

> A norm is a maxim that governs the behavior of the person who seeks to comply with it. However, for the person who appraises behavior in terms of the norm, it is a criterion for the correctness of this behavior. In other words, it is for him a definition, or part of a definition, of correct behavior of a particular type.[25]

Since business research is concerned with studies of both physical entities and people, a broad meaning of "standard" will serve as the starting point for differentiating this term from the other. H. W. Robb of General Electric has stated:

> Standardization is the organized solution of common problems, and standards are the records of such solutions to avoid waste of creative effort in the repetitive consideration of the same problems.

[25]Felix Kaufmann, *Methodology of the Social Sciences* (New York: Humanities Press, Inc., 1958), p. 49.

A standard is the means by which measurement may be made possible. A standard can apply to a process, an object, or an abstract concept (such as time). Once a standard, such as length of one foot, has been established, there is no need to repeat the problem of developing a unit of length for future measurements. Once a standard product has been designed, thousands may be produced without redesigning each one. When a standard of work output per day has been established, the standard provides a means of measuring the output of individual workers. Standards represent arbitrary solutions in the case of the physical sciences and in the behavioral sciences, standards represent human judgments of performance or behavior which should be attained. A standard set above the norm is sometimes called a "high standard" and one set below the norm is called a "low standard."

The business researcher who is concerned with physical standards such as are the subject matter of quality control and packaging should become aware of the services of the American Standards Association and the National Bureau of Standards as well as industry standards established by appropriate industry associations.

Standards may be established by authority, custom, or general consent. Legal weights and volume standards, labeling requirements, or minimum quality established by law are examples of standards based upon authority. The baker's dozen and discount for cash payments to the manufacturer are established by custom. Standards set by trade associations, psychological testing groups, and the American Standards Association are adopted by general consent of the members of the group or of industry.

"Criterion" is closely related to "standard." While a standard is a generally accepted measurement or process, a criterion may be established by anyone on an *ad hoc* basis; a criterion may be used but once or it may become generally accepted and become a standard. A criterion is arbitrary; it is any rule or test used for judging or evaluating. In social science, the beginning of measurement is the formulation of a criterion for possession of an attribute and the separation of those who possess the attribute (possess it in a high degree) from those who don't possess the attribute (possess it in a low degree).

The two basic uses of criteria are:

1. To compare alternate attributes, processes, or courses of action and to appraise a single attribute, process, or course of action.

2. To use criteria as the objective and then "research" or develop a process, system, or set of inputs which will lead to meeting the criteria. This working backward from a specified output to a set of generating conditions is a common type of applied research problem.

It was noted that criteria sometimes serve as objectives as well as measures for evaluation. Objectives are by definition objects or ends to be obtained and not primarily measurement devices. An objective is considered the end of action, as for example, the objective of the research project. While a goal is sometimes considered to be an objective, a fine distinction is that goals are intermediate or short-range ends to be attained on the way to attaining the final goal, the objective. Ackoff states, "In purposive behavior the alternative courses of action are frequently called *means* and the common property of the outcome is called an *end* or *objectives*."[26] Ackoff distinguishes between qualitative *objectives* and *quantitative* objectives. A qualitative objective is an outcome of a choice of course of action which is specified as either successful or not successful. A qualitative objective is thus described as one of only two possible numbers or events. A quantitative objective is achieved in various degrees; it is a set of outcomes differentiated from each other by values along a specified scale.

Objectives may be either tangible or intangible. A tangible objective may be the construction of a new store, factory, or warehouse. It could be the development and design of a new line of products. An intangible objective might be the achievement of a certain market position or establishment of a brand image.

SETS, VARIABLES, PARAMETERS, CONSTANTS, AND FUNCTIONS

In research, it is often necessary to employ symbols which represent numbers or to refer to the nature of some number or group of numbers involved in relationships. The mathematical meaning of "set" is essentially the same as the everyday meaning: A set is a collection or aggregate of objects of any kind such as people, products, points, numbers, or companies. In logic and mathematics, and hence occasionally in research, the usefulness of sets is derived from rules of working with sets to make deductions.

A variable is simply a symbol which represents a quantity or a set of numbers. Variables are referred to as *independent variables* if their values are given, or are exogenous, arbitrarily chosen, or believed to influence a second variable of interest. The "dependent variable" is a variable whose value depends upon the value of the independent variable according to some rule, functional relationship, or probabilistic relationship. Independent variables are sometimes called *decision variables* if they may be assigned values at the discretion of the decision maker, and *exogenous variables* if they are uncontrollable variables representing inputs to the particular analysis being conducted.

Parameters are often confused with variables and constants since all are often represented by symbols. Sometimes parameters are defined as the constraints of the system; they are the quantities whose values are limited in range by their nature. They may be either controllable or they may be noncontrollable and determined by nature. Parameters are symbols whose values remained fixed over the analysis of a given problem. The problem is solved, however, for each of a set of values of the parameter in order to obtain a possible range of solutions. The constant differs from the parameter in that the value of the constant stays fixed once it is determined for a problem set.

A function is a statement of the relationship between the dependent vari-

---

[26]Russell L. Ackoff *et al., Scientific Method, Optimizing Applied Research Decisions* (New York: John Wiley & Sons, Inc., 1962), p. 159.

able and the independent variable which involves constants and/or parameters. If for each value of the independent variable X there is one value of the dependent variable Y, then Y is a single-valued function of X. In terms of set nomenclature, a function is a rule that relates each element of a set called the domain to one and only one element of another set called the range.

ASSUMPTIONS, AXIOMS, POSTULATES, AND PREMISES

The terms *assumption, axiom, postulate,* and *premise* have been used interchangeably by various writers, and yet some writers have made careful distinctions between them at times. A triple identification is given by "The laws that serve as the premises of these deductions are called the axioms of the theory; those which appear as conclusions are called its theorems."[27] Ernest Nagel uses *axiom* and *postulate* interchangeably. The following eclectic definitions are suggested:

Assumption. In formal noninterpreted (no connection with the real world) systems, an assumption is a selected proposition, usually one of a set, put forth as the basis of a deductive system. In interpreted (empirical) systems, an assumption is a proposition which seems to be a plausible description of a real-world condition and is stipulated for the purpose of development of a theory.

Axiom. An axiom is a primitive statement or "convention" in formal deductive systems, or a "self-evident" proposition in an empirical science.

Postulate. A postulate is the stipulation of a proposition, similar to an axiom but not necessarily one of the fundamental set of propositions of the system.

Premise. A premise is any statement forming part of a proof which contains some of the evidence from which the conclusion of the proof is derived.

Manley Howe Jones has written a widely accepted book on decision making which develops an extended definition of premise. His concept is worth noting. It would be difficult to distinguish between his *premise* and the concept of hypothesis except in terms of palatibility to a business practitioner:

> A premise is a statement containing a description of both a cause and a result which we deem pertinent to the alternative we are examining. . . . A premise is really composed of three elements: a cause, a *result and* the *causal connection* which we believe exists between the cause and result.[28]

In logic, the syllogism consists of a *major premise,* a universal statement which indeterminately contains the conclusion, and a *minor premise* which applies to the major premise in order to determine the conclusion.

[27]Gustav Bergmann, *Philosophy of Science* (Madison, Wis.: University of Wisconsin Press, 1957), as cited in Paul H. Rigby, *Conceptual Foundations of Business Research* (New York: John Wiley & Sons, Inc., 1965), p. 31.
[28]Reprinted with permission from Manley Howe Jones, *Executive Decision Making* (Homewood, Ill.: Richard D. Irwin, Inc., 1957), p. 57.

CONCEPTS AND CONSTRUCTS

Concepts and constructs have been discussed in Chapter 1 where their importance to theory development was brought out. With the current emphasis on the development of graphic and mathematical models to represent a higher level of concepts, an understanding of these basic building blocks of science by both researchers and businessmen has become essential.

Concepts are creations of the mind which represent meanings. "Concepts are logical constructs created from sense impressions, percepts or even fairly complex experiences. The tendency to assume that concepts actually exist as phenomena leads to many errors. The concept is not the phenomena itself. . ."[29]

Since phenomena and concepts are distinct, concepts must be defined for the purpose of communication. Concepts are therefore related at the first or lowest level to meanings of phenomena. Concepts at higher levels are defined in terms of lower-level concepts. "The really crucial problem of human behavior apparently is that of forming complex concepts which in turn require *abstraction*. Abstraction utilizes higher order conditioning as applied to concept formation, in which successive levels of concepts are further removed from the original sensory base."[30]

Concept formation starts with observing and noting similarities and differences among discrete stimuli. Concepts are created in the mind to distinguish among groups or categories whose elements have common properties. This requires the abstracting of a common property of a group of objects, processes, events, or situations.[31]

In business research, formation of a concept is a necessary early step to provide means for guiding the research. From the problem symptoms the concept of the problem must be developed. Concepts of solutions in terms of observations, processes, environment, and potentialities must be formulated. Such concepts require creativity if acquired concepts are not to dominate new concept formation. Concepts of solutions serve to guide the researcher further in developing his research methods and organizing and analyzing his observations.

ANALYSIS

While the fundamental bases for the search for truth in the empirical sciences are experiments and statistical sampling, much research in business is founded upon observation and recorded source material. Raw data is usually

---

[29]William J. Goode and Paul K. Hatt, *Methods in Social Research* (New York: McGraw-Hill Book Company, Inc., 1952), p. 43.

[30]Reprinted with permission from Alfred Kuhn, *The Study of Society, A Unified Approach* (Homewood, Ill.: Richard D. Irwin, Inc., 1963), p. 126.

[31]For a further discussion, see T. S. Kendler, "Concept Formation" in *Annual Review of Psychology* (1961), p. 447, and Paul H. Rigby, *Conceptual Foundations of Business Research* (New York: John Wiley & Sons, Inc., 1965), pp. 12–36.

vague and meaningless until it has been analyzed. Analysis consits of breaking the information down into component parts so that it may be presented in a meaningful way. For this reason, analysis often appears in the form of a structured description, an outline, a listing, or a table. Analysis thus specifies clearly what is only known or perceived as a confused whole. Analysis lays bare the relationships among processes, form, and structure. Analysis seeks similarities, differences, and connections. Robert T. Livingston states:

> Analysis is purposive. It is not done for its own sake but rather to
> 1. Discover or isolate fundamental internal functions
> 2. Explore their relationships
>   (a) External
>   (b) Mutual
>   (c) Internal
> 3. Act as a precedent to synthesis[32]

The third objective could be modified to include the statement that analysis may also be followed by interpretation of data to yield greater generality or extend the range of concepts. Selltiz *et al.* state that analysis and interpretation are inextricably interwoven. This discusses the following steps in analysis and interpretation:

> 1. Establishment of categories
> 2. Application of categories to the raw data through coding (assigning on observation or response to a particular category)
> 3. Tabulation of responses
> 4. Statistical analysis of data
> 5. Drawing inferences about causal data
> 6. Use of nonquantified data[33]

Carter Good and Douglas Scates describe analysis in terms of questions to be asked in the inward process of discovering the nature of things:

> 1. Of what are they composed?
> 2. What is their structure?
> 3. What are the substructures or the special organizations that occur here and there as units within the larger structure?
> 4. How are all these individual parts and unit assemblies or organs integrated into an internal system?
> 5. What are the forces that hold them together, and the strains that tend to tear the system apart?
> 6. 'What makes the system work?
> 7. How is it regulated?

---

[32]Robert T. Livingston, *The Engineering of Organization and Management* (New York: McGraw-Hill Book Company, Inc., 1949), p. 135.

[33]Claire Selltiz *et al, Research Methods in Social Relations* (New York: Holt, Rinehart and Winston, 1962), p. 391.

8. From the point of view of continuing research, what new questions are brought to light by analytical work which will serve as guides for further research?[34]

Henry S. Leonard lists analysis among the four primary valid grounds for belief—observation, actualization (bringing about a state of affairs to permit observation), analysis, and inference. Analysis is drawing out the answer from the present situation or problem; no previous information or no observation is required. Inference and analysis are the two modes of reason and are distinct. Inference is a more specific of formalized method of interpretation in that it is based upon rules of logic.[35]

It appears from the above discussion that analysis must be an ingredient of research. It is a necessary step in transforming raw data into meaningful form in order to draw conclusions.

HYPOTHESES, THEORIES, LAWS, AND PRINCIPLES

In Chapter 1, theories and types of propositions were discussed in regard to the fundamental building blocks of science. Since the development of theory is a central objective of science, the nature of theory will be further elaborated on here by the presentation of two additional views.

Sherman Krupp gives a more holistic definition of theory which is useful in understanding the implications of theory.

> We will take theory to mean several related things. It is a way of explaining observations, but it also suggests and channels us to these observations. It is a method of simplifying so that implications may be drawn. Theories are not always formulated into clear and developed systems, nor are they neatly arranged for scrutiny. They are usually informally arranged. The empiricist, for example, creates theory while he believes himself merely to be reporting data; he is a theorist in the way he orders his observations.[36]

Carl Hempel considers a scientific theory as consisting of a set of sentences expressed in terms of a specific vocabulary. The vocabulary consists of terms outside the language of logic, so that many of the terms are defined by means of others. The only way that circularity can be avoided is to have (1) *primitive* terms for which no definition is specified and (2) *defined* terms. Similarly for sentences—they fall into two groups: primitive sentences or postulates or axioms, and derivative sentences or theorems. Hempel adds, "The theory will always be thought of formulated within a linguistic framework of a clearly

---

[34]Carter V. Good and Douglas E. Scates, *Methods of Research* (New York: Appleton-Century-Crofts, 1954), pp. 283–284.
[35]Henry S. Leonard, *Principles of Right Reason* (New York: Henry Holt & Co., Inc., 1957), p. 64.
[36]Sherman Krupp, *Pattern in Organization Analysis* (New York: Holt, Rinehart and Winston, 1961), p. 54.

specified logical structure, which determines, in particular, the rules of deductive inference."[37]

MODELS

The purpose of models in the development of theory is (1) to define and delimit the fundamental assumptions of the theory, (2) to relate (in some instances) abstract concepts to more familiar elements and properties, (3) to substitute for costly experimentation the manipulation of the model and its parameters, and (4) to provide a source of ideas for extending the scope and application of the theory. Models are used in *applied* research and problem solving (1) to define and limit the description of the problem, (2) to develop solutions for various values of the parameters, and (3) to suggest modified and more refined models for future similar problems. The researcher is concerned with four aspects of models: (1) their development, (2) the derivation of solutions, (3) the testing of the model in terms of the real world, and (4) establishing control over the model to determine when the model must be revised.

The closeness of meaning of model and theory is indicated by Krupp:

> Mainly there will be little need to separate a theory from a model. We will normally use the two words interchangeably. However, the formal differences between a theory and a model suggest a way for examining the structure of a theory. Accordingly, a model is a highly formalized theory, a particularized body of propositions selected from a theory, one interpretation of a theory. A model is a construction, a design, an heuristic device to order, explain, predict, or control a particular segment of reality.[38]

The various classifications of models indicate the characteristics of models which are significant to the researcher.

Classification I

1. *Iconic* models retain some of the physical characteristics of the things they represent. Scaled mock-ups and representative drawings are examples.

2. *Analog* models are based on the substitution of one property for another or one process for another. Thus an electrical system could parallel a production flow system, colors could be used to identify different projects on a scheduling board, or a water channel system could represent a traffic flow pattern. Block diagrams are a particularly useful analog form.

3. *Symbolic* models substitute symbols, usually mathematical or logical in character, for the variables in the system.

---

[37]Carl G. Hempel, *Aspects of Scientific Explanation and Other Essays in the Philosophy of Science* (New York: The Free Press, 1965), pp. 182–183.

[38]Sherman Krupp, *Pattern in Organization Analysis* (New York: Holt, Rinehart and Winston, 1961), p. 54.

Classification II

1. *Static* models demonstrate relationships under the assumption that they are not changing with time. Models of plant layouts, flow charts, or mathematical relationships between two variables of marketing are examples.

2. *Dynamic* models are those in which time is an independent variable. They represent changes in conditions over a period of time. As an example, a sales response to advertising model may allow the research to try out constant advertising input, pulses of advertising, or an intensive one-shot advertising campaign for comparison.

Classification III

1. *Deterministic* models are those in which a given input will lead invariably to the same solution. Deterministic models describe an environment in which relationships among variables are "mechanically" related and decisions can be made with certainty as to the consequences. "A deterministic decision structure (decision structure under certainty) has the property that the adoption of a particular policy (choice of a set of values) for the decision variables is either known to lead—or assumed to lead—invariably to one specific outcome and value of the objective function."[39]

2. *Probabilistic* models are statistically based models which deal with decision making under conditions of risk. The outcomes of actions cannot be stated with certainty, only with a probability of occurrence.

3. *Game theory* models treat decision making under conditions of uncertainty. The likelihood of possible outcomes of actions is unknown.

Classification IV

1. *Theory* models, also characterized as descriptive, predictive, positive, or phenomenological models. These models are generalizations of the behavior of phenomena and represent laws and theories.

2. *Decision* or normative models. These models are based upon two types of inputs or independent variables: (1) those which appear as natural exogenous variables beyond the control of the decision maker, and (2) those subject to determination by the decision maker. The purpose of such models is to inform the decision maker of the consequences of various alternatives and to guide him in selecting an optimum.

SUMMARY

This chapter has discussed the meanings of a variety of concepts which appear in the literature of business and social science research. Views of scholars have been presented to show points of divergence and problems of explanation. The purpose of presenting such a set of concepts is to encourage the reader to

---

[39]Charles R. Carr and Charles W. Howe, *Quantitative Decision Procedures in Management and Economics* (New York: McGraw Hill Book Company, Inc., 1964), p. 9.

give more attention to the basic concepts which he himself uses in his research so that his thinking and explanations will be sharpened.

QUESTIONS AND TOPICS FOR DISCUSSION

1. How would you distinguish between terms in a research report which require explicit definition and those for which implicit definition might be permissable?

2. Select a word in your field of interest and see how many different, as well as conflicting, definitions you can find in the literature. Define the word yourself.

3. Would a technical dictionary of business terms be valuable, or would it hinder the development of the scientific aspects of business?

4. Since any empirical science must be based on real-world events, should a "name" such as "fact" or "observation" be assigned to such phenonema? Could you define such real-world events on an interpersonal basis?

5. Are words and concepts the same thing? Why or why not?

6. Is there any relevance of the type of definition used to the purpose of the researcher?

7. Select a journal article and try to find an example of as many as you can of the ten types of definitions which Henry Leonard categorizes.

8. Select a recent report of your own. Can you find technical words whose meanings are ambiguous or vague and which you have not defined?

9. Do you think the "contextual" type of definition is a good means for advancing social sciences?

10. Give an example of a nominal, ordinal, interval, and ratio scale which a business manager or researcher might have occasion to use.

11. Give an example of each of four of the broad areas of measurement of concern to businessmen. Can you think of any which the author has omitted?

12. What are the conditions that measures of attributes of individuals must satisfy?

13. Ackoff, in his book cited in this chapter, writes, "The four critical properties of relations that are significant from the point of view of measurement are *reflexivity, symmetry, transitivity,* and *connectivity.*" What does he mean by each of these terms? Can you think of any measurements made by businesses, such as in sample survey work, which do not meet these criteria?

14. Can you list any different ways in which *reliability* is used than those given in the text?

15. What is meant by *precision of measurement?*

16. How would you interpret "reliable employee," "reliable test of mechanical aptitude," "reliable information," and "reliable information system"?

17. If numerical data are being manipulated and processed, is the final answer apt to be as accurate as, less accurate than, or more accurate than the input data?

18. Is bias in the determination of consumers' preferences likely to occur because of consumers' prejudices, the selection of the sample of consumers questioned, or both?

19. Five reasons for errors resulting from a single measurement are given in the text. Can you think of any which have been omitted?

20. With so many meanings or concepts associated with the term *validity,* can this term ever be used meaningfully without classification? Compose a list of labels and definitions for all concepts of validity which you can think of.

21. Distinguish between a norm and a standard of job performance in a manufacturing plant, using a specific example to illustrate.

22. Distinguish between a standard and a criterion of good job performance in a manufacturing plant, using a specific example to illustrate.

23. Are company objectives and accepted standards of achievement the same?

24. Select a mathematical model of a business problem in a journal article and identify examples and "sets" if given, and examples of parameters, constants, and functions.

25. Select a journal article. Does the author state his assumptions, postulates, and premises explicitly? Give an example of an *implicit* assumption, preferably one that might not be evident to most readers.

26. A common term in the literature is *conceptual framework.* How would you interpret this?

27. Besides the claim that this is the Age of Synthesis, it also appears that is is the Age of Models. Are these statements inconsistent? Has analysis any part of either of these "Ages," and if so, what?

28. What would a "theory of management" consist of? How would a "theory of the firm" be structured? A "theory of business"? Would or should such theories be identical if they are directed toward helping understand what business managers *should* be doing?

chapter 4

Types of Inquiry in Business Research

INTRODUCTION

The unifying purpose of all research is to discover answers to questions raised by scientists and decision makers. For these people, the classification of types of inquiry is irrelevant; the inquiry is determined by the problem. The business scientist, who resides almost exclusively in the university, is well aware of the gaps in his field and the needs for new knowledge at the frontiers. The decision maker always operates in an environment of inadequate knowledge so that his problem is one of allocating his limited resources to problems whose priority he establishes.

There is another large group of researchers whose problems are quite different. This group consists of the neophytes in the universities who are assigned the task of conducting research for a course, a thesis, or a "dissertation." Quite commonly, these students do not have a "problem" and they are not certain what "research" means. Frequently their approach is to take some broad topic such as "business organization," read about it, and then write an organized description of some sort. The nonpurposive essay on textbook material is the mistaken substitute for research.

For those assigned to "do research," their first question might well be, "What constitutes research?" If they know the answer to this question, they can recognize a problem situation or an inquiry which calls for research. This chapter is written for these people in search of a problem.

Business research may be concerned with answering questions about relationships among variables, about complex historical trends, about economic institutions, about specific business problems, about research methodology, and about needs for research. Thus hypothesis testing is not the only purpose of research. There are many other purposes for orderly and systematic investigation which contribute to the fund of business knowledge and theory and lead to answers to operational business questions. This viewpoint is shared by other social science research practitioners. For example, several authorities state:

> Each study, of course, has its own specific purpose. But we may think of research purposes as falling into a number of broad groupings:

(1) to gain familiarity with a phenomenon or to achieve new insights into it, often in order to formulate a more precise research problem or to develop hypotheses; (2) to portray accurately the characteristics of a particular individual, situation, or group with or without specific initial hypotheses about the nature of these characteristics; (3) to determine the frequency with which something occurs or with which it is associated with something else (usually, but not always, with a special initial hypothesis); (4) to test a hypothesis of a causal relationship between variables.[1]

Thus there are a number of investigative purposes which require logical and evaluative methods, not necessarily quantitative in nature. The would-be investigator who has a potential topic may be able to examine a list of such purposes and determine whether his project qualifies as research within the broad framework of investigation characteristic of business research in its present stage of development.

BASIC BUSINESS RESEARCH CLASSIFIED BY PURPOSE

Since the business researcher should be goal-oriented rather than method-oriented, the classification of business research by general purpose will be presented here. The methods which may be employed to achieve the purposes are many. The researcher may be apt to develop a better and more original method if he is concerned with his goals rather than with application of a traditional sterotyped research method. The types of research discussed below are concerned with theory development. In some cases, analogous goals are sought for applied research.

"Needs" Research

In the development of a theory of the firm or a theory of management of business enterprises, researchers have usually selected problems of interest in their own particular specialized area of knowledge. Before a general theory can be developed, exploratory study should be undertaken to determine what the theory ought to encompass. If the construction of theory has already been developed by bits and pieces, there is a need to appraise what has been done and investigate what needs to be done.

A need is a lack, or a want, demand, or desire on the part of theory builders which initiates or triggers the problem-solving sequence. The satisfaction of the need is the end or goal of the research.

"Needs" research in theory formulation has as its purpose the definition of needs in terms of data, concepts, and relationships for advancement of the theory as a whole. In addition, needs research must direct investigators by giving

---

[1]Claire Selltiz et al., *Research Methods in Social Relations* (New York: Holt, Rinehart and Winston, 1962), p. 50.

priorities to problems whose solutions are needed. It is quite possible that, as in the physical sciences, there is some critical problem whose lack of solution is impeding progress on a wide scale.

An interesting example, if not the only one, of attempting to describe the present state of a number of fields related to business is Rollo Handy and Paul Kurtz's *A Current Appraisal of the Behavioral Sciences* (Behavioral Research Council, Great Barrington, Mass., 1963). For each field the authors present a working definition; other specifications of the field; schools, methods, and techniques; results achieved; contemporary controversy; problems of terminology; and comment and evaluation. The confusion, controversy, and problems described in the related business fields of economics, sociology, psychology, political science, and decision theory will serve to suggest needed research for years to come. This small volume is not, however, encyclopedic in scope, so that further needs research is required to delineate more specifically the major problems and their priorities.

Another analytical and taxonomic inquiry into basic research needs deals with the development of a prescriptive theory of business planning. The authors state:

> The purpose of this paper is to outline a program of research which is needed to improve the state of the art of business planning. We have approached this task by relating planning to management science on one hand, and to certain areas of descriptive knowledge on the other. From these relations we have constructed a comprehensive program for research on planning.[2]

Much needs research is based upon opinion and provides conclusions which are so general as to provide little guidance to those who wish to select pressing problems for investigation. For example, one author states:

> The development of a systematic normative theory will require distinct conscious effort in the following directions:
> 1. The formulation of goals. . . .
> 2. We need to formulate decision rules running from the goals, as defined to every nook and cranny of the firm. . . .
> 3. We need to test such rules for workability in living situations or simulations thereof. . . .
> 4. We need to make the results of such tests generally available by publishing them in appropriate learned journals.[3]

Without doubt there are more problems in construction of a theory of business and management than can be listed. The needs questions that research

[2]H. Igor Ansoff and Richard C. Brandenburg, "A Program of Research in Business Planning," *Management Science* (February 1967), p. B219.
[3]Avery B. Cohan, "The Theory of the Firm: A View of Methodology," *Journal of Business* (July 1963), pp. 222–223.

can answer are: What is the structure of the theory to be developed? What are the critical problems? What are some of the smaller, less critical problems whose solutions would fill in gaps in the theory?

Descriptive Research

A distinction needs to be made between "reporting" and descriptive research. Government agencies typically gather data and publish it without evaluation, analysis, or prediction. A number of business and trade publications perform similar tasks in gathering marketing data, labor data, and technical data. Descriptive research is distinguished from reporting because it goes beyond mere presentation of facts. The business researcher seeks to deduce patterns which explain why, how, or when. He may gather such data for purposes of generalization or specific prediction. He may gather such data for purpose of developing hypotheses. Descriptive research may involve gathering data to refute or lend more credence to hypotheses which are not easily tested in rigorous fashion.

Descriptive research is probably most common to sciences and portions of scientific knowledge which are quite undeveloped. The emphasis at this stage is on the gathering of data without much advance knowledge of where it will lead. The gathering of data is directed by priorities of needs-to-know about specific aspects of the field. The early development of marketing theory provides an excellent example of descriptive research. Around 1900 there began to be some slight conceptualization of marketing processes, but there was a tremendous dearth of factual knowledge. In 1912 C. S. Parlin visited all cities of over 50,000 population to estimate the volume of business done in department stores, wholesale dry-goods establishments, and merchant tailoring operations. On the basis of this data, Parlin contributed the concept of "convenience goods, emergency goods, and shopping goods." In later fact-finding studies he provided analysis and recommendations for successful lines and prices.

The above form of descriptive research is analogous to prospecting in new territory. The prospector does not know in advance exactly what he will find, but when he does find something he must evaluate it and seek an application.

The gathering of data for the purpose of uncovering and describing patterns is characteristic of functionalism. "Functionalism is that approach to science which begins by identifying some system of action, and then tries to determine how and why it works as it does."[4] In marketing, much effort has been devoted to gathering data for taxonomic purposes of system development. It is by means of classification (description plus conceptualization) that the parts of the system may be identified. While functionalism goes far beyond classification of knowledge of individual events, just as chemistry goes far beyond such research outcomes as the periodic table, description and classification represent the first research efforts. As F. M. Nicosia points out, there has been a shift from efforts

---

to pinpoint *properties of individual entities* to properties stemming from the modes by which entities mutually relate, i.e., *properties of systems.*[5]

When fact gathering is guided by theory rather than the need to prospect, its purposes are specific and the purpose of the research falls under one of the other categories which follow:

If the development of a science is considered to progress in stages (usually overlapping), then descriptive research falls into an early stage. F. S. C. Northrup expounds upon this theme of stages in the development of a science after stating:

> Thus inquiry, as it proceeds, exhibits at least three major stages: (1) the analysis of the problem which initiates inquiry, (2) the Baconian inductive observation of the relevant facts to which the analysis of the problem leads one, and (3) the designation of relevant facts.[6] The important thing to note is that the second stage of inquiry begins with immediately apprehended fact and ends with desired fact. Facts in these two senses must not be confused. Only fact in the former sense is fact independent of all concepts and theory.[7]

A fascinating and continuing descriptive research project is the study of the interindustry structure of the United States. Originally conceived and developed by Wassily W. Leontief of Harvard University, this matrix description of the buying and selling of goods among industries may lead to valuable practical and theoretical results.[8] As classifications are improved and as data are obtained and improved over a period of years, many insight may be gained leading to hypotheses to be tested.

Another interesting descriptive research project covered the philosophies and creeds of large business enterprises.[9] The background of the study was a review of the changing environment of business, corporate power, and the need for a philosophy of management. The researcher collected and analyzed published statements of corporate heads and wrote many corporate presidents directly. The results of such research could suggest many hypotheses and provide a starting point for much more research.

Exploratory Study for Uncovering Hypotheses

Often the researcher observes two events occurring in close relationship or sequence to each other, formulates a hypothesis of cause and effect, and then proceeds to test it. In the complex social environment, the speculative formation

---

[5] F. M. Nicosia, "Marketing and Alderson's Functionalism," *Journal of Business* (October 1962), p. 403.

[6] F. S. C. Northrup, *The Logic of the Sciences and Humanities* (Cleveland: The World Publishing Co., copyrighted by Macmillan, New York, 1947), p. 29.

[7] *Ibid.*, p. 35.

[8] For a report of input-output, see U.S. Department of Commerce, *Survey of Current Business* (November 1964).

[9] Owen C. Sweeney, "The Philosophies of Large Business Enterprises" (unpublished research report, State University of New York at Albany, School of Business, 1965).

of hypothesis can be very inefficient in that either many hypotheses are rejected or the conclusion that one event is caused by another may not represent the complete situation. This is especially true in business research where it is usually difficult or impossible to design carefully controlled experiments.

Throughout the history of economics the hypothesis that the quantity of a good purchased was primarily dependent of the price formed a basic tenet in economic theory. This is an instance of failure to seek other hypotheses. With the advent of marketing in advanced societies, many new hypotheses have been uncovered and tested in an attempt to describe and predict consumer behavior.

An example of a search for hypotheses, both theoretical and applied, relates to the theory of the small business firm. In the preface, the authors make clear their objectives:

> Several studies of small business problems which we conducted in recent years made us increasingly aware of the limitations of reliance on statistical data alone for the analysis of business growth and survival. . . . Our study was exploratory in character and, for that reason, began without rigid hypotheses. We preferred to give fairly free rein to our curiosity and made certain only to cover all those areas which prior studies had already suggested as relevant.[10]

Test of a Hypothesis

Once a possible answer to a problem has been found, or once a relationship among variables is surmised, a proposition is framed which is tested by whatever ingenious means the researcher can conceive. In business research, the neat, controlled experiment is usually not possible. The researcher must attempt to devise means of testing the truth, generality, or even just the utility of a hypothesis by whatever methods appear "logical." The research may lead only to greater plausibility or probability of the hypothesis and rejection of some leading alternative explanations.

The test of a hypothesis is not synonymous with either research or scientific method. It is one of several phases of research and development of science. In many areas of business, the hypothesis is not known in advance since so little theory is available. Research often consists of altering variable or injecting perturbations in a situation to see what will happen. This is analogous to applying heat to a pan of water, observing the boiling of water, and considering as tested the hypothesis that heat causes the boiling. The conclusions drawn from the experiment become hypotheses which have then passed a sort of preliminary testing. Thus hypotheses may be assumed to be tested after formulation in some cases or prior to formulation in other cases.

When a hypothesis is to be tested, the investigator should clearly formulate

---

[10]Kurt B. Mayer and Sidney Goldstein, *The First Two Years: Problems of Small Firm Growth and Survival*, Small Business Research Series No. 2, Small Business Administration (Washington, D.C.: Government Printing Office, 1961), p. v.

the hypothesis at the beginning of his research. For example, in a report of a study of consumer behavior, the author set forth his hypothesis in two parts as follows:

1. In a consumer decision-making situation where no objective standards are present, individuals who are exposed to a group norm will tend to conform to that group norm.

2. In a consumer decision-making situation where no objective standards are present, individuals who are exposed to a group norm, and are induced to comply, will show less tendency to conform to the group judgment.[11]

Another presentation of the test of a hypothesis indicates how already available date may be used instead of constructing an experiment. The hypothesis is introduced at length by a discussion of the background, but the researcher makes clear his proposition thus:

There have been periodic suggestions in the literature that concentrated industries may tend to pay exceptional wages. . . . This paper attempts a new, direct test of the "monopoly wage" hypothesis using the 1/1000 sample of the 1960 Census of Population.[12]

Historical or Genetic Study (Vertical Time Span)

Historical research might at first glance appear to have little in common with science and the construction of theory. Science has as an objective the establishment of general laws, whereas historical research is concerned with establishing the occurrence of unique events. Although one phase of historical research consists only of determining past events, the ultimate phase deals with the interpretation of such events in the past and present, the establishment of pattern of relationships, and the starting point for projecting trends. Historical research is essential for both basic and applied research in business, because if nothing is known of the past, nothing is known. Explanations of the present derived from historical inquiries are sometimes called "genetic" studies.

Ernest Nagel deduces that the natural sciences are no more free of "singular" statements than historical research is barren of general laws:

It would be a gross error, however, to conclude that singular statements play no role in the theoretical sciences or that historical inquiry makes no use of universal ones. . . . No conclusions concerning the actual character of specific things and processes can be derived from general statements alone; for theories and laws must be supplemented by initial conditions (i.e., by statements singular or instantial in form) if those general assumptions are to serve for explaining or predicting any particular occurrence. . . . Even the pure natural sciences can assert

---

[11]M. Venkatesan, "Experimental Study of Consumer Behavior Conformity and Independence," *Journal of Marketing Research* (November 1966), p. 385.

[12]Leonard W. Weiss, "Concentration and Labor Earnings," *The American Economic Review* (March 1966), p. 96.

their general statements as empirically warranted only on the basis of concrete factual evidence, and therefore only by making use of singular statements.[13]

Some of the possible objectives of historical research are:

1. Filling the gaps in business and economic history.

2. Study of the history of individual companies for interpretation of their impact on economy.

3. Study of the history of individual companies to generalize on good and ineffective patterns of management.

4. Study of "great business leaders" as a theory of cause of events.

5. Study of economic and geographic factors as the cause of business or industrial progress.

6. Study of technological progress and the development of the theory of management.

7. Study of institutions as a source and result of change in the business world.

8. Study of historical, sociological, and anthropological forces as a cause of current business behavior.

9. Study of pluralistic, political, or psychological forces as a cause of current business behavior.

Historical research, like all other research, is not just concerned with digging up facts. Evaluation and interpretation are integral parts of legitimate research. The historical researcher must concern himself with (1) critical evaluation of source documents in terms of authority, content, and meaning, and (2) interpretation of records in terms of general laws, trends, or hypotheses.

Comparative Study (Vertical or Horizontal Time Span)

One purpose of research may be to compare institutions, concepts, practices, trends in significant economic variables, economics of different countries, and the like over a period of time. For example, channels of distribution for manufactured goods and farm goods might be compared in terms of differences, similarities, trends, legal aspects, costs, volume of goods or other factors.

The history of socialistic and capitalistic economics might be compared in terms of growth of national product and trends in operation by evaluating the economics of specific countries. Not only may comparative studies be made for a historical period of time or for particular period of time, but comparisons may be made of factors or situations which never coexisted. For example, a study of leadership was made by examining great "leaders" at different times in history in order to compare their methods and styles.[14]

---

[13]Ernest Nagel, *The Structure of Science* (New York: Harcourt, Brace & World, 1961), p. 548.

[14]Eugene E. Jennings, *An Anatomy of Leadership* (New York: Harper & Brothers, 1960).

Eclectic Research and Theory Construction

Business research may consist of a study of various theories and empirical data for the purpose of building upon the strongest aspects of each theory and reconciling apparent differences. This has been particularly true in the field of organization theory, where many approaches have been used in an attempt to build a theoretical structure.

In economics, organization theory, marketing theory, and in some portions of financial and accounting theory, different schools of thought exist and views of scholars diverge. Research may have as its purpose the comparison of divergent representations and critical evaluation in terms of empirical justification and internal validity.

A major research effort to synthesize the views of experts into a rudimentary theory of behavior was carried out as a group effort by nine sociologists and psychologists. The results were published in a book, *Toward a General Theory of Action.*[15]

A briefer case of comparison of experts' views and the development of a synthesis is that dealing with fair rates of return in regulated industries. The investigator compared two apparently dissimilar models for fair rates of returns under conditions of growth. He then showed that both of these models can be derived from a third, more general model. He compared the usefulness of the models and the behavioral assumptions which underlie the model.[16]

Model Building and Testing

Models, as discussed earlier, are abstractions which in basic management science represent theories. They are thus more complex than the usual propositional hypothesis and are quantitative in nature in their most useful form. An important goal of business research is to construct quantitative models which show the interrelationship among many variables. Model building and empirical testing go hand in hand, since models must be checked for their predictive value. Without such testing the researcher must fall back on plausibility arguments or previously developed laws to substantiate his model until further research subjects it to predictive testing.

An excellent nontechnical description of a generalized marketing model for short-term prediction of consumer sales was developed by Samuel G. Barton. This is a conceptual model which identifies the marketing variables and their structural relationships for the manufacturer of nondurable goods who does not fully control his own distribution system. The result of the research is summarized in a large and elegant block diagram.[17] In contrast is a model for repre-

---

[15]Talcott Parsons and Edward A. Shils (eds.), *Toward a General Theory of Action* (Cambridge, Mass: Harvard University Press, 1951). Paperback reprint, Harper & Row, 1962.

[16]F. T. Sparrow, "Mathematical Models of Growth Allowances for Public Utility Regulation—A Synthesis," *Management Science* (February 1967).

[17]Samuel G. Barton, "A Marketing Model for Short-Term Prediction of Consumer Sales," *Journal of Marketing* (July 1965).

senting the response of sales to advertising. This highly quantitative model was based upon three general assumptions about advertising which are the parameters of the model: sales decay, saturation level, and sales response function. The quite general model was tested for several products and appeared to be realistic.[18]

Research on Improving Research Methods

Much research in business is concerned with the behavior of people in business organizations or the behavior of people in roles external to business organizations (i.e., as consumers, stockholders, or in private conflicting roles). Therefore much research on business and its environment involves the study of human behavior and attitudes. There is a great need for improved methods of measurement so that the researcher does not interact with the environment he is concerned with. A discussion of this problem and some unique solutions is given in a valuable little book by Eugine J. Webb and others, *Unobtrusive Measures: Nonreactive Research in the Social Sciences* (Rand McNally, Chicago, 1966).

Considerable research is continually in progress to improve sample surveys as a source of consumer behavior. Panels have also been used extensively in marketing research and the search for weaknesses and improvements continues. An example of a type of such research is concerned with the possible conditioning effect of repeated questioning of the same people which make up a panel. An experiment was set up to compare responses on four separate interviews dealing with estimates of home alterations. The conditioning effect by type of question and by classification of respondent was evaluated.[19]

An approach for comparative research in marketing is the subject of an interesting analytical and descriptive research paper (see Exhibit 10-1). It could well provide a guide for other types of comparative studies.

APPLIED BUSINESS RESEARCH CLASSIFIED BY PURPOSE

The goal of applied business research is to aid business decision makers to make better decisions by supplying him with useful information when he needs it. While basic research is concerned with the development of science, applied research is concerned with the application of science to singular situations. Applied research may well yield a contribution to business, however, since it is the ultimate test of the theoretical structure and general propositions. Thus there is an overlap, and neither type of research is independent of the other.

"Needs" Research

"Needs" research in the development of business theory centered on needs for knowledge. In applied research, needs research is concerned with the needs

---

[18] M. L. Vidale and H. B. Wolfe, "An Operations Research Study of Sales Response to Advertising," *Operations Research* (June 1957).

[19] John Nater and Joseph Waksberg, "Conditioning Effects from Reported Household Interviews," *Journal of Marketing* (April 1964).

of customers which often may be undefined by them. Needs research is directed toward uncovering the opportunities for the firm's products and services and the effort (planning and mobilization) of capabilities required to match these.[20] The needs researcher investigates the following:

1. General objectives of the firm
2. Market characteristics and trends in competition
3. Customers' objectives
4. Environment and trends in the environment
5. Capability profiles of the firm and potential for change
6. New concepts, including products, for matching effort to opportunity

Descriptive Research

Since research within a company is decision-oriented, descriptive research occurs only to provide a basis for evaluation and action. Most descriptive research is centered on industry-wide subjects: general behavior of customers, characteristics of firms, advertising patterns and techniques, and the like. For example, a descriptive study of the chemical industry was sponsored by the Manufacturing Chemists' Association and conducted by a highly respected university professor.

The chapter headings of this 90-page monograph are:

1. Industrial chemical defined
2. Patterns of competition
3. The number of competitors
4. Structure of the chemical industry
5. Competitive products
6. Price competition
7. Nonprice competition
8. Patents and competition
9. Foreign competition
10. Competition and intercompany relationships
11. Summary and conclusions.[21]

The data, description, and conclusions of this descriptive study provide the individual companies with a basis for further research or for policy decisions.

Another typical descriptive study sought to provide the answer to loss of supermarket shopping loyalty and the reason for more frequent shopping by supermarket customers. Data were gathered for Cincinnati showing store loyalty

[20]See for example Donald J. Smalter, "The Managerial Lag," *Chemical Engineering Progress* (June 1964); Arthur D. Hall, *A Methodology for Systems Engineering*, Chap. 6, "Needs Research" (Princeton, N.J.: D. Van Nostrand Co., Inc., 1962); Wroe Alderson, *Marketing Behavior and Executive Action* (Homewood, Ill.: Richard D. Irwin, Inc., 1957), pp. 355-365.

[21]Jules Backman, *Competition in the Chemical Industry* (Washington, D.C.: Manufacturing Chemists Association, 1964).

of consumers, frequency of shopping, advertising readership, and trends in saving of trading stamps and discount store competition.[22]

Forecasting and Planning

Research for the purpose of forecasting sales potential and planning company strategy is an important and frequently repeated type of research for most companies. Such research may involve investigation of economic conditions, industry trends, market potential, and competitive moves. The scope of such research has been described in some detail on a number of occasions by a former International Business Machines corporate planner, Robert S. Weinberg.[23]

Industry sales forcasting research offers many opportunities for those in academic institutions who are seeking a useful applied topic which draws upon principles developed in all areas of business. Quite different approaches are required for different industries and considerable ingenuity is required on the part of the investigator.[24]

Program Development Research

Programs may be approved and initiated on the basis of either a general formulation or of a set of specifications for results. Research may be required to determine alternative courses of action and to develop a specific program. The program is a formulation of employment of resources, establishment of milestones (major subtasks), and estimate of time and cost in the desired trade-off proportion. The refinements of program budgeting and cost-effectiveness analysis by both industry and government have put program development research on a much more sophisticated plane.

Operations Research (Specific-Problem Solving)

Research into operating problems and the search for more efficient methods of business operations has received considerable attention since the second World War. Operations research in business has generally been identified with solving quite specific problems using scientific method and quantitative techniques. "Operations research is the art of giving bad answers to problems to which otherwise worse answers are given," according to T. L. Saaty, with more truth than jest.[25] While many researchers are concerned with development of methods, the industrial operations researcher is usually concerned with application of methods to solve the pressing or critical problems of his firm.

[22]Ben L. Schapker, "Behavior Patterns of Supermarket Shoppers," *Journal of Marketing* (October 1966).

[23]Robert S. Weinberg, "Multiple Factor Break-even Analysis: the Application of Operations-Research Techniques to a Basic Problem of Management and Control," *Operations Research* (April 1956).

[24]See Robert G. Murdick and Arthur E. Schaefer, *Sales Forecasting for Lower Costs and Higher Profits* (Englewood Cliffs, N.J.: Prentice-Hall, Inc., 1967), for examples of company sales forecasting and market forecasting at the industry level.

[25]Thomas L. Saaty, *Mathematical Methods of Operations Research* (New York: McGraw-Hill Book Company, Inc., 1959), p. 3.

Model Building (Generalized Problem Solving)

For large-scale business problems which justify considerable research effort, complex models may be constructed which permit variation of parameters to handle changes appropriate to specific problems over a fairly long period of time. Sales forecasting models, advertising models, inventory control models, production control models, and capital investment models are appearing much more frequently in the sophisticated companies. Perhaps one of the most advanced models is Du Pont's mathematical model of its Corfam (trade mark) venture. This model combines all major aspects of marketing, production, and risk. It requires tremendous amounts of data, and data processing must be carried out by a computer. A very simple, nonquantitative, and conceptual description is available.[26]

Development of Hypotheses

If a business problem does not yield to hypotheses conceived by the management, the company may conduct research for the purpose of uncovering new hypotheses. There are many techniques for such exploratory research, one of the best known of which is "motivation research." This type of research is aimed at discovering possible explanations for behavior or consumers. In one instance, Jewel Tea Company investigated means for determining how more customers could be acquired and how present customers can be made more satisfied. By means of depth interviews, the relationship between the housewife and the Jewel Tea salesman, the consumer's attitude toward Jewel Tea, and the husband's role in the housewife-Jewel Tea relationship were investigated. Factors which influenced these relationships were brought out and hypotheses resulted which provided a guide to company action.[27]

Another motivation research project dealt with people's attitudes towards eating candy. A very few of the many findings were that candy eating may create personal problems of ambivalence or feelings of guilt; candy was rarely given as a gift to men but rather to older female relations; candy-giving in courtship was associated with the old fashioned type of courting and sitting home.[28]

Test of a Hypothesis

The test of a hypothesis as an objective of research is not limited to theory construction. Although in the past, businessmen have made vital decisions on the basis of untested hypotheses, the trend is toward more emphasis on research. Some reasons for this are that (1) managers are better educated, (2) research

[26]Staff article, "Mathematical Model Becomes Marketing Tool," *Chemical and Engineering News* (January 2, 1967).

[27]"Jewel Tea Company Home Service Routes," Case Study AM 74, Harvard Graduate School of Business Administration, 1957.

[28]"Young & Rubicam, Inc. (A)," Case Study ICH2M83, Harvard Graduate School of Business Administration, 1957.

techniques are more advanced and widely known, (3) there are more trained researchers available, (4) competitive pressures require more sophisticated countermeasures, (5) the cost of failure of many projects relative to the cost of some minimum research has grown enormously, and (6) research also pays off when the results will be used again and again over a long period of time.

An interesting illustration of the rejection of a hypothesis involved the future of a company formed to develop and market a new special-purpose desk-size typewriter-computer. The computer had a limited memory and was being designed to perform invoice computations, payroll computations, and prepare sales reports which were expedited by the electric computer-guided typewriter. Part of the research was an investigation of possible applications for the equipment. The other part of the study was a cost comparison with manual methods and competing equipment. This involved methods analyses and time studies for performing a variety of chores. As the computer prototype was developed, the research showed that the cost per function performed was not competitive except in some unusually high volume instances. The hypothesis that this project would be commercially successful was therefore rejected by the researcher.

Testing hypotheses for new products or for changing present products has been carried out using statistical experimental design techniques. One company tested the null hypothesis that sales of frozen orange juice to fountain managers was not affected by varieties of jugs and dispensers.[29]

Methodology and Methods Improvement

Businesses continually work at devising better methods for market researh, advertising, and sales forecasting. They seek improved methods for researching employee attitudes and behavior and measurement of performance. New management science techniques are sought for researching and solving information problems, logistics problems, and inventory and production problems.

A large-scale research project for developing improved methods of long-range planning was carried out by International Minerals & Chemical Corp. Methods of the Department of Defense under Robert McNamara were studied for application to corporate planning. A method for Project Exploratory Planning and econometric models for some of the products were developed.[30]

QUESTIONS AND TOPICS FOR DISCUSSION

1. This chapter presents business research as either basic or applied research. Do you believe that this is a simplification and that much research has as its purpose both theory development and solution of current business problems?

[29]Seymour Banks, *Experimentation in Marketing* (New York: McGraw-Hill Book Company, Inc., 1965), p. 118.

[30]The results of this research were reported by Donald J. Smalter in "Six Business Lessons from the Pentagon," *Harvard Business Review* (March-April 1966), and in "Influence of Department of Defense on Corporate Planning," *Management Technology* (December 1964).

If so, find several examples from the literature which lie in the basic-to-applied research spectrum.

2. Can you think of other purposes of research projects than those given in this chapter?

3. Many articles have appeared recently which summarize the status of some aspect of business theory. Do these represent "research?"

4. What would be the result if the rules of scientific evidence excluded as invalid all purposes of research except the testing of hypotheses?

5. Why is there a need for research on improved methods of business research? Can you think of specific needs? Can you find examples of such research outside of the field of marketing?

chapter 5

Business-Research Communication Modes

THE ROLE OF COMMUNICATION

Without communication, organized knowledge and planned action would be impossible. Charles Morris classifies communication as designative (signifying characteristics), appraisive, prescriptive, or informative. Scientific discourse is the most specialized form of designative-informative discourse. He says further,

> Scientific discourse is therefore made up of those statements which constitute the best knowledge of a given time—that is, those statements for which the evidence is highest that the statements are true . . . . Any statement which cannot be confirmed or disconfirmed has no place in scientific discourse.[1]

Scientific communication (in a restricted sense) is thus concerned with the transfer between people of information of a special type.

The manner in which such information is transmitted is called a *channel of communication*. The channel with which this book is concerned is the printed page. The form in which the information is transmitted in writing depends upon the objective or objectives of the research and the institutional requirements. Thus for example the form for an applied research project in business is different than the form for a doctoral dissertation in an educational institution or journal article dealing with a theoretical investigation.

Research results must be stored if they are to be added to the fund of man's knowledge. Even applied research results must be stored for at least a short period of time to be of value. The basic information cycle is shown in Exhibit 5-1.

When information is first generated it must be stored, otherwise it ceases to exist and hence is destroyed. Storage may be only in the mind of an individual,

[1] Charles Morris, *Signs, Language, and Behavior* (New York: George Braziller, Inc., 1955), pp. 118–126.

EXHIBIT 5-1
Basic Information Cycle

```
  ┌───────┐        ┌──────────┐
  │ Store │ ─────► │ Retrieve │
  └───────┘        └──────────┘
┌──────────┐     ┌──────────┐     ┌────────────┐     ┌─────────┐
│ Generate │ ──► │ Evaluate │ ──► │ Manipulate │ ──► │ Utilize │
└──────────┘     └──────────┘     └────────────┘     └─────────┘
  ┌─────────┐
  │ Destroy │
  └─────────┘
```

but by the nature of science, the output of research requires longer storage and wider dissemination. The information should be easy to retrieve, but unfortunately this is not the case. The business organization or the academic researcher who requires certain information is limited by the time and cost of searching for information which may not even exist. This problem has implications for those who are writing about research. It suggests that good titles, good abstracts, good organization of material, lucid writing, and wide dissemination in indexes are valuable if the work is not to be wasted. It suggests that communication with others, not oneself, is a prime objective.

In academic institutions so much reference is made to the vehicle of communication (the term paper, report, thesis, or dissertation) that the student often mistakes the vehicle for the purpose of the project. His purpose is to conduct research of some type and quality, and this is what he should devote his attention and intellect to. The communication of his intellectual effort provides him with an exercise in mechanics and exposition. The role of the communication vehicle in academic institutions, then, is to train the graduate student in expressing his ideas to others and to disseminate the results of his research. In industry, the research report is not usually looked upon as a training device, although it may serve this purpose for young executives.

Communication modes for business research differ from those for academic research. Academicians have clung to the traditional modes evolving from the thesis and dissertation characteristic of the humanities. The influence of the empirical nature of business and modern economics has led to a modification of purpose of the communication mode without a resulting change in identifying terms or format. These inconsistencies will appear in the discussion of modes that follows.

TERM PAPER

The term paper is an academic report which may have one of several objectives. In the field of business it is an informative, evaluative, or argumentative form of exposition. It is the most limited in scope of all the various communication modes. Generally the term paper is based on a library investigation of some topic and rarely involves laboratory work. In schools where both opportunity and encouragement make it possible, the student may make a field study of a problem in one or more business firms. An intermediate level of investigation might be based on correspondence with business firms or small sample surveys which can be carried out conveniently in a semester.

In the case of a library project, the term paper project may have the purpose of determining the state of the art of a narrow subject; evaluating processes or institutions; organizing, classifying, and interpreting business data such as historical expenditures for advertising; or presenting and comparing viewpoints of authorities on a topic. The term paper in such a case is primarily a record of library search and intelligent analysis of readings on a single subject.

The term paper is short enough so that it does not require the formal preliminaries of contents, preface, or appendix common to longer expositions. Ten to thirty typed double-spaced pages covers the range of most papers. The term paper is used to acquaint the student with systematic, careful, and accurate gathering and presentation of information. It is not supposed to be a series of quotations tied together by an occasional linking sentence by the student.

The organization of the term paper tends to follow the logic of the exposition of the particular subject. There should, however, be a clear statement of the purpose at the beginning of the paper. The main body of description or analysis should be organized to provide continuity of thought, with headings dividing the text into the main ideas. While there cannot be any rule for the length of material following a heading, a term paper which extends for 20 to 30 pages with no headings is apt to lose the reader unless it is written in masterful style. Two or three headings on every page is apt to make the reading too choppy, while text extending regularly beyond five or six pages without guideposts begins to put a burden on the reader. Proper use of headings forces the writer to organize his thoughts and prevents rambling and repetition so commonly found in term papers.

The style should be directed toward the reasoning rather than the emotional processes. To accomplish this, impersonal sentence structures are used. An acceptable deviation in some term papers which makes for easier reading is the use of the first person plural "we." This is sometimes favored throughout term papers when the author wishes to bring the reader with him through an involved explanation.[2]

BUSINESS RESEARCH REPORT

The business research report is usually a report of applied research. It is the most common type of report prepared in business firms, since firms conduct research primarily to solve specific problems rather than to advance the theory

---

[2] A helpful paperback book on the subject of preparing term papers is that by Gilbert Kahn and Donald J. D. Mulkerne, *The Term Paper: Step by Step* (New York: Doubleday & Co., Inc., 1964).

of management. Quite frequently this research is conducted by specialists or professionals in staff positions to aid management to make decisions. Marketing research and labor relations research are typical of these studies.

Since managers do not always have time (in proportion to the value of all activities they must carry out) to read highly technical reports in detail, the good business report gives the answer first. The business research report generally follows this sequence of ideas:

1. Statement of problem
2. Conclusions and recommendations
3. Description of procedure
4. Results and analysis

The busy executive thus needs to read only the first two relatively brief parts given above. If he has a desire to check further, he may conveniently read the latter two parts. An industry study which was made to forecast demand for textiles, and hence textile machinery, is *A Look at the U. S. Textile Industry through 1970* prepared by Whitin Machine Works (Whitinsville, Mass.), 1963. The table of contents is as follows:

The Long-Term Outlook (contains a description of the problem and conclusions of the study)
Determinants of Textile Consumption
Forecast of Fiber Usage
Outlook for Cotton Systems
Outlook for the Woolen and Worsted Systems

The Machinery and Allied Products Institute conducted research and published a report *Equipment Replacement and Depreciation—Policies and Practices* (1956). The major headings in the contents are:

Introduction (describes background of the problems and needs for the study)
Summary of Results
Scope and Method of Study
Bibliographies

The above order of presentation is the reverse of the usual academic order. The academic sequence of topics follows the pattern of logical reasoning and chronological development of the research. In the business environment the academic sequence is not appropriate. The question that must be resolved, therefore, is whether to teach business-report practices to the business student or to let him be retrained when he enters the business world. The latter approach has a serious drawback. First, the business school graduate may never find out that management doesn't like to read his academic format reports, doesn't read them, or prefers to keep him in a position where someone else reports on the work he does.

The arguments for the academic sequence are that it has always been used in the past and that it represents training in logical thinking. This latter objection can be met by having the student prepare his draft in the logical sequence and then rearrange the order. James Souther's prescription for technical report writing is equally applicable to other business reports.

> In addition to being clear and understandable, the material must be organized so as to be most useful to the reader, and the writer must constantly keep the needs of the reader in mind if his report is to be effective. The growing demand for abstracts and summaries in industrial reports stems from their usefulness to people who use the reports. The effective report writer will place the material which is of greatest interest to the reader at the beginning of the report, *for very often the order in which the writer gathered his material, or the order in which the test was conducted is not the most satisfactory arrangement for the report which covers them.* The results and conclusions in most cases, are far too important to be placed at the end of the report, and the efficient report writer places them in a position of emphasis, near the beginning.[3]

The business research report may vary in length from a few pages to a lengthy volume. In the former case, the title page may be the only preliminary material. In the latter case, title page, routing page (showing who receives a copy), contents page, list of figures and tables, abstract, preface, and introduction may all be found separate from the body of the report.

THE PROFESSIONAL PAPER

The professional paper is directed toward either a basic research problem or an applied research problem. If it is concerned with applied research, it is distinguished from the business research report by its wider application and generality. The applied research report solves an operating problem for a particular company at a particular time. The professional paper, if it does this at all, is such that the problem is one which faces many companies and the solution presented may be adapted by many companies.

An example of just such paper is Carl Vreeland's description of a short-range forecasting technique developed specifically for Jantzen, Inc. The approach to forecasting sales of seasonal style goods is of interest, however, to many other manufacturers of seasonal style goods.[4]

The professional papers as they appear in the professional business journals vary considerably in purpose as listed below with examples of each:

1. *Basic Research–Conceptualization*
   Milton H. Spencer, "Uncertainty, Expectations, and Foundations of the Theory of Planning," *Journal of the Academy of Management* (December 1962), pp. 197-206.

---

[3]James W. Souther, *A Guide to Technical Reporting* (Seattle: University of Washington Press, 1953), p. 7.

[4]Carl Vreeland, "The Jantzen Method of Short-Range Forecasting," *Journal of Marketing* (April 1963), pp. 66–70.

2. *Basic Research—Model Building and Testing*
   Seymour Levy and Gordon Donhowe, "Exploration of a Biological Model of Industrial Organization," *Journal of Business* October 1962, pp. 335-342.
3. *Review of the State of the Theory*
   Donald Austin Woolf, "The Management Theory Jungle Revisited," *Advanced Management Journal* (October 1965), pp. 6-15.
4. *Analysis*
   Daniel Teichroew, et al., "An Analysis of Criteria for Investment and Financing Decisions Under Certainty," *Management Science* (November 1965), pp. 151-179.
5. *Methodology*
   James Rothman, "Formulation of an Index of Propensity to Buy," *Journal of Marketing Research* (May 1964), pp. 21-25.
6. *Applied Research—Single Firm*
   M. S. Gadel, "Concentration by Salesmen on Congenial Prospects, *Journal of Marketing* (April 1964), pp. 64-66.
7. *Applied Research—Industry*
   Arch Patton, "Deterioration in Executive Pay," *Harvard Business Review* (November-December 1965), pp. 106-118.
8. *Prescription*
   Myles L. Mace, "The President and Corporate Planning," *Harvard Business Review* (January-February 1965), pp. 49-62.
9. *Description*
   Abe M. Tabir, Jr., "Marketing Government Surplus Property," *Journal of Marketing* (October 1963), pp. 27-30.
10. *Speculative Prediction*
    John Diebold, "What's Ahead in Information Technology," *Harvard Business Review* (September-October 1965), pp. 76-82.
11. *Essay*
    Philip Lesly, "Effective Management and the Human Factor," *Journal of Marketing* (April 1965), pp. 1-4.

The professional business papers as they appear in the journals appear not to follow any set form. In view of the many purposes which the articles serve, this is not surprising. The only characteristic that most have in common is that a statement of the objective is given at the beginning. Several journals such as *Management Science, Journal of Marketing Research,* and *Journal of Marketing* publish an abstract of each article at the beginning. The *Publication Manual* of the American Psychological Association advises authors preparing articles: "The organization of an article that reports an experiment has now become fairly standard. The principal divisions of such an article are Problem, Method, Results, Discussion, and Summary."

From the above discussion of the professional paper, it is evident that Business Schools which offer a course culminating in a professional paper need to identify for the students what is acceptable. Generally such courses are designed to offer the student an opportunity to conduct a small research project to gain experience in research and research reporting. The professor guiding these projects may be hazy about alternative organizations or may be dogmatically inclined toward the traditional report of experiment. It might be wise to ask which type of organization is easiest for the business manager to read and advise the student of this alternative. That is, have the student organize the report to give the answer first.

MASTER'S THESIS

The thesis has had a long history of development in universities from being a test in disputation to a scientific test of hypothesis required for a degree. John Almack states succinctly:

> A thesis today is commonly regarded as a coherent report of research, in which both the process and the results are given. Its origin is a problem; its central proposition is an hypothesis.[5]

The master's thesis as a requirement of graduate education represents the culmination of mature investigation of a relatively narrow and specific problem. It may have as its objective any of the purposes discussed in Chapter 4. In its narrowest sense, it has been considered the substantiation of a specific point of view. This is typical of the library-based research on some conceptual controversy in business or economic theory. The concept of the thesis in business schools has been evolving into a broader one as the representation of the solution of a problem. As a result, solution of empirical problems, quantitative analyses, and other forms of "hard" research are becoming more typical of the work underlying the master's thesis in the better schools. The thesis in the business school is a more rigorous report of an investigation than a discursive essay demonstrating skill in rhetoric. In short, the business school master's thesis is becoming more of a scientific document.

Various scholars have attempted to spell out standards of performance for the thesis. Although it is easy enough to specify minimum requirements of form and style, it is another matter to define the minimum acceptable quality level. For example, the following portion of discussion of performance standards by Paul Koefod indicates the difficulty of conveying what is really acceptable:

> Having selected a project suitable as a basis for a Master's or Doctor's essay, the prospective writer faces his first substantive requirement. He must have sufficient clarity, and assurance about his project to be able to make clear to others what it is. . . .

[5] John C. Almack, *Research and Thesis Writing* (Boston: Houghton Mifflin Co., 1930), p. II.

> The second requirement in the substantive category is that the writer's argument be clearly expressed. . . . The analysis of his problem or subject must be clear and unquestionable as well as adequately incisive, penetrative, and completely dissecting. His synthesis must be coherent and logical.[6]

Although Professor Koefod elaborates and continues further in one of the most careful attempts to describe criteria and standards, it is apparent that application of such generalities must be highly subjective. Another standard which has been set forth, also mentioned by Professor Koefod, is that the thesis must be of a level suitable for publication. While at first thought this might be a reasonably useful standard, it does not state the kinds of periodicals for which it is suitable. It is one thing to write at a level suitable for the *American Economic Review* or *Journal of Marketing Research* and quite another to write an essay suitable for one of the dozens of obscure business or trade publications. Further, a thesis might be very well done and have no publication value. An example of such a thesis would be an economic and marketing analysis to determine if a certain company should enter into design and production of unit residental transformers.

The pragmatic solution to communicating the minimum quality level of theses may be simple. A group of faculty members could rank a number of theses subjectively as enough theses could become available. A range of another half dozen representing average level of quality could also be selected. Graduate students could then examine these two groups to orient themselves and guide their own efforts. It would undoubtedly be useful to point out to the students some of the outstanding theses so that some might be motivated to aim high.

A characteristic of the master's thesis is a fairly well established form of organization. This includes preliminary parts and references sections similar to the form for a book. This extension of form serves to further differentiate it from a term paper. The organization is shown in Exhibit 5-2.

In business research, length of the thesis is not in question. If the research problem is acceptable to the advisor, then the thesis need simply cover the results in the form of Exhibit 5-2. The development of a mathematical model and its rationale might require only 20 pages. On the other hand, a comparative study might well run well over 100 pages. The thesis is, after all, only the documentation of the intellectual work; it is not the substance of thought.

DISSERTATION

The doctoral dissertation has long been a project in search of its purpose. The meaning of dissertation is to argue from the viewpoint of the expert in the

---

[6]Paul E. Koefod, *The Writing Requirements for Graduate Degrees* (Englewood Cliffs, N.J.: Prentice-Hall, Inc., 1964), p. 106.

EXHIBIT 5-2
Organization of the Thesis

I. The Preliminaries

   1.   Title Page
   2.   Preface and/or Acknowledgments (optional)
   3.   Table of Contents
   4.   List of Tables
   5.   List of Illustrations

II. The Body

   1.   Introductory chapter or chapters giving a complete statement of the problem, the background of the problem, the need for solution or the significance of the problem, the general approach to the problem, and the limitations of the work.
   2.   Report of the research which may include separate chapters on apparatus used (if any), procedure, results and analysis, and discussion.
   3.   Conclusions and generalizations drawn from the study.
   4.   Recommendations for implementation of results or for future research.

III. The Reference Sections

   1.   Appendix
   2.   Bibliography
   3.   Index (if appropriate)

field. Paul E. Koefod describes the dissertation thusly:

> The dissertation represents a species of essay different from the thesis. Its function is to provide systematic discussion of a subject or topic. Its scope usually is broader than that of the thesis, and its style is less rigorously formal. The purpose of the dissertation is to establish a criticism, clarification, or refinement—that is, to establish an arguable view. To dissertate is to discourse, or argue, in a learned manner. In contrast to the formal, scientific logic of the reasoning in the thesis, the dissertator treats his topic or subject more or less didactically.[7]

Although even an abstract of Professor Koefod's scholarly and thorough exposition of the nature of the dissertation cannot be given here, some further comments are appropriate. Professor Koefod gives the view that the dissertation should convey the results of experience and profound meditation. It is a formal essay in the analysis, interpretation, or evaluation of a subject or body of knowledge. As an attempt at establishment of a point of view, it may be critical, normative, conjectural, or speculative.

It is apparent from examination of "dissertations" in those fields of knowledge which lay claim to being sciences that those dissertations are not dissertations as described by Dr. Koefod. Rather, the doctoral dissertation has been transformed into a research report. This is particularly true in the social science field of business administration. In fact, the tendency is for the research to be an applied research project based upon gathering data in the field. With the growth of emphasis on the quantitative approach to business problems, there have ap-

[7]*Ibid*, p. 20.

peared some doctoral dissertations consisting of development of mathematical models. The emphasis on scientific method in modern times has led to dissertations which are based on measurement and carefully constructed deductive or inductive reasoning leading to a new contribution to knowledge. There has been, in the business schools, a retreat from the philosophical, speculative, and argumentative essay. This suggests that the current product should be labeled not a dissertation but rather a research report.

Actually it is the substantive intellectual effort (and implementation of research plans in the case of field research) which should be the primary focus of attention. If only research projects are currently being accepted, then the criterion should be that the work makes a really original contribution to man's knowledge. It may be a contribution to basic theory or to an actual business problem. The combination of the research project and the research report in the business administration field should have the three fundamental purposes:

1. Measure the ability of the candidate to conduct research which makes a real contribution to man's knowledge.

2. Train the candidate in scholarly writing.

3. Determine whether the candidate has the ability to continue to educate himself after his formal course work is concluded and his degree has been granted.

The doctoral research report is a formal document following the same organization as the master's thesis. It deals with a more substantial problem drawing upon more breadth of knowledge and skill with research and analytical techniques. The author knows that his problem, his research methods, his reasoning, and the scope of his work will have to stand up against the critical evaluation of a faculty committee.

Because of the scope of the doctoral project, the doctoral research report is usually considerably longer than the master's thesis. A length of 120 to 200 pages is fairly typical. Many faculty members believe that greater conciseness should be encouraged so that the doctoral report be kept considerably shorter. More faculty members could read it and criticize it, and the advisor would be able to read the report more often and more thoroughly. The result should lead to higher quality, and the student should derive more value from this experience.

RESEARCH MONOGRAPH

The research monograph is a research report covering a fairly large research project on a single subject. It is usually a form of communication among scholars in a particular field, and as such, has a limited audience. Since the monograph is usually longer than an article but shorter than a book, publication of the business research monograph is usually supported by a university press, a bureau of business research, a research foundation, or the author himself.

The research monograph has historically been a very scholarly treatment of some aspect of theory, written by a single author. The business research monograph, and other social science research monographs, often now deviate considerably from this pattern. The monograph may be highly theoretical, as for example, *Strategic Planning: A Conceptual Study,* which deals with concepts, principles, and ideas in the strategic planning process, and only indirectly with broad procedural aspects.[8] In contrast, a highly empirical study covered the results of investigating the capital-expenditure decision-making process in large corporations. A part of the study covered the forms and manuals used by the participating firms.[9]

Another theoretically based research monograph is distinctive because it consists of a set of papers on the same subject, i.e., the problem of "functionalism" in social science theory and method. The central theme is the strength and limits of functionalism; the authors apply this theme to anthropology, economics, political science, and sociology.[10]

The organization of the business research monograph does not follow any set form. Usually there is a table of contents, but frequently there is no list of illustrations or tables given. Also, there is no index despite the fact that the length of a monograph extends from about 50 to 200 printed pages. Frequently there is a long bibliography on the subject treated.

BOOK

For lengthy research projects which have broad appeal and commercial possibilities, publishing firms may publish the research in book form. In fact, the book itself may have little promise of profit, but the firm may wish to add to its prestige by issuing such a book. A good example of a widely known book covering lengthy and careful investigation of how business managers manage, as seen from a sociological viewpoint, is M. Dalton's *Men Who Manage.*[11]

SUMMARY

The aspects of business research which affect the mode of communication of the research are:

1. Character of the research in the applied-to-basic research spectrum
2. Institutional setting
   (a) Business or industry
   (b) Trade association

[8]Franklyn H. Sweet, *Strategic Planning: A Conceptual Study*, Research Monograph No. 26 (Austin: Bureau of Business Research, University of Texas, 1964).

[9]Donald F. Istvan, *Capital-Expenditure Decisions: How They Are Made in Large Corporations*, Indiana Business Report No. 33 (Bloomington: Bureau of Business Research, Indiana University, 1961).

[10]Don Martindale (ed.), *Functionalism in the Social Sciences: The Strength and Limits of Functionalism in Anthropology, Economics, Political Science, and Sociology*, Monograph 5 (Philadelphia: The American Academy of Political and Social Science, 1965).

[11]Melville Dalton, *Men Who Manage* (New York: John Wiley & Sons, Inc., 1959).

EXHIBIT 5-3

Summary of Characteristics of Research Communication Modes

	Number of Authors	Source	Approximate Length	Organization
Term paper (research)	1	Student	Brief (10–30 typed pages)	Not formal and consists only of body of report
Research report	1 or more	Business, trade association consultant, non-profit research organization, government agency, university	Several pages to several volumes	Adapted to the problem and the audience. Gives the problem, conclusions, and recommendations at the beginning.
Professional paper	1 or more	Universities, nonprofit research organizations, government agencies, consultants business firms	About 3–20 printed pages	Adapted to the problem and generally in chronological sequence.
Master's thesis	1	Graduate student	About 20–100 typed pages	Highly formalized. Chronological order of investigation. Preliminaries but no index.
Doctoral dissertation	1	Graduate student	About 50–200 typed pages	Somewhat formalized. Chronological order of investigation. Preliminaries but no index.
Research monograph	1 or more	University, nonprofit research organization, government agency, trade association, consultant	About 50–200 printed pages	Adapted to the problem. Formal preliminaries and indexing often omitted.
Book	1 or more	Same as above	Over 150 printed pages	Adapted to the audience and the problem. Complete preliminaries and usually indexed.

(c) Nonprofit research organization

(d) Independent contract supported by nonprofit foundations

(e) Government

(f) University

3. Scope and significance of the research

4. Competence level of the researcher

5. Resources available

The characteristics of the modes of communicating and documenting research are summarized in Exhibit 5-3.

QUESTIONS AND TOPICS FOR DISCUSSION

1. What is the distinction between an "essay" and a "research report?"

2. It has been said that a research report is no more than a description of an actual study whereas an essay is a discussion of some problem representing the opinions, often undocumented, of the author. Do you agree that a research report is purely descriptive without discussion, analysis, conclusions, or recommendations?

3. If an essay is made up of opinion and undocumented propositions, can an essay thus defined be considered a thoroughly substantiated contribution to science?

4. Is a different level of intellectual effort required to formulate a problem, conceive of an empirical test, implement the test, and derive conclusions from that required for scholarly speculation about nature?

5. Should term papers in collegiate schools of business be restricted to research reports? Why or why not?

6. Could all forms of business-research communication modes discussed in this chapter be considered business research reports?

7. What might be some weaknesses of research reports actually prepared by people in business firms?

8. Do you think that the format or organization of professional business-research papers should be more standardized for purposes of information retrieval?

9. What are the purposes of the master's thesis in schools of business? What should be the characteristics of the thesis so that these purposes may be achieved?

10. What *are* the purposes of the doctoral dissertation in schools of business? What *should be* the purposes of doctoral dissertation? Should the name of this document be changed?

11. Should all academic business research papers required to meet prescribed educational requirements be modeled after the ideal business research report rather than traditional academic forms?

12. Do you think that "doctoral research monograph" is a more appropriate term for "doctoral dissertation" in collegiate schools of business today?

13. Formal documents are usually not as easy to read and comprehend as

informally written and structured documents. Does formality really provide greater objectivity of research and reporting?

14. With research in business being reported in various unpublished and published documents, it is difficult to find out what has been done and what is being done. Can you think of a grand plan for centralizing all information on business research?

15. Are there other forms of written business research communication modes that have not been discussed in this chapter?

part **II**

THE PRACTICE OF
BUSINESS RESEARCH

chapter 6

Identification, Selection, and Formulation of the Problem

WHAT IS A PROBLEM?

The researcher in industry does not usually trouble to ask what a problem is; he sees himself surrounded by problems which call for solutions. Yet not infrequently, because of this failure to understand the nature of problems and problem definitions, he solves the wrong or irrelevant problem. The neophyte researcher in academic institutions—the graduate student—is in a different situation. He must seek out a problem of appropriate magnitude. He is often in contact with problems in his course work and reading and is unable to perceive these problems. "Defining problems calls for as much creativity as solving them."[1]

In general terms, a problem is a felt need, a question thrown forward for solution. It is a deviation between that which is known and that which is or becomes desired to be known. A problem exists when an individual interacts with his environment and finds himself in an indeterminate situation, questioning, doubt, or uncertainty. He must have in mind some objective or goal, but (1) means for achieving the objective or goal have not been determined, or (2) alternative methods for achieving the objective or goal have been formulated but uncertainty exists as to which method is best. He is faced with a task to be accomplished. A problem arises in a psychological setting where an individual (1) has in mind a set of goals (which may be to establish goals!), (2) has sufficient motivation to respond to the stimulus of events, and (3) the context of the stimulus of events indicates to him that a solution must be sought and that it is time to initiate its performance.[2]

---

[1] Arthur D. Hall, *A Methodology for Systems Engineering* (Princeton, N.J.: D. Van Nostrand Co., Inc., 1962), p. 94.

[2] Based on Robert B. Miller, "Task Description and Analysis," in Robert M. Gagne (ed.), *Psychological Principles in System Development* (New York: Holt, Rinehart and Winston, 1962), p. 214.

There are four broad classes of problems:

1. The search for a primary problem to be solved. The graduate student does this, the scientist in business research must do this, and business firms also must seek primary problems on which to apply their resources to achieve solutions.

2. Diagnosis of the primary problem from the many symptoms of some existing difficulty.

3. The primary problem itself.

4. Secondary problems which are those connected with the methods of solving the above three classes of problems.

Problems may also be classified according to the general method of solution:

1. Conceptual problems which are solved by creative thinking, selection, and synthesis. Heuristic reasoning to a plausible solution would also fall in this category.

2. Logical problems which are solved by deductive methods whereby the solution is implicit in the premises.

3. Empirical problems whereby inductive reasoning based upon observations of phenomena terminates in the verification or rejection of a question of fact.

It is apparent that complex problems involve all three of the above as subproblems.

The nature of problems of business science and business application have sufficient differences that an explanation of the concepts of each should be considered. The problems of business science are questions which lead toward universality of laws, starting with primitive questions about the generality of observed phenomena and cause and effect. At the same time, greater precision of laws is also a problem of science.

Problems in applied business are also identified as "decision problems," since the objective of the solution is to lead to a business decision. A decision problem is one whose solution requires that some action be taken. According to Ackoff, the minimal necessary and sufficient conditions for the existence of a decision problem are:

1. A decision maker, one who has the problem.

2. An outcome or goal desired by the decision maker.

3. At least two unequally efficient courses of action which have some chance of yielding the desired objective.

4. A state of doubt in the decision maker as to which course is best.

5. An environment or context of the problem.[3]

Note that search problems and methods problems have been omitted by this author.

[3] Russell Ackoff *et al.*, *Scientific Method: Optimizing Applied Research Decisions* (New York: John Wiley & Sons, Inc., 1962), p. 30.

The symptoms that a problem exists in a business firm, while not always obvious, are:

1. Performance is *presently* not meeting *present* objectives.

2. It is *anticipated* that performance will not be continuing *present* objectives at some future specific time.

3. Objectives for the future *are changed* and *present* operating procedures, if continued, will not achieve the revised objectives.

An extrapolation and expansion of the applied research problems given by J. H. Lorie and H. V. Roberts provide a useful listing of such business problems:

1. Need to identify policies and operating practices which should be changed in the interest of the business.

2. Need to formulate specific alternatives of the practices and policies which should be changed.

3. Need to choose between alternatives.[4]

4. Need to develop improved research methods.

PROBLEM SEARCH

The search for a problem to investigate consists of two phases: (1) identification of possible problems and (2) selection of a problem.

Identification of Possible Problems

Within a company, identification of possible problems involves a search for symptoms of problems (deviations from standards of performance) followed by a diagnosis of possible problems. This is a vital step since if the primary problems are not identified correctly, solving the wrong problems leaves the company worse off due to cost in dollars and time. It is important for the company to identify a number of problems so that proper selection can be made of the most important ones within the limitation of resources.

The graduate student, and perhaps the inexperienced professor as well, faces a different situation with respect to problem identification. First, he has a vast range of problems which he may scan. He is not restricted to those problems which are causing trouble in a single company. Second, he may identify either basic scientific (theoretical) problems or decision problems. He should identify several problems initially so that he can screen some out by preliminary selection and narrow down to one problem after the remainder have been carefully formulated and again evaluated. The following approaches may be used to find problem areas.

1. *Ask experts* in a particular area of business such as marketing, production, finance, organization, or general management. While this approach may not receive an award for creativity, it may serve to identify some particularly good problems. Creativity may be demonstrated to good purpose at a later stage in the

[4] James H. Lorie and Harry V. Roberts, *Basic Methods of Marketing Research* (New York: McGraw-Hill Book Company, Inc., 1951), p. 67.

research. The student may find a problem in which his professor has a strong interest so that he has someone who will provide worthwhile critical evaluation throughout the research.

If the researcher has an opportunity to attend professional society meetings, he may be able to uncover some good ideas in "corridor conversation." If he is interested in applied research, such meetings often provide an opportunity to quiz practicing business executives about problems which they face.

Finally, the researcher may contact local executives directly, arrange for interviews, and seek to identify problems of mutual interest which he could work on.

2. *Become a specialist.* The researcher may select some narrow area of both theoretical and practical significance and make himself an expert in the field through course work and independent reading. For example, capital-equipment acquisition and replacement is a narrow enough field for a student to become expert in, yet it has many theoretical and practical ramifications.

3. *Search the literature.* Sometimes students have no ideas where the problems lie. The student should read the journals in his major area of concentration and related journals as well. By scanning the scholarly literature, he will find unanswered questions, pioneering research which calls for improvement and refinement, recurring articles on the same problem as various scholars seek solutions, and reports of research currently in progress at other institutions. Masters' theses, doctoral dissertations, university bureaus of business research reports, nonprofit organization (such as RAND Corporation) research reports, and government publications are sources of ideas. Reading of journals in other fields of business than his major interest will often lead to ideas by analogy. Business publications for businessmen rather than scholarly journals may also suggest problems to the researcher.

The student should look for areas of controversy, observations without explanation, apparent inconsistencies between data and theory, opportunities for a more quantitative approach to problems, and statements which arouse his curiosity.

4. *Explore areas of dissatisfaction.* Dissatisfaction is expressed far more frequently than satisfaction. Read replies and criticisms of papers as published in the journals. Listen to professors and colleagues for criticisms of points of view, generally accepted concepts, or of actual business practices. Government legal actions against business such as those published in the *Journal of Marketing* may suggest topics. Critical articles appearing in business periodicals or business newspapers are also sources of ideas.

5. *Look for current developments and trends.* The development of the electronic computer and its growing use suggests dozens of topics. The trends toward numerical control machinery, coalition bargaining, conglomerate mergers, concentration of ownership of companies by pension funds, shorter time from laboratory model to mass-produced product, government influence on pric-

ing, and many others will suggest thousands of topics of all kinds. General business publications such as *Business Week, Barron's, Wall Street Journal,* and *Forbes* are good starting points. Trade publications such as *Steel, Iron Age, Industrial Marketing, Datamation,* and *Supermarket Merchandising* also suggest trends. *Industrial Marketing* has published *Business Publication Guide* (May 1966) which lists 2,450 U.S. and Canadian business publications alphabetically, by industry, and by publisher. The industry listing alone may suggest a broad area in which to seek a problem as well as listing the periodicals in the area.

6. *Maintain an idea notebook.* In the ideal application of this technique, the student carries with him at all times a small diary or notebook in which he jots down questions and ideas that come to him. In his course work, his discussions with colleagues, his contacts with business, his readings, and his meditative moments, the curious and scientifically oriented student will always be wondering and critically evaluating. The researcher should catch the ephemeral questions and problems which fleet by so rapidly in everyday life.

It may not be practical for the researcher to carry such a notebook with him or to take time out to overtly jot down his ideas. He may be better off to maintain a logbook at home or in his office where every evening he conscientiously tries to document ideas which aroused his curiosity during the day. If some very good question arose during the day, he may be well advised to jot it down on any scrap of paper available.

Although this method of searching for questions or problems may appear cumbersome to the modern business student, he should become aware that it is a common practice among physical and natural scientists. Even in the fast pace of the business firm where practicality is the creed, engineers and scientists are requested or even *required* to maintain logbooks of ideas for purposes of future patent protection.

7. *Examine the theoretical structure of the field.* For both theoretical and applied research, the researcher may find problems by reexamining the theoretical structure of the general area of business in which he is interested. He may look for gaps, opportunities for amplification and refinement, or advances at the edge of the field. He may seek new conceptualizations which better explain and predict. Empirical verification is a very fruitful source of research problems.

For applied research, he may seek applications of current theory. The researcher may also look for new methods of applying theoretical concepts or bridging the gap between theory and practice.

Selection of a Problem

The selection of business and economic problems to solve through research is not always made on a rational basis within the firm. Managers who are able to exert the influence and who are most persuasive are apt to secure the most assistance from staff research groups. The staff research group itself may make selections of problems which are interesting to them rather than those which are most crucial to the future of the firm. If the research staff is small, the selection of problems for research is apt to be reduced to meeting one crisis after another.

The selection of problems within the firm should depend simply upon two factors, namely, (1) the expected long-range gain resulting from making the correct decision, and (2) the cost of the research. Generally there are resource constraints of available competent researchers, funds, and time. Since present decisions affect the future, the allocation of resources should be directed toward present decisions. All the implications of a correct or an incorrect decision should be taken into account in evaluating a particular problem. The practical difficulties of selecting an optimum set of problems for research is that some subjective weighting system may be the best available approach.[5]

The selection of a problem for research by academic people involves no priority system, in most cases. The graduate student is usually free to select any problem whose solution will satisfy academic requirements and resource limitations. Therefore the graduate student should be guided in problem selection by the following factors.

1. *High degree of interest in the problem.* Research requires a probing attitude, a tenacity of spirit, and a dedication to thoroughness. If the student has a degree of intellectual or personal interest in the results obtained from the research he will be apt to bring to his project these three virtues. "Personal interest" does not mean a prejudiced wish for a particular outcome of the research, but rather a desire that the result, whatever it is, will be of use to the researcher. If the student has relatively little interest in the problem he is working on, the project becomes sheer drudgery—a chore he seeks to complete with minimum expenditure of time and effort. His report will reflect this on both the student and the school.

2. *Topic of significance.* It is an advantage to work on a topic which is in the mainstream of current applied or theoretical interest. A student working on such an applied problem may attract the attention of local executives of companies whose encouragement will stimulate his interest. The fact that someone will be able to use the results immediately is a strong incentive. If he works on a significant theoretical problem, he may have the opportunity to become acquainted with some of the leading scholars in the field. Exchange of correspondence will likely stimulate both his thinking and his enthusiasm.

3. *Novelty of the idea.* While novelty may be one aspect of significance of a topic, it is not synonomous. A novel problem means that the researcher need not fear following in the footsteps of experienced predecessors. No one else has prior claim to the idea, which otherwise may pose ethical difficulties. A novel problem conceived by the student is also a sign to his advisors of a promising

---

[5] For an operations research approach to evaluating measures of various courses of action, see C. West Churchman, Russell L. Ackoff, and E. Leonard Arnoff, *Introduction to Operations Research* (New York: John Wiley & Sons, Inc., 1957).

researcher. A novel problem may lead to new ways of looking at other problems or lead to unexpected conclusions.

4. *Researcher's resources.* The resources of the researcher are his own intellectual capabilities, training, and experience, his physical facilities and funds, clerical and technical assistance, library resources, and time available. Lack of training and experience may be overcome by diligent effort on the part of the student; indeed, one of the purposes of graduate research is self-education. The limitations of physical facilities such as laboratory and equipment, electronic computer, and special office and drafting equipment, and transportation should be taken into account when the student selects his problem from among those he is considering. The cost of the research, with a contingency fund of 10 to 20 percent, should be compared with funds the student has available. In the case of applied research, the student may be able to obtain modest support from local retailers, advertising agencies, news media, manufacturing plants, or even the Chamber of Commerce, according to who can use the results.

If library resources are poor, it may be necessary for the student to concentrate on problems for which he gathers primary data.

With regard to time, most students underestimate the time involved to conduct their first research project. In a three-semester-hour course given over a number of years, students were asked to estimate the time required as part of their research proposal. At the conclusion of the research it was usually found that the time required was between two and three times that estimated. The rule used in a certain advanced development laboratory for completion of a project seems to apply in business research as well. "Estimate the time required and then double it."

5. *Availability of data.* No matter how well a project is formulated and planned, if the data are not available the research cannot be executed. In the case of research based on library or secondary data, some preliminary investigation will uncover deficiencies. If a survey of people or of firms is contemplated, the respondents must be both *willing* and *able* to answer questions. One student took as a project an inquiry into reasons for failure of a new product, a letter opener with a cigarette lighter built into the handle. He had formerly worked for the firm which produced this as a gift item. He felt confident that the cost, market, and sales data which he had worked with were in storage and his former coworkers would cooperate in supplying the data and their own knowledge. After considerable planning and correspondence, he discovered that many organizational shifts had taken place since he had left the previous year. The new people knew nothing of the project and the data had been scattered around in different offices, much of it destroyed as obsolete.

"Sensitive" data such as sales and profit information or union-management relations is often difficult to obtain because the parties are unwilling to divulge it. On the other hand, a housewife may be *willing* to state how many bottles of soft drink she purchases in a year but may be *unable* to give the information.

6. *Benefits from solving the problem.* A strong motivation is provided if special benefits accrue from completing research on a particular problem. An intellectual or personal satisfaction may be obtained from solving a difficult problem. Another problem may yield professional recognition from the researcher's colleagues or professors within his institution. Another problem might have publication possibilities and consequently lead to external recognition by scholars. Some problem solutions have an immediate monetary value for the researcher, as for example, those subsidized by foundations or universities. Others lead indirectly to greater compensation through professional advancement. Service to the profession, the institution, or the community may provide an incentive to work on certain types of problems.

FORMULATING THE PROBLEM

Need For Careful Formulation

In mathematics or in quantitative business models it is obvious that every variable must be defined, that assumptions be clearly expressed, and that the desired relationships sought for must be specified. With this sort of blueprint to start with, the research is well defined. Most business problems do not lend themselves to the degree of abstraction required by mathematical representations. There remains, however, the necessity for carefully expressing and specifying the problem. There are seven reasons for such careful formulation.

1. Proper formulation of the problem provides a sense of direction to the research. It indicates the starting and end points. It is a skeleton of the research which must be filled in by the researcher. Although a problem well formulated is not a problem half solved, formulation may prevent the wrong problem from being solved.

2. Another purpose of problem formulation is to specify the scope of the research. Almost every business problem has many ramifications which are relevant. Even if the ramifications are limited, problems may be pursued in depth far beyond economic and time justifications. Problem formulation provides the boundaries.

3. Problem definition implies definition of terms which clarify the problem. If common language terms or the researcher's own meanings are used in expressing the problem, the researcher becomes aware of the need for clarification of these terms to achieve clarification of the problem. The looseness of meaning of many common business words was illustrated in Chapter 3.

4. Problem formulation to some extent indicates the limitations of the research itself. For example, the problem may be limited to determining sales response to advertising in a test market area because limitations of the time and money prohibit a nationwide study.

5. The major assumptions should be clearly established by the problem formulation. Too often, assumptions are not considered by the researcher so that he has difficulty with his analysis. He then implies some assumptions in the

middle of the research report which further confuses the reader. Many times, controversy about research results is caused by neither party stating their assumptions and both using different ones. Once again, operations research or quantitative models have the advantage of forcing the researcher to state his assumptions.

6. Problem formulation includes an expression of the context of the problem. Problems do not exist in a vacuum, nor are they solved in a vacuum. A business problem is a situation which is part of a larger situation. Each business problem has many interfaces with other business and environmental systems. While it may be impossible to describe all interfaces of the problem, a description of the background and environment places the problem in context. It may serve to identify major external factors impinging on the problem which should be considered in the research.

7. Problem formulation provides economy in research. By thinking through the problem formulation, the researcher is forced to recognize assumptions, key factors, limitations, and resources required. By setting the direction and scope of the research by proper problem formulation, the researcher will save much time from recycling the process of problem definition, research, and back to redefinition of the problem again. Good problem formulation will enable him to determine if he is repeating work already done, because he will be able to make better initial comparisons of his problem with previous research. It will guide him immediately toward the data he will need so that he will not gather too much data or irrelevant data.

Methods for Developing the Definition of the Problem

There are, perhaps, two basic methods for the student to approach the job of formulating his problem. In the first and simplest case, he has conceived of a problem area and needs only to develop and refine the problem statement. This process is indicated in Exhibit 6-1. Note the three possibilities for zeroing in on the problem:

1. Narrowing down from general and vague to more specific statements.
2. Oscillating between overbroad and overnarrow.
3. Broadening a narrow specific question into a broader significant problem.

In this method, the student follows this kind of questioning:

1. What are the unknowns? What data are available or obtainable? What are the constraints?
2. Can a solution be found which satisfies the constraints? Are the constraints sufficient, redundant, or contradictory? Can any restraints be modified or removed?
3. Can a diagram, flow chart, or geometrical figure be drawn to represent inputs, outputs, constraints, transformations, or flows?
4. Establish verbal and then symbolic representations of the various parts of the problem. Write down relationships among the parts of the problem.

EXHIBIT 6-1
Development of a Problem Definition

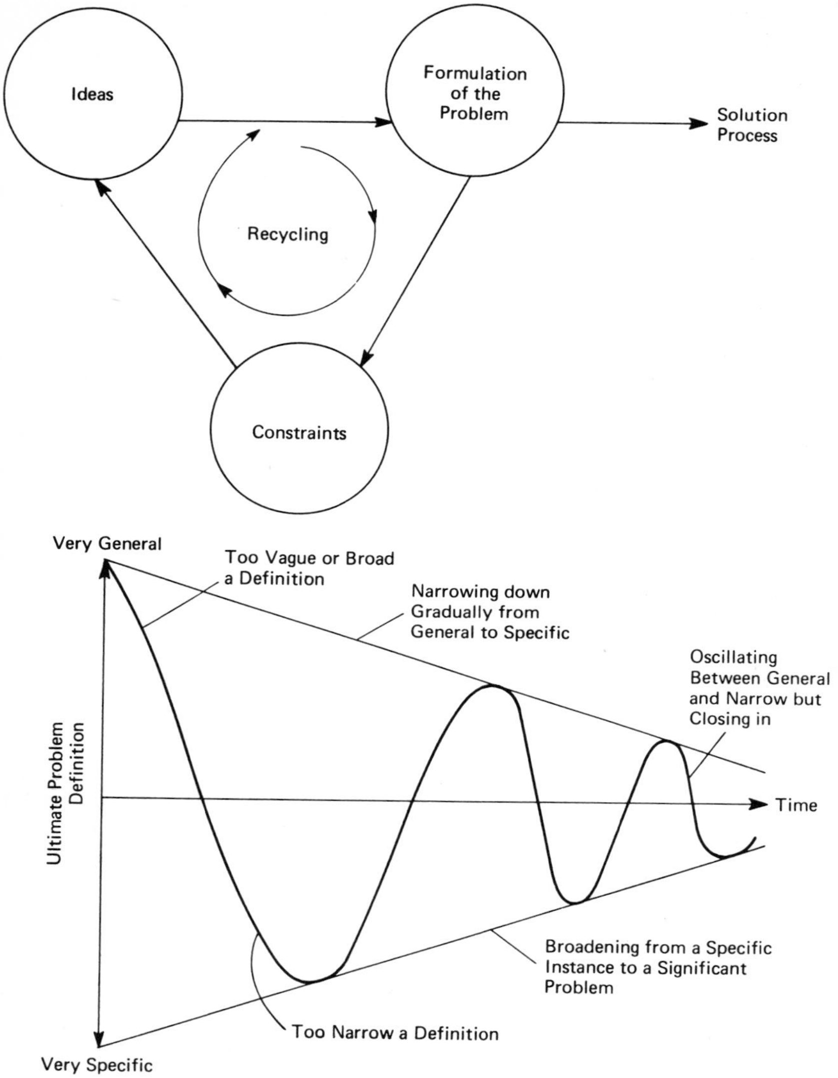

With this approach, the inputs (given conditions or data) are set forth, the conditions or restraints of the problem in terms of desired processes and outputs are specified, and subproblems, sketches of system relationships, and other contextual information is developed. The problem statement is redefined again and again as explicitness of ideas, conditions, or restraints is achieved. This process has also been described in step-by-step outline form by other scholars as follows:

1. Analysis of the major problem or problems in terms of subordinate problems.
2. Statement of the limits or scope of the study.
3. Orientation of the problem.
   (a) An historical account, remote or recent.
   (b) A survey of previous studies or related studies.
   (c) An analysis of previous studies or related subjects.
   (d) Preliminary survey.
4. Description of the general nature of the problem.
   (a) Type
   (b) Source
   (c) Procedure
5. Statement of limitations of technique employed.
6. Recognition of assumptions and implications.
7. Importance, value, or significance of study to business theory or practice.
8. Definition of terms.[6]

An application of this method in a business situation is outlined in Exhibit 6-2.

EXHIBIT 6-2
Defining a Marketing Problem

Symptom of the Problem: A continuing decline in sales volume on Dell-O Margarine.

Dimensions of the Problem: Time: very urgent. Profit: very important. Facilities: within company, none; outside (advertising agency), complete.

A. Subdivide problem into major elements:
   1. Industry elements
   2. Competitive elements
   3. Market elements

B. Examine existing hypotheses within organization:
   1. Company sales decline reflects lower industry volume
   2. Company sales decline result of growth in volume of lower-priced margarines
   3. Company sales decline result of low butter prices

C. Decision made to explore industry elements, with emphasis on stated hypotheses. Informational objectives include:
   1. Size and trend of industry volume
   2. Dell-O market share and trend in that market share
   3. Price-class division of industry volume and trends in that division
   4. Influence of butter prices, consumer incomes, and other economic factors on industry volume

Source: Richard D. Crisp, *Marketing Research,* (New York: McGraw-Hill Book Company Inc., 1957), p. 294.

[6] A. S. Barr, William H. Burton, and Douglas E. Scates, *The Methodology of Educational Research* (New York: Appleton-Century-Crofts, Inc., 1941), p. 86. Item 7 has been revised from the authors' text to apply to business instead of education.

EXHIBIT 6-3

Student's Diary of Formulation of a Problem

SESSION	STATUS
1	Specific idea in mind.
2	Topic will involve a comprehensive survey and I have been gathering data pending personal interviews with various companies.
3	Original topic would involve too much time and expense. New topic—Franchising. Specific area not yet determined.
4	I would like to restrict the topic to the area of Restaurant and Food Service Franchising. There appears to be an informational gap between the franchiser and prospective franchisee and I would like to conduct a survey in this area. I have mailed 35 letters to various companies in the food service franchising area and to date have received 6 replys which have been very informative. In the final report, I expect to include approximately 50 companies. I then hope to interview several franchise holders and correlate their reactions with the companies' examples as used in their selling proposals.
5	Prepared draft of project proposal.
6	I am conducting research in library and to date have material from <u>Franchising Magazine</u>, <u>Merchandising Week</u>, <u>Opportunity Magazine</u>, <u>Journal of Marketing</u>, <u>Restaurant Management</u>, etc. To date approximately 15 articles have been found. Survey of companies to date have provided material from 55 firms. All publications in the field have been written for and received. This includes material from the National Better Business Bureau, The Small Business Administration, Boston University, and the National Franchise Association.
7	I have confined the problem area to that of distorted information. I have incorporated this in my revised project proposal together with an overall objective. The survey has been extended to 25 "independents" so that more conclusive data will result. Eighty-five companies have responded to date.
8	Rewrote proposal, defined objectives, completing outline.
9	Project proposal (Problem Statement)

TITLE:

An Evaluation of the Opportunities and Limitations of Franchising in the Food Service Industry

BACKGROUND:

Though franchising remained a relatively stagnant field during the first ten years after its inception, it has grown greatly in a series of successive "leaps and bounds" in the past twenty years.

The first impetus of any magnitude took place during the post World War II years when returning GI's and middle-aged couples worried about augmenting retirement incomes, invested in small mom-and-pop roadside ice cream and hamburger franchises started by little-known but expanding companies. Slowly, fed by a series of successful operations, the idea caught on. With the advent of the annual "Start Your Own Business Exposition" in the New York Coliseum, interest also greatly increased.

Though the industry has experienced its share of failures, as of 1965 over 400 companies were operating in the franchise field, offering every type of franchise imaginable.

Today, franchising has become a major industry in its own right with sales of approximately $15 billion a year. Furthermore, recent studies indicate that at least 10,000 new franchised outlets are opening every year with this amount increasing steadily.

Perhaps the one most significant type of franchising, however, lies within the food service area. The vast majority of companies which grant franchises fall into this category. Most franchises, regardless of area, are quite similar in nature, and, in view of the fact that food-service franchising affords the greatest representation in the field, the topic has been restricted to this area.

EXHIBIT 6-3 (*continued*)

OBJECTIVES:

Although there are several magazine articles and some company literature on the subject of franchising, as well as a periodical and some very limited reports produced by the Small Business Administration, to date there is only one book published in the field. This seems rather astonishing in view of the size of this industry.

Furthermore, the published information presently available invariably utilizes as a nucleus company literature that for the most part comes from the industry leaders. Thus the objectivity of such information is questionable. For an initial objective, data to fill this "informational gap" is in order.

Secondly, the franchise, by its very nature, tends to appeal to a specific audience partially because certain capital and credit requirements must be fulfilled. Little has been established as to who comprises this audience. Thus one might ask the question: "To whom does a franchise afford opportunity?" Another objective of this research is to find this answer.

Third, the extent to which one might pursue opportunity within a franchise operation is definitely limited, and an evaluation of these opportunities and limitations is in order.

Fourth, the risks involved in entering a franchise agreement need to be analyzed. Though many succeed, research to date uncovered sixteen company failures in the past two years, indicating that a risk factor is present, one that must be analyzed.

The overall objective, then, is to evaluate the basic field of food franchising, citing its operational aspects and opportunities in the light of its obvious and more hidden limitations.

An illustration of how a student developed his idea for a three-semester-hours course is produced in Exhibit 6-3. This example was not chosen because of a brilliant attack upon problem formulation, because of a polished and edited report of his thought processes, or because the ultimate problem was a particularly good one. It was selected to show from original notes jotted down at the beginning of each session the thought processes of a student in formulating a problem. Note the typical approach of so many students to research as an application of a particular technique rather than a search for an answer to a question.

The second method is used to guide the student to identification, selection, and formulation by a systematic narrowing-down process. The student is asked a sequence of questions:

1. What is your major field of interest or your concentration of courses? The answer may be a functional field such as marketing, or it may be an interdisciplinary theoretical area such as organizational behavior or operations research.

2. Specify several subfields which you have found to be interesting to you while taking courses. The student who first named marketing might indicate an interest in selling or advertising or both.

3. Would you like to investigate some theoretical aspect of this subfield or an applied problem?

4. If you choose a theoretical aspect, are you familiar with the theoretical writings in the field? If the student is not aware of the current theoretical structure in this narrowed-down area of knowledge, he is guided to the literature.

EXHIBIT 6-4

Formulation of a Problem by Narrowing Down from a Broad Area

SESSION   STATUS

1   I really had no idea as to what field or topic I was going to write on.

2   I've decided to write in the area of accounting. I've read some articles in the field but I haven't decided my research topic as of yet.

3   In the area of accounting I've been doing some more reading. A couple of fields have interested me in this area:
     (a) Pension Plans
     (b) Extraordinary Gains and Losses
     (c) Accounting Ethics

4   I've narrowed my topic down to pension plans. I have been reading articles in this area but have not narrowed this topic down to anything specific as of yet.

5   Tentatively, I plan to find out what the trend is as pertains to the financing and accounting for pension plans. Due to the increasing importance of pension plans and the increasing costs of these plans to companies, management has come to realize the need for planning of present and future funds. Specifically, I want to find out how companies are financing and accounting for their pension plans. Are their methods being contested by the internal revenue? Is the Accounting Principles Board of the AICPA setting up special ways of accounting for pension plans? (As was suggested in class, I plan to look into "portable" pension plans and the affect of this type of plan on company costs and the effect of this plan on accounting records.)

6   I have done more reading on pension plans. Specifically, I've read most of the magazine articles in the library which pertain to this topic. I tried to locate articles on the "portable" pension plans but could only find one article that even mentioned this aspect of pension plans.

7   I've written up my research project proposal for today. My topic is, Accounting and Financing For the Cost of Private Pension Plans.

8   After discussing my research project proposal in class I have narrowed my topic down to the financing of pension plans. I have written up a new research project proposal for today's class.

9   Research project proposal and outline

10   Outline as follows:

THE FINANCING OF PENSION PLANS

I.   Introduction
       A.   The growth of pension plans
       B.   The importance of pension plans

II.   Pension Financing Environment
       A.   Objectives of company as pertains to financing
       B.   Minimum standards for financing
       C.   Obligations of financial manager
            1.   Need for responsibility and control
            2.   Consideration of "escalator effect"

III.   Specific Methods of Financing Pension Plans
       A.   Characteristics of each method
            1.   Advantages and disadvantages of each method
            2.   Examples using figures to compare methods
                 (a) Statistics concerning the methods
                 (b) Charts and graphs to emphasize differences

EXHIBIT 6-4 (*continued*)

IV. Investment Policies Used with Pension Plan Financing
    A. Common stock investment
        1. Growth of investment
        2. Risk involved with investment
        3. Rate of return on investment
    B. Fixed income investments
        1. Growth of investment
        2. Risk involved
        3. Rate of return on investment
    C. Investment strategies
        1. Mixture of the two types of investments
        2. Utility function of the policy
        3. Reliability of cash inflow
        4. Predictability of cash outflow
V. Funding Agencies for Financing Pension Plans
    A. Trust funds
        1. Trust agreements
        2. Advantages and disadvantages of using a trust fund
    B. Insurance companies
        1. Contracts with life insurance companies
        2. Advantages and disadvantages of using an insurance company
VI. Summary and Conclusions

5. If you choose to work on an applied problem, have you come across such a problem in your experience or reading? If the student cannot think of an applied problem to work on, he may discuss possible problems with local executives or professors in this narrowed-down area.

Actually the professor may play a large part in this incubation process by asking the above questions, acting as a prober and questioner to stimulate the student's thinking, and generally getting the student to follow his own interests and special capabilities. Exhibit 6-4 shows in raw form the notes a student made describing his thoughts as he developed his problem over a number of weeks.

FORMULATION OF ILL-STRUCTURED PROBLEMS

There are problem situations which are so complex, have such vague and so many inputs, constraints, and goals associated with them, that different researchers may formulate completely different problems in the same circumstances. These "ill-defined" or "ill-structured" problems are at the other end of the continuum from well-defined problems where the objective or task is specific and either the input or the process for transforming the input is given. As W. R. Reitman says,

> To the extent that a problem situation evokes a high level of agreement over a specified community of problem solvers regarding the referents of the attributes in which it is given, the operations that are permitted, and the consequences of those operations, it may be termed unambiguous or well defined with respect to that community. On the

other hand, to the extent that a problem evokes a highly variable set of responses concerning referents of attributes, permissable operations, and their consequences, it may be considered ill-defined or ambiguous with respect to that community. [7]

There appear to be a broad domain of problems which involve the *transformation* or *creation* of states, objects, or collection of objects. Let I and E stand for initial and terminal states or objects, respectively. Let T denote a process, program or sequence of operations. A problem situation may then be represented by the three-component vector

$$[I, E, T]$$

A vector $[I, E, T]$ is called a *problem vector* if it has associated with it a *problem requirement* that another vector $[I', E', T']$ is to be found such that I', E', and T' are elements of I, E, and T and so that T' applied to I' will yield a unique E'. Finding the I', E', and T' in this situation is called solving the problem identified by the problem vector and problem requirements. When the sets I, E, and T are not defined or are ambiguous, the problem is ill-structured. There are many solutions, so that the objective of the researcher is to generate just *one* complete and particular solution, i.e., just one $[I', E', T']$ which satisfies the problem requirement.

Perhaps the most definitive approach to tackling ill-structured problems of an applied nature is the following.

A. Analyze the relevant operations and the communication system by which they are controlled.
  1. Identify and trace each communication related to operations under study.
  2. Identify each transformation of information and decision process.
  3. Identify each step in the relevant operations.
  4. Drop from consideration each communication or transformation which has no effect on operations (e.g., billing in production operations).
  5. Group operations between control points.
  6. Prepare a flow chart showing:
    (a) Control points and decisions made.
    (b) Flow of pertinent information between control points and time consumed.
    (c) Flow of materials and time of grouped operations.

[7]Walter B. Reitman, "Heuristic Decision Procedures, Open Constraints, and the Structure of Ill-Defined Problems," in Maynard W. Shelly, II, and Glenn L. Bryan (eds.), *Human Judgments and Optimality* (New York: John Wiley & Sons, Inc., 1964), p. 285. The successive concept of *problem vector* is drawn from the same source. The student is urged to read this entire contribution by Reitman.

B. Formulate management's problem.
 1. Identify decision makers and the decision-making procedure.
 2. Determine the decision makers' relevant objectives.
 3. Identify other participants and the channels of their influence on a solution.
 4. Determine objectives of the other participants.
 5. Determine alternative courses of action available to decision makers.
 6. Determine counteractions available to other participants.
C. Formulate the research problem.
 1. Edit and condense the relevant objectives.
 2. Edit and condense the relevant courses of action.
 3. Define the measure of effectiveness to be used.
  (a) Define the measure of efficiency to be used relative to each objective.
  (b) Weight objectives (if qualitative) or units of objectives (if quantitative).
  (c) Define the criterion of best decision as some function of the sum of weighted efficiencies (e.g., maximum expected return, minimum expected loss).[8]

SUMMARY

To a great extent, the most important step in research is the identification, selection, and formulation of the problem. A problem properly identified and formulated, even if never subjected to research, has more value than the solution to the wrong decision problem. Quantitative approaches to research require precise formulation of the problem and thus are attaining greater favor among researchers and decision makers. There remains considerable difficulty, however, both in stating and solving "ill-defined" problems.

From the viewpoint of the university student, finding and formulating a problem is too often an ill-structured problem for him. Some suggestions for guiding the student in this endeavor without restricting his creative thinking have been outlined in this chapter.

QUESTIONS AND TOPICS FOR DISCUSSION

1. Distinguish between an essentially scientific theoretical problem and an applied problem. Describe the nature of a problem which falls in between these two extremes.

2. Should there be a distinction between identification of a problem and selection of a problem? Given reasons for your answer.

---

[8]C. West Churchman, Russell L. Ackoff, and E. Leonard Arnoff, *Introduction to Operations Research* (New York: John Wiley & Sons, Inc., 1957), p. 132.

3. Can several different problems of a business produce the identical symptom or symptoms? What would be the implications for the researcher if such were to be the case?

4. If you are faced with a problem, what alternatives do you have which will lead to a resolution of your situation?

5. Usually in business, one big problem consists of many subproblems. The cost of the problem is often prohibitive. What should the company do when it is faced with such a situation?

6. If you are a student with a major field of concentration or interest, prepare an outline showing major problems businesses face in your functional field and subdivisions of these problems.

7. Take an article from the business literature reporting on basic research in business. Criticize the author's formulation of the problem. Reformulate the problem.

8. What are major weaknesses of business-problem formulation which you have observed from experience and reading?

9. Take a major topic in this chapter and write a critique, an amplification, or a revision of it.

10. Can you develop a different systematic method for a student to develop a problem for research?

11. Design forms which could be printed and given to students so that they end up with a formulation of a problem. This could consist of a set of questions to answer or a series of steps to perform. The last form sheet could consist of line items, which when filled out represent a complete specification of a problem.

12. In your own words, give a complete definition of an ill-structured problem. What are some actual examples from business which you have read about or experienced?

13. How do operations researchers handle or "digest" ill-structured problems?

14. Give five or six concrete examples from business in terms of "problem vectors" and "problem requirements."

chapter 7

Preparing the Research Proposal

WHAT IS A BUSINESS RESEARCH PROPOSAL?

A business research proposal is a bid or offer to undertake an investigation of some business problem. Business research proposals may be classified as:
1. Internal proposals.
2. External—solicited or unsolicited—proposals
   (a) Directed to a private firm for its own commercial purposes.
   (b) Directed to a trade association.
   (c) Directed to a nonprofit institution such as a hospital, non-profit research organization, or university.
   (d) Directed to a government agency.
   (e) Directed to a prime contractor or subcontractor for government work.

Internal proposals within business firms are likely to be unstructured and somewhat informal. A letter may be all that is required to propose a market research project, for example. Within academic and other bureaucratic types of institutions, a more formal approach is usually required.

External proposals are those prepared for an organization other than the one that employs the researcher. The solicited external proposal is prepared in response to a formal or informal request. It may be requested as a bid against other proposals.

The unsolicited external proposal is initiated by a company or individual for another organization or individual. The proposer, because of his technical competence and ability to identify the needs of a commercial organization, government agency, or institution, advances a proposal on a speculative basis. The unsolicited proposal has the advantage of not facing competitive proposals.

NEED FOR A RESEARCH PROPOSAL

The research proposal serves two basic needs. In the first case, it provides a document to the potential sponsor of the research for evaluation relative to his needs. It permits him to evaluate both the proposed research design and the researcher or research team. By comparison with other proposals submitted, if any, he may then decide which is likely to yield the best result for his investment.

In the second case, the preparation of a research proposal satisfies the need of the researcher to think through and plan his research carefully. Even if he is doing the research without a sponsor, the preparation of a proposal is a valuable exercise. The research proposal, when prepared for a sponsor, forces the researcher into a thorough criticism and structuring of each aspect of his proposed research. He must ask himself at each step, "If I were a potential sponsor, why would I want to spend money on this proposed research?" If too subjective a view is taken by the researcher, he will likely have his proposal rejected with a consequent waste of time and effort. This does not mean that all good proposals are accepted, but that carefully prepared proposals are more likely to be accepted than those amateurishly prepared.

STUDENT'S RESEARCH PROPOSAL

Research Paper and Master's Thesis Research

For research term papers and for the common three-semester-hour graduate research course, the research proposal need not be elaborate. It should also be brief so that the student is not discouraged at the start from getting his research under way. The minimum requirements which suffice well for a proposal at this level of academic work are:

1. Tentative title
2. Statement of the problem
3. Research strategy and outline of method
4. Problems anticipated in carrying out the research
5. Resources required
6. Nature or form of the results

A typical example of a student's business research proposal is shown in Exhibit 7-1. While such a proposal could be improved by further reworking, it served its purpose in requiring the student to think ahead. In particular, thinking about problems which may prevent his completing this particular project has proved worthwhile.

Generally, student proposals lack one important ingredient found in professional proposals, namely a time schedule. Since students are faced with a deadline for completion of the work, the scope of the research is usually tailored to the time available.

Doctoral Research

Doctoral research involves a heavy commitment of time, effort, and sometimes money by a highly educated individual. It also requires the valuable time of several professors on the student's doctoral committee. In these circumstances

EXHIBIT 7-1
Student's Project Proposal

TITLE: Stan Celebucki

The High Cost of Medicaid

OBJECTIVE:

The objective of this study is to show if the cost of Medicaid to New York State taxpayers is far in excess of the benefits being gained. The study will further show that if a compulsory health insurance law were passed, a substantial saving would accrue to the tax-payers. The comparison between Medicaid and compulsory health insurance will take into account the cost of health insurance for those presently receiving welfare assistance.

PROPOSED APPROACH:

The cost of health insurance equivalent to Medicaid will have to be found. Next, the number of New York State residents presently receiving welfare assistance will have to be determined. From these figures the cost of compulsory health insurance to New York State taxpayers may be computed.

The above cost will then be compared to the cost of Medicaid presently accruing to New York State taxpayers. The cost of Medicaid will then be broken down into both direct and indirect elements for further analysis.

Required for Study:

1. Knowledge of what Medicaid covers.
2. Contact with insurance companies to find thd cost of equivalent health insurance.
3. Knowledge of the number of people receiving welfare assistance in New York.
4. Knowledge of the average direct cost per patient covered by Medicaid.
5. Knowledge of the number of people receiving medical assistance under Medicaid for a specified time period.
6. Knowledge of the total cost of Medicaid to New York State taxpayers for a specified time period.
7. About 120 hours of available time.

Problems Anticipated:

1. All of the data may not be available.
2. Interviewing may be required to determine the average direct cost per patient covered by Medicaid.

Expected Results:

The study should prove or disprove that Medicaid is costing New York State taxpayers more than it's worth.

a carefully worked out research project proposal should be required. In fact, the student should be required to defend (1) his problem as one of sufficient scope, and (2) his proposed method as one that will provide adequate evidence for his conclusions. In some respects, defense of the plan of action is as important as a defense of the finished report; for if the research design does not meet the standards of the doctoral committee, the finished work will not.

SMALL-SCALE PROFESSIONAL RESEARCH PROPOSAL

A small-scale professional research project is usually one conducted by a professional worker, perhaps with some technical and clerical assistance with a total cost of about $25,000 or less. A consultant or university professor might be the director of such a project. A small-scale research proposal may contain the following sections.

1. *Introduction*

Start with a concise background of the problem, the problem statement, and the significance of the problem to the sponsor, or to scientific development in the case of basic research. A realistic estimate of the cost and time required may be appropriate at this point.

2. *Qualifications of the Researcher or the Research Director and His Research Team*

Most research is supported on the basis of the people involved. Thus an individual who can demonstrate past successful experience is more apt to obtain a grant than an unknown. This means that the neophyte researcher must usually start as an associate of an accepted researcher. If the proposal is offered only by an inexperienced researcher, he should transpose the sequence of this section with the following section (3).

3. *Research Strategy and Method*

The researcher's understanding of the problem, previous attacks upon it, and alternative approaches should be briefly covered. He should indicate why his approach is the best and modifications of it which will ensure a solution in the face of possible difficulties.

The specific research method should be outlined, the equipment and facilities which are required should be listed, and a detailed schedule presented. (Often this section precedes section 2.)

4. *Budget*

A detailed budget should be presented in a form desired by the potential sponsor. For example, the sponsor may not allow expenses for travel or for clerical help. In such case these expenses would be included under some other heading such as salaries or fees for the research directors. Limitations on travel, per diem rates, and purchase of capital equipment are other points which should be anticipated in the proposal.

The researcher should consider carefully all possible costs. For example, he should not forget the cost of publication of the final report *and* the number of copies to be produced. A more obscure cost in the case of most federal grants is that of maintaining records over a number of years. For example, one agency states:

> Each grantee shall provide for keeping accessible and intact all records pertaining to the Grant: (1) For 3 years after the close of the fiscal year in which the expenditures are liquidated; or (2) Until the Grantee is notified that such records are not needed for program administrative review, or (3) Until the Grantee is notified of the Federal fiscal audit.[1]

An illustration of the format which might be used for a budget is shown in Exhibit 7-2. A simpler budget format adapted from an actual proposal is repre-

---

[1] U.S. Department of Health, Education, and Welfare, *A Manual For the Preparation of Proposals* (Washington, D.C.: Government Printing Office, March 1967), p. 76.

EXHIBIT 7-2
Budget Format

RESEARCH PROGRAM BUDGET

		Rate	Total Man-Days or Man-Weeks or Man-Months	Total Dollars
A.	Salaries			
	1. Director...			$
	2. Associate or assistant			
	director			
	3. Technical assistants			
	(or graduate students)			
	4. Secretarial and clerical......................................			
	Subtotal for Salaries.....................................			$_____
B.	Other Costs			
	5. Employee services and benefits			$
	6. Travel...			
	7. Office supplies...			
	8. Rent...			
	9. Reproduction and storage			
	10. Equipment			
	Subtotal of other costs..			$
	11. Total of Direct Costs			
	12. Federal Support (percent of line 11).................................			$
	13. Institutional Support (percent of line 11)			$
	14. Federal Funds Requested			$

EXHIBIT 7-3
Sample Budget

BUDGET

Research Director
Kent Gordon, Professor of Management, State U.
  2 months at half time during summer... $ 2,500

Associate Director
Karl Delmar, Professor of Management, State U.
  2 months at half time during summer... 2,200

Research Assistants (2)
  Academic year... 7,840
  Summer, 9 weeks, 40 hr/wk @ $3.00/hr... 2,160

Clerical Expense (1)
  480 hours @ $2.00/hr... 960

Travel 1,500

Telephone and office supplies 500
  Subtotal $17,660
Overhead at 40% 7,064
  Grand Total... $24,724

sented in Exhibit 7-3. Salaries for professors must be based on their annual academic rate. Note that an allowance of 40 percent is shown for payment to the university for general administration and facilities.

LARGE-SCALE PROFESSIONAL RESEARCH PROPOSAL

In preparing a proposal for a large research project, it is essential that the researcher uncover through personal communication as much as possible about the objectives of the sponsor. Even when specifications have accompanied a request to bid, further probing is important. The problem in developing a proposal is getting enough information, not in getting too much. In parallel with such a dialogue, the research team should (1) review previous successful and unsuccessful efforts to solve similar business problems and (2) attempt to develop new, economical, and technically sound approaches to the research problem.

When time runs out so that preliminary research and the process of obtaining information from the sponsor must terminate, the preparation of the proposal gets underway. Generally, although the sequence may vary, the content of the large-scale research proposal is:

1. Introduction
2. Proposed method of approach (and problems anticipated)
3. Qualifications of researchers
4. Facilities available
5. Budget
6. Schedule
7. Management of the project
8. Conclusion

Introduction

The Introduction contains a clear, concise statement of the problem or technical specification, what is involved in solving the problem, the proposed method of approach, and the form of the expected results. Define and delimit the area of the research. A realistic time estimate, a conservative cost estimate, and a statement of the research team's qualifications and willingness to devote its resources to the proposed research should also be included. The purpose of the introduction is to present a brief overall look at what the research team is offering and to capture the interest of the reader immediately.

Proposed Method of Approach

The method of reaching a solution should be developed, using as many chapters as there are significant parts or phases to the method. Relation to related previous research as a basis should be shown. Obvious alternative approaches should be mentioned briefly to show that they have been considered and that the proposed method is superior. Point out realistically problems that may arise in reaching a solution and how they might be dealt with. Modifications of method required by such obstacles as inability to obtain certain information should be included.

Outline briefly the personnel assignments, facilities or location of work, procedures, and milestone schedule. Establish the fact that the research team has a realistic and sophisticated approach to the problem and will be able to deliver results worth the money expended.

Qualifications of the Researchers

The qualifications of the researchers generally start with academic degrees held. The highest degree held is particularly significant if it is a Ph.D., since this is an indication of research training. Another very important (if not most important) qualification is experience in carrying out previous research. Therefore a concise description of such experience should be included. Finally, actual experience as an executive or employee in business carries considerable weight if the sponsor is a business enterprise. Top managers are often dubious about the ability of armchair professors to solve practical problems. For each researcher, the relevant business and technical societies he belongs to also helps identify his fields of interest.

There is a question as to whether the age of each researcher should be included. If all the researchers are older men or all are very young men, a listing of ages could be disadvantageous. On the other hand, if there is a good mixture of ages which can be represented as a combination of experience and imagination, there may be an advantage to showing ages.

Facilities Available

It is an advantage to show that appropriate modern facilities are available for the research. Depending upon the research, such facilities as printing and reproduction equipment, a machine shop, a special research laboratory, various perceptual and other physiological and psychological equipment, and electronic computers may be an asset. The proposal should carefully list any possible relevant facilities, including office facilities for researchers and technicians.

Budget

The budget format may follow generally that discussed under the small-scale professional research project. For a large-scale project, it is advisable to show quarterly or even monthly expenditures so that the reviewer may check costs against scheduled performance. Budget refinements and details are indicative of careful planning.

Schedule

One way of scheduling is to identify major phases or milestones of the research and estimate completion times from time of start. The convenient

EXHIBIT 7-4
Gantt Chart for Research on Merchandising of Dairy
Products in Public Eating Places

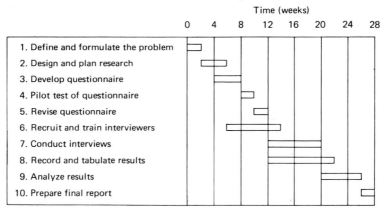

format for presentation of this type of schedule is the type of bar chart known as the Gantt chart. See Exhibit 7-4.

If the project is a very large and complex one, perhaps involving several major but related objectives, a critical path method of scheduling may be effective. In its simplest form, major milestones and tasks are identified. Starting with final milestones, the completion of the research, the schedule is developed by working backward to show each event which must directly precede the achievement of a particular event. Events are indicated by circles, and activities that must be carried out to complete an event are shown as arrows connecting two or more events. (See Exhibit 7-5.) The time required to complete each activity is estimated and shown on the network diagram.

Each path is traced from starting event to end event and the times for each path are individually accumulated. The longest time path is called the "critical path," because the delay in activity in this path delays the entire project. Statistical methods for arriving at "expected" times for activities are widely discussed in books and articles under the heading PERT (Program Evaluation and Review Technique) and CPM (Critical Path Method).

Management Section

The purpose of the management section of the research proposal is to convey to the potential sponsor the vital message of exactly how the research team plans to implement the project. The management section should touch upon the following subjects in varying detail:

1. Master plan for doing the research
2. Organization for conducting the research
3. System of management procedures and controls for execution of the plan

EXHIBIT 7-5

Critical Path Diagram for Research on the Nature of Product Planning in Industry

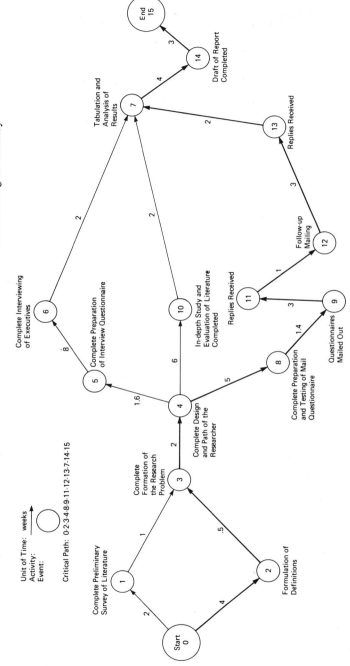

   4. Management and technical reports
   5. Research team relationship with the sponsor
   6. Financial responsibility
   7. Management competence

A master plan is required for large complex research projects to show how the researcher will tie together all phases and all tasks involved, the scheduled dates, the economic considerations, and approaches to problems for which no precedent exists. Tables, charts, and illustrations aid considerably in presenting such material in a form that can be readily grasped by the reader.

Where a number of people are involved in a research project, the various interrelationships must be formally identified. The sponsor needs to know that the director of research is an individual with the personality, ability, and experience to coordinate and inspire the members of the research team. In turn, the qualifications of the management team, as presented in a separate section or in the section, under consideration, must instill confidence in the sponsor that they are capable team workers as well as problem solvers.

For complex projects with a number of people involved, management procedures for information processing become essential. Members of the team need to know what each of the others is doing if the work is to be integrated and coordinated. Record control, flow-of-work procedures, control of financial expenditures, and schedule control are critical to the successful operation of such projects.

The relationship between the potential sponsor and the research team or the institution conducting the research may sometimes lead to disaster. The major cause for this is failure to define carefully the part to be played by each. For example, the direction of the research may come from either the sponsor or the institution proposing the work and it should be clearly understood which it is. The type and frequency of progress reports should be spelled out so that the sponsor is not subject to a big surprise at what has been done when the project is over. The sponsor's limits on control or "interference" during the research process needs to be delineated. Such control relates both to the work performed and the money expended.

How payments to the research organization will be made is another point to be specified. Should they be regular monthly payments, progress payments, or lump-sum payment at the conclusion? Is the sponsor expected to provide information, services such as clerical or printing, or facilities? Who will have the authority to speak for the sponsor and who for the research institution? Who shall have the right to publish results of the research and when? These and other relevant questions should be thought about in developing a proposal.

Financial responsibility and overall management competence are requisites for the conduct of expensive research projects. Obviously the sponsor must be convinced that the proposing group possesses both. Ability to plan excellent research does not guarantee performance in implementation. The nature of the research proposal as a whole provides a clue to the management sophistication of the research director.

PROPOSALS TO GOVERNMENT AGENCIES

It is common practice for government agencies responsible for expenditure of large sums of money on research to establish a formal project proposal outline. This is particularly true when many research projects must be carried out in support of a program that must show readily discernible results. An example of such a proposal format and instructions for preparing a proposal are shown in the appendices to this chapter.

EVALUATION AND REASONS FOR REJECTION OF PROPOSALS

Both formal and informal methods have been used to evaluate research project proposals. The formal methods consist essentially of establishing desired criteria and weights (points) for each criterion. Each proposal is evaluated in terms of each criterion, and the proposal obtaining the greatest number of points is awarded the contract. This formal approach is most apt to be applied in the case of competitive bidding.

The informal approach is based upon the judgments of the decision makers in the sponsoring agency as to whether a research proposal best meets their needs. The principal needs are understood, but not necessarily ranked, weighted, or documented. In practice, the positive aspects of the evaluation include:

1. The background of the researchers and personal relationships between sponsor and research director.

2. The responsiveness of the proposal as a whole to the needs of the sponsor.

3. The cost of the project relative to the funds available.

4. The balance between the gains which are promised and the risk inherent in the conduct of the research.

5. Clarity of presentation of the proposal.

6. A good schedule for completion.

7. A follow-up proposal to a previously successful project.

Negative aspects which may lead to rejection of a proposal are:

1. Failure of the proposal to meet the sponsor's requirements.

2. Insufficient funds available at the time the proposal is made.

3. Inadequate review by the potential sponsor.

4. Technical deficiencies in the approach and method given in the proposal.

5. Poor presentation of the proposal. While a beautifully illustrated and handsomely bound proposal will not overcome technical deficiencies, a sloppy, unclear, and unprofessional-looking proposal will almost surely defeat whatever merit the concept itself may have.

QUESTIONS AND TOPICS FOR DISCUSSION

1. Should there be a different presentation of information for solicited proposals and unsolicited proposals? Explain.

2. Would you advocate the preparation of a research proposal for a master's thesis? For a term research paper?

3. Do you think that there would be fewer unsuccessful doctoral "dissertations" written in economics and business if a formal research proposal were required to be prepared in advance and defended by the candidate? Discuss.

4. Select a report of research from a business journal and construct a research proposal for the research as if it had not yet been performed. Make estimates of time and costs as best you can. Does the cost or time required seem high?

5. Obtain a research proposal from a government agency and analyze it.

6. In evaluating a research proposal, would you place more weight on the clarity, logic, and completeness of description in the proposal or on the background of successful research of the research team? Discuss.

7. Design a form for a business research proposal which could be completed rapidly for small projects and which would be complete enough for large proposals. Do you think the federal income tax forms represent good analogies?

8. Contact a high-level business executive and inquire about the format of proposals for research on business problems in his company. If only memos or letters are used, obtain his opinion about advantages and disadvantages of a more formal approach.

9. Contact a research foundation or a government agency and inquire about reasons for their rejection of past research proposals.

10. Make a brief search for studies of why research proposals are rejected. (See for example the National Science Foundation report, *A Case Study of Support of Scientific and Engineering Research Proposals,* NSF 63–22.) What conclusions do you reach?

APPENDICES

FORMATS FOR GOVERNMENT RESEARCH PROPOSALS

APPENDIX A

U.S. DEPARTMENT OF LABOR

Office of Manpower, Automation and Training

DL—MT—201
Budget Bureau No. 44—R 1216

INSTRUCTIONS FOR

PREPARING AND SUBMITTING A PROPOSAL FOR A RESEARCH PROJECT UNDER THE MANPOWER DEVELOPMENT AND TRAINING ACT, PL 87-415

These instructions are in three parts:

A. General instructions,

B. A specific outline to be used in describing the content and procedure of the research project, including personnel and facilities, and

C. An outline for an estimated budget.

There is *no printed* form to be used.

A. GENERAL INSTRUCTIONS

1. Proposal Submission

The first page of the proposal must show the following information in the order indicated.

PROPOSAL SUBMITTED TO THE DIRECTOR, OFFICE OF MANPOWER, AUTOMATION AND TRAINING, U.S. DEPARTMENT OF LABOR, FOR THE CONDUCT OF A RESEARCH PROJECT UNDER THE PROVISIONS OF TITLE I OF THE MANPOWER DEVELOPMENT AND TRAINING ACT, PL 87–415

Project title:	(Be concise, descriptive, and as specific as possible. Avoid obscure technical terms. Include key words under which project may be indexed.)
Submitted by:	(Name of organization, institution, agency, or individual hereinafter referred to as "organization.")
Address:	(Of organization.)
Telephone number:	(Of organization. Include area code.)
Initiated by:	(Full name and position of individual who is initiating project, ordinarily the director or chief investigator.)
Transmitted by:	(Full name and position of official who is approving the submission of the proposal. This must be someone with authority to commit the organization to the proposed project. The proposal should be signed by both the initiator and the transmitter on the original or master copy.)
Date:	(Date transmitted.)

2. Mailing Address for Proposals

Send all proposals to: Director
Office of Manpower, Automation and Training
U.S. Department of Labor
Washington, D.C. 20210

3. Scope and Substance of the Proposal

The initial proposal should be complete enough to communicate all the information necessary for a sound evaluation. Excessive length should be avoided. It should encompass the following:

a. *Area of Study*

(1) The proposed research should seek to develop new knowledge or new applications of existing knowledge which give promise of furthering the objectives of the Manpower Act. The objectives of the Manpower Act as stated in title I of the act may be summarized as follows:

(a) To develop and apply the information and methods needed to deal with the problems of unemployment and other malutilizations of manpower resources.

(b) To accomplish technological progress while avoiding or minimizing individual hardship and widespread unemployment.

(c) To raise the skill levels of the Nation's work force, to increase the Nation's productivity, and to provide the manpower resources needed for the advancing technology.

(2) The project should be focused primarily on significant manpower problems.

(3) The anticipated results of the project should have broad national interest. Projects may be limited to special areas *only* where such studies can be shown to provide a basis for generalized conclusions, or to have application over a wide area.

(4) The project should not duplicate ongoing research; nor should it duplicate completed research the results of which provide currently valid applications.

b. *Research Design*

(1) The problem with which the research proposes to deal should be clearly defined.

(2) The proposal should reflect an adequate knowledge of other research related to the problem.

(3) Questions to be answered or hypotheses to be tested should be well formulated and clearly stated.

(4) The proposal should outline fully the procedures to be followed and wherever applicable, include information on such matters as sampling procedures, controls, types of data to be gathered, and statistical analyses to be made.

c. *Personnel and Facilities*

(1) The director or principal investigator must be someone who has previously done successful research in the the area involved or who has clearly demonstrated competence for performing or directing work in that area.

(2) The organization or individual submitting the proposal must have facilities and staff available which are adequate for carrying out the research.

(3) Where applicable, as, for example, for a research proposal involving a casework study of a training program, the proposal should indicate the agreed interest and intended cooperation in the program on the part of all local agencies whose interest and cooperation are necessary for the successful accomplishment of the research project.

d. *Economic Efficiency*

(1) The suggested approach to the problem must be reasonable in terms of overall cost as compared with the cost of other possible approaches.

(2) The suggested approach to problems involving the analysis of statistical data must utilize, to the extent feasible, data already available or being collected through government and other sources.

(3) The total proposed expenditure must be justifiable in terms of the probable value of the results of the proposed research.

4. Preparation of Proposal Statements and Reports

Generally, initial proposals should run about 8 to 10 pages in length. More detailed and lengthier statements may be required for proposals during negotiation.

a. *Number of Copies Required*

Proposals should be submitted in 30 copies, typed or otherwise reproduced on white paper of standard size on one side only.

b. *Submission and Review Dates*

Proposals may be submitted at any time, and will be reviewed as expeditiously as possible. Acknowledgment of receipt will usually be made within 15 days. Processing, review by research specialists, and evaluations of comments received usually require 60 days from receipt of proposal.

5. Approval

Notice of approval for negotiation (or disapproval) will be given as soon as possible following review and evaluation. Final approval for contracting will depend on negotiations, and will require agreement on content, structure and budget of the project by both the organization and the Office of Manpower, Automation and Training.

NOTE: As required by the Office of Statistical Standards, Bureau of the Budget, any research contract entered into will include the following clause: "The Researcher shall submit to the Secretary or his designated representative copies of all proposed questionnaires and survey plans for clearance in advance of the use in accordance with the Federal Reports Act of 1942."

B. OUTLINE OF PROPOSAL CONTENT AND PROCEDURE

Follow the outline below in describing the proposed project. Identify each section by number and title as indicated in the outline.

1. Abstract

On a *single, separate* page submit a summary of the proposal under two main heads: (1) Objectives and (2) Procedures.

2. Problem

Give a brief statement of the problem to be investigated explaining its importance and significance in relationship to the objectives of the Manpower Act.

3. Objectives

State the hypotheses to be tested or the specific questions to be answered.

4. Relationship to Other Research

Discuss the proposed study in relation to previous or ongoing research in related areas, and indicate how the proposed study will extend the body of knowledge about the areas. Point our what will be distinctive or different about the proposed research as compared with previous research, and in what ways it may suggest or lend support to programs for action in the manpower area.

5. Procedure

Describe the procedure in detail listing the steps to be followed. Where pertinent, be sure to include specific information on each of the following:

a. *Populations, samples, experimental and control groups, if any.*

Indicate their origin, composition, purpose, use, numbers involved, types of data to be collected on each, sampling plans, etc.

b. *Experimental design and methods to be used.*

c. *Data.*

Describe types to be gathered and methods to be used. Indicate extent to which the data analyzed will be from existing sources, such as Department of Labor or Census Bureau. Describe questionnaires, interview guides, tests, and other research instruments to be used.

d. *Analyses.*

Indicate methods of statistical and other analyses to be used in testing the hypotheses or achieving the objectives.

e. *Phasing.*

Indicate approximate time schedule for various aspects or phases of the project.

f. *Expected endproduct.*

This should include preliminary reports of findings periodically during the course of the project, and a final report.

6. Personnel

Give name, title, and a brief statement of the research experience of the principal investigator, and of other key personnel if possible.

7. Facilities

Indicate special facilities and similar advantages, including research staff resources, available to the organization.

8. Duration

Estimate total time for project and indicate beginning and ending dates.

9. Other Information

Indicate other information pertinent to the proposal, including the following:

a. Extent of agreed cooperation in project by agencies whose support is necessary for the successful accomplishment of objectives. Include names and titles of officials of such agencies giving assurance of cooperation. For example, in a training-research project, cooperation of State employment security agency may be vital to the success of the project.

b. Amount of financial or other support available for this project from other sources.

c. Whether this proposal has been or will be submitted to any other agency or organization for financial support.

d. Whether this proposal is an extension of or an addition to a previous project supported by the Department of Labor or other government agency.

e. Whether this project or a similar one was previously submitted to the Department of Labor or other government agency.

C. BUDGET

Include a section on estimated costs of the project to be covered by contract with the Department of Labor. Start this section on a new page, identifying it in sequence with previous sections as "10. Budget."

The cost of performance of a contract includes the costs of necessary direct items of expenditure incurred in the performance of the contract; it may also include an amount for overhead or indirect costs to be determined by negotiation.

Following the categories as shown in the outline below, and rounding all amounts to the nearest dollar, list anticipated requirements for all items of expenditure. If the project is expected to extend beyond the end of the fiscal year (June 30), indicate amounts required for each year and in total.

1. Direct Costs

a. *Personal Services*

(1) Include salaries and wages of all personnel which are directly attributable to actual performance under this contract, whether on a full- or part-time basis. (List personnel by title, man-months and dollar amount.)

(2) Include, in connection with the above, but identify separately, allowances for vacation, holiday, and sick-leave pay. Also include employee benefits if customarily granted.

(3) Include consultants as required.

b. *Materials and Supplies*

List all materials and supplies which are directly expended by the contractor in performance of the contract.

c. *Travel*

Include subsistence during travel, in accordance with the contractor's established policy.

d. *Communications*

Include telephone and telegraph charges.

e. *Services*

Include those not specifically covered under personal services. When a study involves securing information through Federal agencies (as U.S. Bureau of the Census) or State agencies (as State employment service), the costs of such services should be included.

f. *Other*

Itemize by category and amount.

2. Indirect Costs or Overhead

Include pro-rata share of administrative costs. Give basis for the determination of the proposed overhead rate and reference to other current Government contracts, if any. Overhead rates may be fixed during the negotiation of a contract, or may be determined provisionally, with final settlement made at the conclusion of the contract.

If the division between direct and indirect costs as outlined above differs from the contractor's established accounting system and procedures for allocating such costs, the contractor's system may be followed and the differences will be considered in negotiating an equitable percentage to be applied in the contract. It is most important that all items of cost be readily identifiable regardless of whether they are shown as direct or indirect.

The proposed budget will be reviewed against applicable Federal regulations as part of the initial review. Where changes are necessary for projects which are otherwise approved for negotiation, these changes, as well as decisions concerning the determination of overhead rate, will be made during the negotiation of the contract.

APPENDIX B

CAP-RDT FORM 1
DEC 64

OFFICE OF ECONOMIC OPPORTUNITY

Form Approved
Budget Bureau No.
Approval Expires

```
┌─────────────────────────────────────┐
│  Project No. (Do not Use This       │
│            Space)                    │
└─────────────────────────────────────┘
```

NOTICE OF TRAINING OR DEMONSTRATION OR RESEARCH PROJECT

Submitted to: Community Action Program, Office of Economic Opportunity, Washington, D. C.   20506

Type of Project: ☐ Demonstration   ☐ Training   ☐ Research

Give names, departments, and official titles of PROJECT DIRECTOR and ALL MAJOR PROFESSIONAL PERSONNEL engaged on the project:

Name or title of project (10 words or less):

Name and Address of Applicant:

Summary of Proposed Project — (200 words or less.) In the Science Information Exchange summaries of proposed projects are exchanged with governmental and private agencies and are forwarded to interested investigators. Your summary will be used for these purposes.

Signature of
Project
Director _____ Date _____

Do Not Use This Space

Amount of Grant: $ _____
Grant Period: From _____ to _____
Grantee Support: $ _____

OFFICE OF ECONOMIC OPPORTUNITY
COMMUNITY ACTION PROGRAM

Form Approved
Budget Bureau No.
Approval Expires

Leave Blank
Date Rec'd _____
Application No. _____
Date Ack'd. _____

Leave Blank
Action _____
Action Date _____
Grant No. _____

PROPOSAL FOR DEMONSTRATION OR TRAINING OR RESEARCH GRANT

P.L. 88-452   Title II A   Section 207

Type of Project: ☐ Demonstration   ☐ Training   ☐ Research

A. Amount *(for the grant period shown in item B)*

$ _____

B. Duration of Grant Period *(12 months or less-See instructions.)*
_____ through _____
Mo.   Day   Year   Mo.   Day   Year

C. Type of Proposal *(Check one box only)*

☐ New Proposal

☐ Continuation of Grant Number _____

D. Estimated Duration of Project after the first grant period
_____

E. Estimated Total Cost of the project beyond the first grant
period _____

F. Project Director

Name _____

Mail Address of Project _____
_____
_____
_____ Tel. No. _____

G. Applicant Agency or Department

Name _____
_____

Mail Address _____
_____
_____

H. Financial Officer

Name _____

Title _____

Mail Address _____
_____
_____ Tel. No. _____

I. Designation of Payee *(Treasury check will be drawn as follows)* _____

J. Official Authorized to Sign Proposal for agency

Name _____

Title _____
_____

K. Personal Signatures (in ink)

(1) Project Director (Same as "F" above)_____ Date _____

(2) Authorized Official (Same as "J" above) _____ Date _____

Mail Completed Application to:
Community Action Program
Office of Economic Opportunity
Executive Office of the President
Washington, D.C. 20506

CAP-RDT FORM 2
DEC 64

Page 1

PROPOSED BUDGET

Use this form to itemize the expenses of the project in the grant period from _____

_____ to _____ (Same as period shown on page 1,
Mo.   Day   Year   Mo.   Day   Year

item B) The total amount requested in item i of column(2) must be the same as shown on page 1, item A.

(1)	(2) Funds requested from OEO (Omit cents)	(3) Grantee Contribution (Omit cents)
a. Personnel List all positions. Indicate time devoted to project and basis of compensation (see instructions).	$	$
Total Personnel	$	$
b. Trainees (Itemize): Applicable to Training Projects Only: (1) Subsistence	$	$
(2) Travel	$	$
c. Permanent Equipment (Itemize) Total	$	$
d. Consumable Supplies (Itemize by major types) Total	$	$
e. Travel (Itemize) Total	$	$
f. Miscellaneous Expenses (Itemize) Total	$	$
g. Totals — Direct Costs (Sum of categories a through f)	$	$
h. Indirect Costs (See Instructions and *Conditions Governing Grants*)	$	
i. Totals (Sum of categories g and h)	$	$

CAP-RDT FORM 3   Page 2
DEC 64

I. ESTIMATED BUDGET FOR SUBSEQUENT GRANT PERIOD(S)

A. Use the form provided below to give estimates of budget category totals for each grant period being requested. If support beyond the period requested in item B of page 1 of the application is not required, enter the word none in the appropriate column(s).

BUDGET CATEGORIES	SECOND GRANT PERIOD			THIRD GRANT PERIOD		
	___ to ___ Mo. Day Year Mo. Day Year			___ to ___ Mo. Day Year Mo. Day Year		
	OEO	Applicant Organization	Other (specify)	OEO	Applicant Organization	Other (specify)
a. Personnel						
b. Trainees: (Training Projects Only) (1) Subsistence						
(2) Travel						
c. Permanent Equipment						
d. Consumable Supplies						
e. Travel						
f. Miscellaneous Expenses						
g. Total Direct Costs (Sum of lines a-f)						
h. Indirect Costs						
i. Total Budget (Sum of lines g-h)						

B. Use the space below to explain and justify any unusual expenses. (Use continuation pages if necessary).

II. PREVIOUS AND CURRENT SUPPORT OF PROJECT (complete applicable lines only if this is an application for a continuation grant)

GRANT NUMBER	GRANT PERIOD	AMOUNT OF GRANT
	First Grant Period	
A.	From ___ to ___ Mo. Day Year Mo. Day Year	
	Second Grant Period	
B.	From ___ to ___ Mo. Day Year Mo. Day Year	

CAP-RDT FORM 4
DEC 64

Page 3

BIOGRAPHICAL SKETCHES

Provide brief sketches for all major professional personnel already selected who are to be actively engaged in this project. Begin with the Project Director.

A. 1. Name: _____ 2. Date of birth: _____
    3. Title of position in program: _____ 4. Sex: _____
    5. Education:
        Degrees conferred. (Begin with baccalaureate degree. Identify honorary degrees under field.):

DEGREE	INSTITUTION CONFERRING	FIELD(S)	YEAR

    6. Experience, especially that establishing qualifications in area covered by this application:

NATURE	YEAR(S)

    7. Fields of present professional interest, in order of choice:

    8. List publications in area related to project emphasis. (No more than five.):

B. 1. Name: _____ 2. Date of birth: _____
    3. Title of position in program: _____ 4. Sex: _____
    5. Education:
        Degrees conferred. (Begin with baccalaureate degree. Identify honorary degrees under field.):

DEGREE	INSTITUTION CONFERRING	FIELD(S)	YEAR

    6. Experience, especially that establishing qualifications in area covered by this application:

NATURE	YEAR(S)

    7. Fields of present professional interest, in order of choice:

    8. List publications in area related to project emphasis. (No more than five.):

CAP-RDT FORM 5
DEC 64

RESEARCH OR DEMONSTRATION PROJECT PLAN AND SUPPORTING DATA

Please describe your proposal in accordance with the following outline:

1. Research or Demonstration Project Plan

    The criteria governing the award of demonstration or research project grants are listed in The Demonstration Grant Guide or The Research Grant Guide. The information to be supplied in response to Items A through H below will be interpreted and evaluated by the reviewing groups in the light of these standards.

    A. A description of the specific problems to be addressed in the project.

    B. A precise identification of the hypotheses the project is going to test, including a clear explanation of the assumptions on which the demonstration or research is based.

    C. A detailing of the form of organization to be used in conducting the program. If organizations other than the applicant are to be closely related to the project, evidence of their agreement to cooperate should be submitted.

    D. Resources available for the project. In addition to the information on the budget requested as part of the application form, a description of the resources available should include a listing of the personnel available to staff the demonstration or research project.

    E. Specification of the form of organization to be used in conducting the program. If organizations other than the applicant are to be closely related to the project, evidence of their agreement to cooperate should be submitted.

    F. Detail the physical facilities which will be required for the projects, and evidence as to their availability.

    G. A full description of the evaluation procedure. Where the applicant plans to contract for evaluation, evidence of the contractor's skills and interest in the project must be presented.

    H. Other activities and grants of the applicant which relate to the proposed demonstration or research.

2. Supporting Data

    Provide copies (if possible) of any material which you consider to be useful to the review group and to the Director of the Office of Economic Opportunity, in making their determinations. List and concisely summarize this material below.

TRAINING PROJECT PLAN AND SUPPORTING DATA

1. Training Project Plan

The criteria governing the award of training grants are listed in the Training Grant Guide. Please review carefully before submitting the application. The information to be supplied in response to Items A. through G. below will be interpreted and evaluated by the reviewing groups in the light of these standards. The relationships between previous grant period(s), the grant period currently being requested, and any subsequent grant period(s) desired should be thoroughly explained.

Please describe your proposal in accordance with the following outline:

A. Purpose - Indicate the specific aims of the training program, and in what way it proposes to make a contribution to the training area. State the problem(s) the training program will address.

B. Scope and Method - Describe in detail the type of training program proposed: For example - (1) a training center grant to establish the administrative structure of a training center which includes staffing and the development of plans for future programs; (2) a program for curriculum development; (3) individual programs of in-service training, workshops, seminars or institutes. Indicate also the specific instructional content, procedures, and techniques which will be used to implement the program. For each objective listed in Item "A", show how the training program is intended to fulfill it.

C. Trainees - Where relevant describe jobs in which trainees will be placed.

D. Organization - Indicate the organizational structure of the staff of the training program.

E. Evaluation - Show how the training program will be assessed.

F. Current Related Activities - Include a description of any activities currently being conducted in areas related to the proposed training program. List related grants and contracts, including amounts, funding agency, and purpose. Indicate whether this or a similar proposal has been submitted to another funding source (public or private) and current status of such application.

2. Supporting Data

Provide copies if possible of any material which you consider to be useful to the review group and to the Director of the Office of Economic Opportunity in making their determinations. List and concisely summarize this material below.

CAP-RDT FORM 7
DEC 64   Page 7 (Training)

Office of Economic Opportunity

APPLICATION FOR A COMMUNITY ACTION PROGRAM

Demonstration, Research or Training Grant

CAP-RDT.8. ELIGIBILITY OF APPLICANT
(This form is to be filled in by the applicant agency's counsel)

NAME OF APPLICANT AGENCY	DO NOT FILL IN: *(For Administrative Use)*

4.1 TYPE OF APPLICANT	4.2 PUBLIC AGENCY *If public, indicate whether applicant is:*			
☐ PUBLIC	☐ STATE(S)	☐ COUNTY(IES)	☐ CITY(IES)	☐ INSTITUTION(S) OF HIGHER EDUCATION
☐ PRIVATE NONPROFIT	☐ TRIBAL COUNCIL(S)	OTHER *(Specify)*		

If applicant is a public agency, proceed to item 4.5; do not answer items 4.3 and 4.4.

4.3	INSTITUTION OF HIGHER EDUCATION

☐ Check here if applicant is an institution of higher education as defined in Section 401(f) of the Higher Education Act of 1963, Public Law 88–204. If this is the case, proceed to item 4.5; do not answer item 4.4.

4.4	PRIVATE NONPROFIT ORGANIZATION

If applicant is a private nonprofit agency other than an institution of higher education, answer all of the following questions.

4.4.1 NONPOLITICAL	4.4.2	NONPROFIT STATUS		
IS APPLICANT A POLITICAL PARTY?	HAS FEDERAL TAX EXEMPTION BEEN APPLIED FOR?	IF YES, GIVE DATE	STATUS OF APPLICATION	
☐ YES ☐ NO	☐ YES ☐ NO		☐ GRANTED ☐ DENIED ☐ PENDING	

4.4.3 IF TAX EXEMPTION WAS GRANTED		4.4.4 *If Federal tax exemption has not been applied for, or if it was granted but is not currently in effect, explain on an attached statement the reasons for such action. Check here if statement is attached.* ☐
GIVE DATE	IS IT CURRENTLY IN EFFECT? ☐ YES ☐ NO	

4.4.5 *If Federal tax exemption has not been applied for, or if such application is currently pending, do you certify to the best of your information and belief, applicant is a nonprofit agency, which is defined as an agency (other than a political party) no part of whose earnings inures or lawfully may inure directly or indirectly to the benefit of any private member, shareholder, or other individual?*

☐ YES   ☐ NO   *If you wish to explain your answer to this question, attach a statement and check here.* ☐

4.4.6	CORPORATE STATUS	
INCORPORATED ☐ YES ☐ NO	IF YES, GIVE DATE AND STATE OF INCORPORATION	IF NO, GIVE DATE OF ORIGIN

4.4.7	CONCERN WITH POVERTY	
YEAR APPLICANT AGENCY CREATED	IS IT AN AGENCY WITH PRIOR CONCERN WITH PROBLEMS OF POVERTY? ☐ YES ☐ NO *(see below)*	IF YES, SPECIFY YEAR SUCH CONCERN BEGAN.

TYPE OF ACTIVITIES UNDERTAKEN AT THAT TIME AND SUBSEQUENTLY

4.4.8 IS APPLICANT AGENCY SPONSORED BY A PUBLIC AGENCY?

☐ YES   ☐ NO

If so, specify name(s) of agency(ies), and indicate nature of sponsorship in such terms as: ex officio representation on governing body, naming of members of governing body, official resolution authorizing creation of applicant, etc.

NAME OF PUBLIC AGENCY	NATURE OF SPONSORSHIP

4.4.9 IS APPLICANT AGENCY SPONSORED BY AN INSTITUTION OR ORGANIZATION WITH A PRIOR CONCERN WITH PROBLEMS OF POVERTY?

☐ YES   ☐ NO

If sponsored by an institution(s) or organization(s) with prior concern with problems of poverty, specify names of institution(s) and organization(s), and nature of sponsorship in such terms as: ex officio representation on governing body, naming of members of governing body, official resolution authorizing creation of applicant, etc.:

NAME OF INSTITUTION OR ORGANIZATION	NATURE OF SPONSORSHIP

4.10	CERTIFICATION OF AUTHORITY

I, the undersigned, as a duly licensed attorney at law, hereby certify that to the best of my information and belief, the applicant agency has the authority, under applicable principles of law, to carry out the program described in this application.

TYPED NAME OF COUNSEL	SIGNATURE
ADDRESS	

CAP-RDT FORM 8 DEC 64

GSA DC 65- 11217

chapter 8

Business Research Design—The Strategy

THE PROBLEM OF CONFIRMATION

The strategy of business research design as opposed to the tactics or techniques is the general approach used in the collection and analysis of data for the purpose of explanation and confirmation. Nagel describes four types of explanation, listed here in a modified form.

1. *The deductive model.* In this model the formal structure of deductive argument is followed and the conclusion is a necessary consequence of the premises.

2. *Probabilistic explanations.* The premises and the conclusions contain statistical assertions.

3. *Functional or teleological explanations.* Explanation indicates the functions or dysfunctions which a component or subsystem performs in a larger system.

4. *Genetic explanations.* Historical inquiry determines why certain characteristics or relationships exist by tracing the historical evolvement of the current status.[1]

The difficulty in providing explanations is that of confirmation of relationships by means of induction. Since business research is concerned with the empirical world, generalizations must be based upon a limited number of observations or cases. Such generalization from a few to all implies a uniformity in nature. It was David Hume who raised the question as to whether any connection between facts can be shown, since any case which has not been examined may not fit the explained connection.

If the philosophical problem is handled on a pragmatic basis, however, research is concerned with strengthening belief in an explanation. Consistent with scientific thought, every relevant test which fails to overthrow a hypothesis strengthens belief in the hypothesis for purposes of explanation and prediction. The *strategy* of research should be concerned with planning an optimum method

[1] Ernest Nagel, *The Structure of Science* (New York: Harcourt, Brace & World, 1961), pp. 21–25.

of attacking a problem to gather relevant data on which to base the strongest inferences possible with due regard for costs.

STRATEGY AS A SYSTEMS APPROACH AND OVER-ALL PLAN

Once the problem has been formulated, the researcher should establish a plan for his investigation. The plan takes into account the formulation of the problem, the nature of the confirmation or test to be employed, the means of gathering data, and the theoretical concepts to be used. These are all related to form a research system. Therefore the choice of any one influences the nature of the others. For this reason it may be necessary to reformulate the problem by asking the question in a different way, if better and more economical methods are possible through such reformulation. The ultimate objective of the research remains invariant, of course.

In a greatly simplified example, the question might be asked, "How do small groups arrive at decisions?" In trying to devise a strategy for such research, the investigator may think that observation and questioning of individuals may both be required. Asking people about their thought processes may not be considered valid evidence. The researcher may then reformulate his question as, "What factors affect problem solving by small groups?" His strategy might then be to actualize a small-group situation, supply problems to the group, and vary such factors as the method of intercommunication among members, level of intelligence, experience, age, problem difficulty, and the like. He would observe characteristics such as number of communications involved, communication centers, or time required for solution.

It has often been stated that when a problem is well formulated, the problem is half solved. While this may be true, the final formulation may be the result of speculation about the research strategy which leads in turn to a reformulation of the problem. The most general method of science must be used in developing the strategy for the research in order to tie together all components of the research system. This method is simply to think hard about the total system problem.

Strategy is concerned primarily with:

1. *Identification of general approaches* to the problem. The general approach is distinguished from a technique or data-collection procedure by the fact that various techniques may be utilized to carry out a general approach. For example, general approaches to determining consumer brand preferences might be (a) ask the consumers, (b) observe the consumer at point of purchase, (c) determine relative market shares, or (d) examine trash from homes to find out the brand and quantity used. Thus techniques for asking the consumer might be structured or unstructured personal interviews, mail surveys, or "voting" machines at point of purchase. Similarly, vaous techniques may be used for the other general approaches.

2. *Efficiency of research design.* The appropriate data must be obtained in a

manner which balances off cost, time, and precision of measurement. The ingenuity of the researcher is called upon to select a strategy to obtain relevant data in time to meet the needs of the sponsor in an economical manner which permits objective analysis leading to a valid solution of the problem.

DEVISING A STRATEGY

Devising a strategy for optimizing the research design calls for ingenuity on the part of the investigator. In most cases researchers tend to seize upon some favorite method for gathering data—usually surveys involving the use of questionnaires. Little attention is paid to the validity of the method which is influenced by the nature of the questionnaire itself and the interaction of the researcher with the respondent. This problem has been high-lighted by E. J. Webb and others who put forth a call for new means of nonreactive research. At the least, they call for "triangulation," the use of differing approaches and comparison of results.[2]

The investigator should allow himself time for free-wheeling type of thinking in generating a strategy. Creative thinking cannot be strait-jacketed to office hours. Reflection, data gathering, analysis, incubation, and further reflection over a period of time are required. Alex Osborne lists the phases of the creative process as follows:

1. Orientation: Pointing up the problem.
2. Preparation: Gathering pertinent data.
3. Analysis: Breaking down the relevant material.
4. Hypothesis: Piling up alternatives by way of ideas.
5. Incubation: Letting up, to invite illumination.
6. Synthesis: Putting the pieces together.
7. Verification: Judging the resultant ideas.[3]

FUNDAMENTAL RESEARCH STRATEGY

Fundamental research, particularly, demands creativity and originality in research in the social sciences. For example, strategies which involve securing a number of people may involve either exorbitant costs for paying participants or an invalid experiment utilizing the nonrandom group of individuals who are willing to give up their time without reimbursement. As another instance, the difficulty of extrapolating laboratory results to field conditions is obvious. Biologists found that results obtained about life habits of animals in the laboratory under carefully controlled conditions were relatively worthless, and they eventually turned to reports of amateurs who studied animals in their natural environment.

The strategy must bridge the gap between the known and the unknown,

[2] Eugene J. Webb et al., *Unobtrusive Measures* (Chicago: Rand McNally & Co., 1966).
[3] Alex Osborne, *Applied Imagination* (New York: Charles Scribner's Sons, 1953), p. 125.

between the data and the solution. The formulation of the problem provides the setting and constraints upon the strategy. If the researcher avoids rigidity of thought with regard to problem formulation, facts, and solution, he is more apt to optimize his research plan. In devising a strategy the researcher might be helped by asking himself such questions as the following:

1. What parallels are there for solving analogous problems in the natural sciences? In other social science fields?

(a) Do I know of similar problems?

(b) Is there something similar I could copy, adapt, or modify?

(c) What analogies exist between the components of my problem and problems in other fields?

2. What parallels are there in the past for solving such problems? What have previous researchers done to solve similar problems in the past?

3. What can I adapt, modify, or substitute? What situation is like this one? What ideas are suggested by the structure of the problem? What ideas are suggested by functions of components of the problem system? How could I modify this by change in process, location, shape, color, time, or substitution of parts? Can I work on the other end, the other side, the after-product, or after-process?

4. What can I add or eliminate? Can I change to a larger group, a larger sample, a larger area, a larger device, a longer time, a longer distance? Can I add more parts, more ingredients, more varieties of people, or situations? Can I add more steps in a process? Can I double, triple, or quadruple some feature or all features? Can I miniaturize, condense, or reduce the number of steps? Can I make something lighter, quieter, smoother, or simpler? What can I eliminate or abstract to reduce cost, to focus on the major variables? Can I divide it into parts and work on it piecemeal?

5. What can I rearrange, reverse, or combine? How else could I arrange this? Should I try several permutations? What if I change the sequence, transpose, reverse, turn upside down, turn inside out? What about a different spatial arrangement, different organization structure, rearrangement of functions? What about a rearrangement of time? What ideas, groups, parts, previous researches could be combined? What processes could I combine? Can I combine combinations?

6. Can I reformulate the problem differently? How could I reformulate the problem to redirect the research and yet achieve the real objectives? Can I restate the problem to permit solution of a part of the problem? Can I modify the problem statement by dropping some of the conditions, adding some assumptions, making it more general, or making it more specific? Can I use higher-level data or intermediate unknowns to bring the data and the unknowns closer? Have I found all relevant data which will help me? Did I omit any essential conditions which will simplify or clarify the problem? Have I talked this over with other people to see if there are ways of interpreting the problem situation I failed to see?

Applied Research Strategy

Applied research strategy dictates a first step that is not likely to be required for fundamental research. This step is to determine if the problem can be avoided completely rather than solved. Another alternative which avoids applied research is for management to seek opinions of experts as to the solution of a problem and to act on these rather than research. The decision process representing the most general stratgey for dealing with applied problems is shown in Exhibit 2-2.

If the decision process leads to the necessity of performing research to solve the problem, the researcher should ask himself the same or similar questions to those given in the previous section. Questions about the objectives and formulation of the problem are especially important in applied research. In addition, the applied researcher should consider to a far greater extent than the basic researcher the following two basic strategies.

1. Divide the research into two or more major phases. After each phase is completed, the following subphases are reconsidered and restructured if necessary. This is a serial approach.

2. Perform parallel lines of investigation.

(a) Completely different approaches may be worked on at the same time or two teams may independently work towards a solution using the same general approach. This research is costly and is used only when time is a vital factor and substantial gains or losses are at stake.

(b) Different parts of the problem are worked on in parallel. Often it is assumed that the answer to one part is available and a successive phase is concurrently investigated. In cases where PERT (Program Evaluation and Review Technique) is employed, parts of the research are linked together to minimize the time required for the whole project.

Examples of Research Strategy

1. Melville Dalton was concerned with the nature of adjustment in business firms between the executives to whom method and procedure are paramount and executives who adapt to achieve results in spite of formal restraints. The strategy adopted was not to send out mail questionnaires, but instead to conduct lengthy in-depth case studies over a decade of managers in four companies and the roles they played. Dalton actually worked for two of these firms. He did not approach top management for formal approval, but worked through close friends employed at the firms. No explicit hypotheses were set up in advance. The nature of the inquiry controlled the method at every step rather than having the method limit the research. The strategy was one of personal involvement with the people who were most familiar with the conflicts and resolutions within the companies.[4]

2. A study by Alfred Politz had as its objective the determination of how

[4]See "Appendix on Method" of Melville Dalton, *Men Who Manage* (New York: John Wiley & Sons, Inc., 1959).

many people perceived posters on the sides of buses in a certain city. The strategy which was evolved was actually count the number of pairs of eyes which looked directly at the poster. The technique used was to take a sample of photographs at random times by means of a concealed camera on the bus pointing out over the poster.

3. A researcher wished to study liquor consumption patterns in a city without package stores. He adopted the strategy of counting empty bottles in the trash being carted away from homes.

4. Various strategies have been employed to study communication patterns and problem solving in small groups. Actualization of a small group and restriction of channels of communication has been one strategy adopted. Another strategy has been to study the flow of correspondence through a communication center in a business, such as a mail room. Another strategy adopted has been to study the correspondence of key executives to see whom they write to and who writes to them. Simulation by construction of models analyzed with the aid of computers is still another strategy.

5. Two researchers performed an experiment to test consumers' preference between two types of canned peas. The researchers also wished to test the results of three variations of strategy. In the first case, the homemaker received two cans of peas and was asked to serve both at the same meal. In the second case, homemakers were asked to serve one can of peas at one meal and the other can several days later. In the third test, one group of homemakers received one type and another group received the other type of the product. The findings showed that the different strategies produced different results. The researchers concluded that market researchers must use common sense and understanding of the problem being studied in selecting the basic research approach.[5]

6. An inquiry was made into the impact of managerial climate on the behavior of work groups. The question was raised as to whether employee-oriented management or task-oriented management lead to higher levels of organizational performance. The investigators used simulated experimentation as the research strategy. A model of a firm was constructed based upon findings of previous research into effects of supervision, group cohesion, and rewards for efficiency. The reasons given for selecting this particular strategy were:

(a) The hypothesis under investigation is difficult to test in an industrial context by a field study.

(b) A controlled experiment of adequate scope and duration would have been very costly and unpractical. In addition, the results would have been confounded by the dynamics of the environment and the effects of uncontrolled internal variables.[6]

---

[5] Roger Bengston and Henry Brenner, "Product Test Results Using Three Different Methodologies," *Journal of Marketing Research* (November 1964).

[6] Eugene E. Kaczka and Roy V. Kirk, "A Simulation Study of Managerial Climate, Work Groups and Organizational Behavior," paper presented at The Institute of Management Sciences American Meeting, Boston, April 6, 1967.

There is a growing awareness of the need for research strategies which increase validity and reduce the effects of irrelevant environmental influences. Strategies are needed to replace those for which the researcher interacts with the environment being studied. Unthinking application of techniques and tools at the implementation level must be replaced by reflective thought about the general approach to problem solution if business research is to develop a science of business.

HEURISTICS AND RESEARCH STRATEGY

Heuristic, a word derived from the Greek for "discover," is concerned with the process of solving problems. Modern heuristic (or heuristics) has come to mean a procedure used to reduce problem-solving effort. A heuristic program is a method based upon rules of thumb which takes the problem solver along the path to a solution. Heuristics are directed toward optimum procedures rather than optimum solutions. Thus *acceptable* solutions rather than *optimal* solutions are sought. Thus very complex problems or problems which even computers balk at may be approached by heuristic methods.[7]

In applied research, heuristic programs have been developed for such problems as assembly-line balancing, warehouse location, job-shop scheduling, plant layout, inventory control, and engineering design. In each case a series of steps are given and at various steps the problem solver must use his judgment in selecting from a number of alternative possibilities.

While it thus appears that the development of a heuristic program represents a strategy for solving a class of applied problems, the question arises as to whether heuristic has any application in solving basic research problems. To some extent the answer may be affirmative. The researcher may divide his research into phases whereby each successive phase is contingent upon the preceding phase. Judgment must be used at each decision point. Thus a rough heuristic program is developed for optimum seeking.

SUMMARY

A distinction has been made between the general approach to solving business problems as well as providing confirmation and the specific techniques and tools used to implement this approach. There are many well-developed tools and techniques at the disposal of the researcher. There is a need, however, for more and better strategies. The development of a strategy requires creative thinking about the problem. Questions have been suggested which may serve to stimulate the researcher in his quest for a research strategy.

[7]See, for example, Jerome D. Wiest, "Heuristic Programs for Decision Making," *Harvard Business Review* (October 1966).

QUESTIONS AND TOPICS FOR DISCUSSION

1. The thesis of this chapter is that a strategy of research can be identified. Take the position that this thesis is false and discuss research methods, techniques, and tools in support of your position.

2. What is meant by "confirmation" in research and science?

3. How is strategy or research design related to confirmation?

4. If you accept the thesis that the research process is a system, identify the components, the inputs, the flows, and the outputs.

5. In devising a research strategy, what things would you have to take into account?

6. Can you develop a list of questions more general or more specific than those in the text *or* a procedure or method to provide a better guide to the development of a strategy for business research?

7. Examine ten journal articles on business research. Identify, if you can, the strategy employed.

8. Some research appears to be so straightforward that there is no strategy to be considered—only an obvious method. Examine ten such research project reports. Can you think of at least two other approaches in each case which might have resulted in stronger confirmation of the conclusions?

9. Is heuristic a means of developing an improved strategy?

10. Do you believe heuristic methods have any application in basic research in business? Explain your position.

chapter 9

Business Information
Search and Retrieval

INTRODUCTION

It is usually considerably less expensive for the business researcher to search for and retrieve information which he needs than it is to expand his research project to include generating all such necessary data. At least a crude analysis should be made in advance to determine whether the cost and risk of a search is greater or less than the cost and risk of operational investigations. The risks attached to a search are (1) the data or information is not in storage, and (2) the information exists but its accuracy, reliability, or validity cannot be ascertained. The risks attached to the generating of information are (1) the failure of the research for such reasons as faulty design or implementation and (2) time and cost explosions.

The cost of search and retrieval may be lowered by the assignment of an individual to the task who has experience and knowledge in the field of interest. Cost may also be lowered for the nonknowledgeable person by the application of systematic instead of random search procedures. Systematic procedures also lower the risk of using poor information since overlapping reports which permit cross-checking are more likely to be uncovered. The purpose of this chapter is to acquaint the reader with the sources and organization of information files and to suggest a systematic approach to searching and retrieving.

Once data has been stored within the company, whether it is external or internal in origin, the problem is one of selectively retrieving it on time and economically. Considerable literature has appeared on storage/retrieval of information and on the central problem of management-information systems.

SOME BASIC DEFINITIONS

The terms "information" and "data" are often assumed to be loosely synonymous. It is useful for search and retrieval, however, to distinguish between two concepts, one of which may be labeled *information* and the other *data*.

Information is the narrower of the two terms and, roughly, may be considered data that has been processed to make it useful to a particular person at a particular time. If data are not relevant to an individual's current activities and do not affect his behavior, they are not considered to be information. Information is a sign (behavior stimulus) which may be either quantitative or qualitative in nature. Such signs are coded representations of concepts integral to either a human sender or receiver. Such signs cause someone to behave as if some entity had, has, or will have certain attributes or characteristics. "Noise" increases information content in the mathematical sense but generally decreases the practical (or semantic) value because noise is spurious information. Thus researchers and decision makers search for information i.e., data which are relevant to their needs and activities; all else are data but not information.

Data may consist of a group of facts or statistics which constitute a record of an observation or event. The word *data,* in the broader sense in which it is used here, also means any recorded report of *processed* data. Processed data might consist, for example, of a report of previous research or speculation. The terms *data bank, data file, storage file,* and *data base* are particularly appropriate terms which have been adopted. "Information storage" is not particularly appropriate unless the material stored is relevant data which are being stored for further processing. "Data storage" would generally be more appropriate. On the other hand, "information search and retrieval" are particularly appropriate terms and are significant because they imply the *selection* of data relevant to an individual's needs. A researcher in business remarked facetiously that in each ton of data there is only one ounce of information.

Retrieval means "bringing back," and hence refers to data which have been stored. A search usually precedes retrieval in order to determine first if the data exists and where it is located if it does exist. In modern times vast amounts of data are recorded and stored in all manner of files and archives for the purpose of being converted to useful information by some researcher or decision maker. Retrieval is getting information out of the file once the search indicates the likelihood that it is in the file.

From the viewpoint of the applied researcher employed in a company, data may be classified as internal data (within the company) or external data (not in company records). The problem of retrieving internal data is related to the problem of prior selection and storage, and both must be considered in the design of management-information systems. Data are usually stored within a company because there is a recurrent need for a particular type of material. The researcher, applied or otherwise, who must search for external data is faced with enormous amounts of published and otherwise recorded data. If he is seeking some specific item, unless he is knowledgeable in his field and skilled at searching, the cost of the search may easily outweigh the value of the information. While there is no unique set of specific steps to follow in searching for information, a presentation of the general system of files, archives, and indexes may be helpful to most potential and practicing researchers.

PRODUCERS OF DATA RELEVANT TO BUSINESS

The scope of business data is extremely broad and includes all or parts of such major fields as economics, sociology, psychology, anthropology, law, history, communications, and preferential behavior. It would be difficult and completely impractical to attempt to identify all possible producers of business-related data. However, it is important to identify in some way the principal producers for the purpose of searching. An outline of these producers is as follows:

I. Government
  A. Federal or national
  B. States or provinces
  C. Local authorities
  D. International organizations (for example, United Nations or Common Market)
II. Nongovernment
  A. Business firms
  B. Business research and service firms
  C. Nonprofit foundations and institutes
  D. Trade associations
  E. Professional associations and societies and nonprofessional associations (labor)
  F. Labor organizations
  G. Universities
  H. Individuals

The methods or places of storing are:
  1. Libraries (published material)
  2. Data banks for specialized information
  3. General information storage/retrieval systems
  4. Files and archives

HOW TO SEARCH "SYSTEMATICALLY"

There are three kinds of searches. In the first, the investigator wants specific data and is willing to stop at the first source of such data. In the second, the investigator wants a check on the data he will use so that he seeks two or more sources for the purpose of cross-checking. In the third type of search, the investigator wishes to survey the literature on some subject as completely as possible. A systematic search in each case should be the type of search which offers a high probability of success at the lowest cost.

In the first case—search for specific data—the researcher might follow the series of steps below until he finds the data.
  1. Based on knowledge of specific sources, search these sources.
  2. Ask a colleague or librarian who is familiar with the field.

3. Search selected indexes, abstracts, and directories.

4. Search all indexes, abstracts, directories, and bibliographies available relating to the field of inquiry.

In the second case it is likely that the researcher should consider placing some limitations on his search. He might for example decide that only literature of the past ten years is significant. Or he may decide that the most significant information has been published in the journals and research sources and not in trade magazines or books. In such cases, he would not search all indexes and directories, but rather only selected ones. In the event a complete search is to be made, the procedure would be as follows:

1. Search *for* guide services which lead to indexes, directories, and bibliographies.

2. Search *for* indexes, directories, and bibliographies. These are usually organized to provide information to source material according to one or more categories:

(a) Subject and/or author

(b) Field of knowledge

(c) Type of producer (government, doctoral dissertation output, universities, or commercial publishers, for example)

(d) Form of storage (microfilm, computer-tape data banks, books, movie films, institutional records, maps)

3. Search the indexes or files in (2) for references that seem relevant. Depending on the type of data sought, the researcher should plan in advance an efficient method of listing references to avoid duplicate listing. Sources which are physically contiguous should be listed or assembled together so that all reference material in a single source may be conveniently retrieved and examined.

4. Examine the sources for the desired relevant data.

5. If possible, check with other authorities on the subject to determine if any major unsuspected source has been overlooked.

The above procedures are in contrast to the random approach so often used. In the random approach the investigator locates a book or article in the field of interest which has a bibliography. This bibliography leads him to other sources and their bibliographies so that he soon picks up many threads in the web of relevant knowledge.

For both of the above-mentioned methods of searching, simple and general, the researcher may proceed more rapidly if he has some knowledge of guides to business indexes and sources. Some of the principal guides are listed or briefly described in the next two sections. The address of the producer of the guide or source is given in appropriate instances. The order of presentation is somewhat arbitrary.

PRINCIPAL GUIDES, INDEXES, AND DIRECTORIES

1. *Guide to Reference Books,* by Constance M. Winshell, American Library Association, Chicago, 1967.
2. *Guide to U.S. Government Serials and Publications*
   Four volumes, U.S. Government Printing Office.
3. *Guide to American Directories*
   Gale Research Company, 1400 Book Tower, Detroit, Michigan 48226.
4. *Measuring Markets, A Guide to the Use of Federal and State Statistical Data (1966)*
   U.S. Department of Commerce, U.S. Government Printing Office, Washington, D.C. (approx. $.50)
5. *Marketing Information Guide*
   Monthly annotated bibliography of government and nongovernment publications, U.S. Government Printing Office, Washington, D.C. (approx. $2/year)
6. *Social Science Data Archives in the United States (1967)*
   Council of Social Science Data Archives, 605 West 115 Street, New York, N. Y. 10025
7. *Executive's Guide to Information Sources*
   Three volumes, Gale Research Company (see 3).
8. *Management Information Guide Series:*
   The Developing Nations
   Public Finance Information Sources
   Textile Industry Information Sources
   Real Estate Information Sources
   Building Construction Information Sources
   Standards and Specifications Information Sources
   Business Trends and Forecasting Information Sources
   Gale Research Company (see 3).
9. *Checklist of Bureau of Foreign Commerce Publications*
   An annotated bibliography prepared by the U.S. Department of Commerce, U.S. Government Printing Office, Washington, D.C.
10. *Checklist of Available Reports in the World Trade Information Service*
    Available only from U.S. Department of Commerce and its field offices.
11. "Research Clearinghouse" in *Business Horizons*
    Indiana University, Bloomington, Ind.
12. *Program of Research on the Management of Research and Development*
    Annual; Department of Industrial Engineering and Management Science, The Technological Institute, Northwestern University, Evanston, Ill. 60201.
13. *Research Program on the Organization and Management of R & D*
    Semiannual progress report, Alfred P. Sloan School of Management, Massachusetts Institute of Technology, Cambridge, Mass. 02139.

14. *Directory of National Trade Associations*
    U.S. Government Printing Office, Washington, D.C.
15. *National Directory of Newsletters*
    Gale Research Company (see 3).
16. *Statistics Sources,* edited by Paul Wasserman et al.
    Gale Research Company (see 3).
17. *Sources of Business Information*
    By Edwin T. Coman, Jr., Berkeley and Los Angeles, University of California Press.
18. *Guide to Business History*
    By Henretta M. Larson, Boston: Canner & Company, Inc.
19. *The Journal of Economic Abstracts*
    Quarterly, American Economic Association.
20. *Monthly Catalog, U.S. Government Publications*
    U.S. Government Printing Office, Washington, D.C.
21. *Applied Science and Technology Index*
    The H. W. Wilson Company, New York.
22. *Business Periodicals Index*
    The H. W. Wilson Company, New York.
23. *Business Publication Guide*
    Industrial Marketing supplementary volume, 740 Rush Street, Chicago, Ill. 60611.
24. *Selected Rand Abstracts*
    The Rand Corporation, Santa Monica, Calif.
25. *American Doctoral Dissertations, Index, and Dissertation Abstracts*
    Microfilm Library Services, Ann Arbor, Mich.
26. *Natural Bureau of Economic Research Publications*
    Annual and cumulative, National Bureau of Economic Research, 261 Madison Avenue, New York, N. Y. 10016.
27. *Index of University Publications of Bureaus of Business and Economic Research*
    Bureau of Business and Economic Research, University of Oregon, Eugene, Oreg. 97403.
28. *Catalog of Publications-Organisation for Economic Cooperation and Development*
    2 Rue André-Pascal, 75 Paris 16e.
29. *Operations Research/Management Science*
    International Literature Digest Service, Executive Sciences Institutes, Inc., Whippany, N. J.

SELECTED SOURCES OF BUSINESS DATA

The U.S. Government issues a wide variety of reports covering almost every phase of economic activity. A brief description of publications covering population statistics, income statistics, industry employment, and sales statistics is given in Exhibits 1-4 at the end of this chapter. A list of commonly used federal government source publications (which overlap to some extent those described in the Exhibits) is given below.

1. *Statistical Abstract of the United States* (annual). This one-volume basic reference source is the standard summary of statistics on the social, political and economic activity of the United States. It selects data from both governmental and private statistical publications and relates data to comparable series in its supplement, *Historical Statistics of the United States from Colonial Times to 1957.*

2. *Survey of Current Business* (monthly) contains basic national income accounts and other business data in considerable detail.

3. *Business Cycle Developments* (monthly) presents economic indicators in convenient form for analysis and interpretation by specialists in business cycle analysis.

4. *Economic Indicators* (monthly) contains data and graphs for items included in national income analyses.

5. *Economic Report of the President* (annual); *Census of Population* (every ten years). *Vol. 1: Characteristics of the Population,* consists of 54 parts; a summary, a part for each state, and a part for the territories. Subjects covered include sex, age, marital status, color or race, nativity, mother tongue, educational and employment status, and related data. *Vol. 2:* Subject reports in individual parts. *Vol. 3:* Selected area reports include data for state economic areas, standard metropolitan statistical areas, size, Americans overseas, and type of place. Supplementary reports include reports on special topics, advance reports, and special-use statistics.

Current population reports (several series). Series P-20: Population Characteristics. Series P-23: Technical Studies. Series P-25: Population Estimates. Series P-27: Farm Population. Series P-28: Special Censuses (of a specified city or area). Series P-60: Consumer Income. Series P-65: Consumer Buying Indicators.

6. *Federal Reserve Bulletin* (monthly).

7. *Monthly Labor Review, Monthly Report on the Labor Force, Handbook of Labor Statistics, Manpower Report of the President,* and *Scientific and Technical Personnel in Industry* (1960) provide detailed data on employment, earnings, work weeks, and the like.

8. *Reviews of Data on Science Resources* and others. National Science Foundation papers and reports, issued irregularly throughout the year. Expenditures for R&D by source of funds, performer, and industry are given. Scientific and technical personnel and salaries are reported. Summary of research results and research projects in progress are other topics covered.

9. *Facts for Marketers,* published in nine regional volumes, is to be a series of 100 Standard Metropolitan Statistical Area market studies. It contains se-

lected data from other government publications in a form useful to marketing researchers.

10. *U.S. Industrial Outlook.*

11. *Construction Review.*

12. *Foreign Commerce Weekly.*

13. *Quarterly Summary of Foreign Commerce.*

14. *International Commerce.*

15. *Foreign Trade Reports.*

16. *Congressional Record.*

17. *Long Term Economic Growth 1860-1965* covers aggregate output, input, and productivity; processes related to economic growth; regional and industry trends; international comparisons; and growth rate triangles.

18. *Federal Reserve Historical Chart Book* (annual) contains long-range charts which supplement the monthly *Federal Reserve Chart Book* on financial and business statistics.

19. *Congressional District Data Book* presents statistical information from recent Censuses of Population, Housing, Agriculture, Business, Manufactures, Mineral Industries, and Governments, and from other sources, for districts of the 88th Congress.

20. *Census of Business* most recent results are available in a series of advance and final reports for retail, wholesale and selected services trade segments. These will subsequently be incorporated into volumes as indicated below:

Vol. 1. Retail trade summary statistics. Consists of six reports, by state, U.S., and standard metropolitan statistical area, giving sales size, employment size, firm size, legal form of organization, and merchandise line sales by large area.

Vol. 2. Retail trade area statistics. Consists of a U.S. summary and a report for each state, giving figures by kind of business for the State and its local areas.

Vol. 3. Major retail center statistics. A report for each of 116 standard metropolitan statistical areas and a U.S. summary.

Vol. 4. Wholesale trade summary statistics. Consists of eight reports, including sales size, losses, sales by class of customer, commodity line, sales by kind of business and area.

Vol. 5. Wholesale trade area statistics. Consists of a U.S. summary and a report for each state, giving figures by kind of business for the State and its local areas.

Vol. 6. Selected services, summary statistics. Consists of seven reports, including size and form of organizations, kind of business and area. Services include laundries, repair services, personal services, sports, advertising, motion pictures, and hotel/motel business.

Vol. 7. Selected services area statistics. Consists of a U.S. summary and a report for each state, giving figures by kind of business for the State and its local areas.

21. *Current Retail Trade Reports.* Weekly, monthly, and annual sales.

22. *Census of Agriculture.* Results of the 1959 Census of Agriculture have been published and results of the 1964 Census of Agriculture have been released.

Census of Governments. The 1957 *Census of Governments* was the first to be taken since 1942. Previously this data was gathered approximately every ten years.

23. *Census of Housing* has been taken as part of the Census of Population in 1940, 1950, and 1960.

24. *Census of Manufactures* has been taken irregularly since 1810. Recently the census has been taken in 1947, 1954, 1958, 1963.

25. *Census of Mineral Industries* has recently been conducted for 1963.

26. *Annual Survey of Manufactures* since 1949 has provided manufacturing statistics for years between censuses.

27. *Census of Transportation* was conducted for the first time in 1963. It covers distribution of commodities by classes of transportation, passenger travel, and a bus and truck inventory.

In addition to data published by the federal government, the individual States, municipalities, and private organizations generate research and reports. A few very useful private publications are listed.

1. *Moody's Manuals* consisting of *Industrials, Banks and Finance, Public Utilities, Transportation* and *Governments* show financial data and executives for organizations in the fields as classified.

2. *Standard & Poor's Standard Corporation Descriptions,* in loose-leaf form, provides continuously updated financial and historical information on U.S. corporations.

3. *Poor's Register and Directory of Executives* provide historical and organizational information on firms.

4. *Standard and Poor's Industry Surveys,* in loose-leaf form, provides updated statistics and analyses of industries.

5. *The Fortune Directory: The 500 Largest U.S. Industrial Corporations, the 50 Largest Banks, Merchandising, Transportation, Life Insurance Companies, and the 200 Largest Foreign Industrial Companies* and *Plant and Product Directory.*

6. *Moody's Handbook of Common Stocks.*

7. *Standard & Poor's Analysts Handbook, Composite Corporate Per Share Data.*

8. Dun and Bradstreet's *Reference Book* provides the name, address, and type of business activity, often with credit rating, of a large proportion of firms in the United States.

9. *Economic Almanac,* published by the National Industrial Conference Board, parallels *Statistical Abstracts* but introduces more data from nongovernment sources.

10. *Handbook of Economic Statistics* published by the Economic Statistics Bureau is an annual volume along the lines of the *Economic Almanac.*

11. F. W. Dodge Corporation monthly reports on construction in the United States.

12. *Facts on File* published by Facts on File, Inc., 119 West 57 Street, New York, N. Y.

13. *Keesing's Contemporary Archives* published by Keesing's Publications, Limited, 65 Bristol Road, Keynsham, Bristol, England, are in loose-leaf form for maintaining up-to-date data on current events, both descriptive and statistical.

14. *International Trade Reporter* (The Bureau of National Affairs, Washington, D.C.) two volumes, loose-leaf, gives updated shipping information and foreign import and exchange controls.

15. *Unted Nations Yearbook of International Trade Statistics.*

16. *United Nations Statistical Yearbook.*

17. *Foreign Affairs* Foreign Affairs Publishing Co., New York. Monthly.

18. *Latin American Business Highlights* (The Chase Manhattan Bank) Quarterly.

19. *Latin American Sales Index* (Dun and Bradstreet) Annual.

20. *Encyclopedia of Associations* (Gale Research).

21. *Research Centers Directory* (Gale Research).

22. *Sanborn Buying Power Maps* and *Sanborn Fire Insurance Maps* provide multicolored detailed maps which locate specific income areas and provide detailed description with location of every building in cities of over 2500 population. (Sanborn Map Company, 629 Fifth Avenue, Pelham, N. Y. 10803.)

23. Forecasting models for the U.S. economy are being employed at the University of Pennsylvania's Wharton School, University of Maryland, University of Michigan, U.S. Department of Commerce, Brookings Institution, Council of Economic Advisors, and the Federal Reserve Board. *Fortune* publishes an elaborate input-output portfolio of charts for the U.S. economy.

24. Besides the data banks listed in *Social Science Data Archives* in the United States, a few of the other computerized data bank services are as follows.

International Telephone & Telegraph. Economic forecasting, and world trade statistics for the United Nations.

Compustat, a service of Standard and Poor's. Tape records on 1,000 companies' stock prices, sales, earnings, dividends, and capital investments.

Selling Areas—Marketing (SAM), a subsidiary of Time, Inc., and Speedata, a subsidiary of Computer Applications, Inc. Gathering and processing of data from food chains and wholesalers.

Bunker-Ramo Corporation. Financial data service with on-line stock prices.

Carnegie Institute of Technology. About 2,000 economic series for economic forecasting stored in a computer with access by Teletype.

F. W. Dodge Company. Construction market data processed by a computer.

EXHIBIT 9-1*
Population Statistics from Federal Sources

Title of Publication	Kinds of Data	Geographic Coverage	Frequency of Data[1]	Frequency of Publication	Issuing Agency
Current Population Reports					
Population Characteristics[2] (P-20 Series)					
Growth of Metropolitan Areas in the United States	Total population in all standard metropolitan statistical areas by age groupings, with total number of inhabitants in central cities and outside central cities	National	Annual (Cumulative from 1960)	Planned annual	United States Department of Commerce, Bureau of the Census, Washington, D.C. 20233
Household and Family Characteristics	Gives number of households, families, sub-families and group quarters and population in these units by age, and characteristics of families and unrelated individuals by type	National	Annual	Annual	Same as above
Households and Families by Type	Number and percent of family units and households by type, color of head and residence	National	Annual	Annual	Same as above
Marital Status and Family Status	Marital status, by age, sex, residence and color; family status by age and sex; families	National	Annual	Annual	Same as above

Mobility of the Population of the United States	and households by type, age of head, and other characteristics Mobility status and type of mobility by color, metropolitan-nonmetropolitan residence, age, sex, employment and other social and economic characteristics	National and regions	Annual	Annual	Same as above
Population Estimates[3] (P-25 Series)					
School Enrollment	Enrollment of civilian noninstitutional population in public and private schools by level of school, age, color and sex and in special schools by age and sex	National	Annual	Annual	Same as above
Estimates of the Population by Age, for States and Puerto Rico	Total resident population by age groups	National, regions, divisions, and States	Annual	Annual	Same as above
Estimates of the Population of Selected Standard Metropolitan Statistical Areas	Total population, births, deaths, net civilian immigration, and net change in number and percent	Standard metropolitan statistical areas, by constituent counties	Annual	Annual	Same as above

*Taken from *Measuring Markets, A Guide to the Use of Federal and State Statistical Data*, prepared by the U.S. Department of Commerce, 1966.

EXHIBIT 9-1 (*continued*)

Title of Publication	Kinds of Data	Geographic Coverage	Frequency of Data[1]	Frequency of Publication	Issuing Agency
Estimates of the Population of States	Resident and civilian resident population	National, regions, divisions, and States	Annual	Annual	Same as above
Estimates of the Population of States, by age	Resident population by age groups	National, regions, divisions, and States	Annual	Annual	Same as above
Estimates of the Population of the United States	Total population including armed forces abroad, total resident and civilian resident population	National	Monthly	Monthly	Same as above
Estimates of the Population of the United States by Age, Color and Sex	Population by age groups, color, and sex. Same data available by single years of age for population under 25	National	Annual	Annual	Same as above
Estimates of the Population of the United States and Components of Change	Total population, births, deaths, net civilian immigration, and net change in number and percent	National	Annual and Semiannual with monthly total population	Annual	Same as above
United States Census of Housing	Occupancy, tenure, color or ethnic group of occupants, persons per room, vacancy status and other housing charac-	National, regions, divisions, States, standard metropolitan statistical areas, urbanized areas	Decennial for years ending in "0"	Every 10 years	Same as above

	teristics on a comprehensive basis. Some types of data (those collected on a sample basis) are not given for smaller areas	urban and rural areas, counties, city blocks and census tracts	Every 10 years	Same as above
United States Census of Population	Sex, color or race, month and year of birth, marital status place of birth citizenship, relationship to head of household and other population characteristics on a comprehensive basis. Some types of data (those collected on a sample basis) are not given for smaller areas	National, regions, divisions, States urban, rural nonfarm, and rural farm areas, standard metropolitan statistical areas, urbanized areas, urban places of 10,000 or more, counties, and census tracts, with summary data for smaller units	Decennial, for years ending in "0"	

[1] In most cases comparative data are given for prior periods.

[2] Other periodic reports in this series, published at infrequent intervals, deal with such demographic characteristics as education attainment and fertility.

[3] In addition to the reports listed in this series, the Bureau of the Census releases Current Population Reports at infrequent intervals providing population projections for the country as a whole by age and sex, projections of the total population for states, and results of special censuses taken at the request and expense of city or other local Governments.

EXHIBIT 9-2*
Income Statistics from Federal Sources

Title of Publication	Kinds of Data	Geographic Coverage	Frequency of Data[1]	Frequency of Publication	Issuing Agency
Current Population Reports (P-28 Consumer Income)	Aggregate and median total money income of families and un- related individuals by income classes, family composition, education of family head, major sources, marital status, sex and color, industry, occupation, etc.	National, farm and nonfarm	Annual	Annual	United States Department of the Census, Washington, D.C. 20233
Statistics of Income – Indi- vidual Tax	Provides data on number of returns, adjusted gross income, sources of income, types of exemptions, taxable income and tax items, all classi- fied by size of adjusted income.	National and State, 100 largest standard metropolitan statistical	Annual Annual	Annual Biennial	United States Treasury Department, Internal Revenue Service, Washington, D.C. 20222
Survey of Current Business	Aggregate personal income by type and major industrial source Disposable personal income Aggregate personal income by type and detailed industrial source	National National National	Monthly Quarterly Annually in the July issue (some exceptions)	Monthly	United States Department of Commerce, Office of Business Economics, Washington, D.C. 20233

	Total and per capita personal income	National, regions and States	Annually in the April issue	Monthly	United States Department of Commerce, Office of Business Economics, Washington, D.C. 20233
	Aggregate personal and per capita income by type of income and industrial source	National, regions and States	Annually in the August issue (some exceptions)		
	Disposable personal income	Regions and States	For selected years		
United States Census of Population	Total money and median income of families and unrelated individuals by income size classes for places with between 2,500 to 10,000 inhabitants with additional detail for larger areas, including family composition educational attainment, marital status, and other characteristics of head of household such as age, sex, color, occupation and industry	National, regions, divisions, States, urban rural non-farm, and rural farm, standard metropolitan statistical areas, urbanized areas, counties, cities, urban places, of 2,500 and over and census tracts	Decennial, year preceding census of population	Every 10 years	United States Department of Commerce, Bureau of the Census, Washington, D.C. 20233

*Taken from *Measuring Markets, A Guide to the Use of Federal and State Statistical Data*, prepared by the U.S. Department of Commerce, 1966.

[1] In most cases comparative data are given for prior periods.

EXHIBIT 9-3*

Industry Employment Statistics from Federal Sources

Title of Publication	SIC Industry Digit Detail[1]	Geographic Coverage	Frequency of Data or Reference Period[2]			Frequency of Publication	Issuing Agency
			Employment	Average Earnings	Aggregate Pay Roll		
Annual Survey of Manufacturers	2·3	National, divisions, and States	Annual (average of 4 monthly figures)		Annual	Annual during inter-censal periods	U.S. Department of Commerce, Bureau of the Census, Washington, D.C. 20233
	2	Standard metropolitan statistical areas with 40,000 or more manufacturing employees	Annual (average of 4 monthly figures)		Annual		
	4	National	Annual (average of 4 monthly figures)		Annual		
	Total industry	National and smaller areas	Annual (average of 4 monthly figures)		Annual		
Area Trends in Employment and Unemployment	Total industry	Major	Bi-monthly			Monthly	U.S. Department of Labor, Bureau of Employment Security, Washington, D.C. 20210
		Small labor market areas	Bi-monthly (from latest bi-monthly report)				

Census of Business: Retail Trade	2-3-4	National, regions, divisions, States, standard metropolitan statistical areas	Workweek ended nearest November 15th	Census year and workweek ended nearest November 15th	Every five years for years ending in "3" and "8" (beginning 1967 for years ending in "2" and "7")	U.S. Department of Commerce, Bureau of the Census, Washington, D.C. 20233
	2-3	Counties and cities with 500 or more establishments	Workweek ended nearest November 15th	Census year and workweek ended nearest November 15th	Every five years for years ending in "3" and "8" (beginning 1967 for years ending in "2" and "7")	
	2	Counties and cities with 2,500 or more inhabitants				
	Total industry	National, regions, divisions and States	Workweek ended nearest November 15th	Census year and workweek ended nearest November 15th		U.S. Department of Commerce, Bureau of the Census, Washington, D.C. 20233
Census of Business: Selected Services	2-3-4	National, regions, divisions, States and standard metropolitan statistical areas	Workweek ended nearest November 15th	Annual and workweek ended nearest November 15th	Every five years for years ending in "3" and "8" (beginning 1967 for years ending in "2" and "7")	U.S. Department of Commerce, Bureau of the Census, Washington, D.C. 20233

*Taken from *Measuring Markets, A Guide to the Use of Federal and State Statistical Data*, prepared by the U.S. Department of Commerce, 1966.

EXHIBIT 9-3 (continued)

Title of Publication	SIC Industry Digit Detail[1]	Geographic Coverage	Frequency of Data or Reference Period[2]			Frequency of Publication	Issuing Agency
			Employment	Average Earnings	Aggregate Pay Roll		
	2-3	Counties and cities with 200 or more establishments	Workweek ended nearest November 15th		Annual and workweek ended nearest November 15th		
	Total industry	National, regions, divisions, States and counties and cities of 2,500 or more inhabitants	Workweek ended nearest November 15th		Annual and workweek ended nearest November 15th		
Census of Business: Wholesale Trade	2-3-4	National, regions, divisions, States, standard metropolitan statistical areas, and counties with 100 establishments or more	Workweek ended nearest November 15th		Annual and workweek ended nearest November 15th	Every five years for years ending in "3" and "8" (beginning 1967 for years ending in "2" and "7")	U.S. Department of Commerce, Bureau of the Census, Washington, D.C. 20233
	Total industry	National, regions, divisions, States, and counties and cities of 5,000 or more inhabitants	Workweek ended nearest November 15th		Annual and workweek ended nearest November 15th		
Census of Governments	(Not applicable)	National, States standard metropoli-	Month of October		Month of October	Every five years	U.S. Department of Commerce,

		tan statistical areas, counties			for years ending in "2" and "7"	Bureau of the Census, Washington, D.C. 20233
Census of Manufacturers	2-3-4	National, divisions States and standard metropolitan statistical areas with 40,000 or more manufacturing employees	15th of a specified month	Calendar year	Every five years for years ending in "3" and "8" (beginning in 1967 for years ending in "2" and "7")	U.S. Department of Commerce, Bureau of the Census, Washington, D.C. 20233
	2-3	Counties with industry groups or with 500 or more employees	15th of a specified month	Calendar year		
	2	National in separate summary tables	15th of a specified month			
	Total industry	National, divisions, States, standard metropolitan statistical areas and counties and cities of 10,000 or more inhabitants	15th of a specified month			
Census of Population	2-3	National, States standard metropolitan statistical areas and counties and cities of 250,000 or more inhabitants	A week during the month of April	For years ending in "0"	Every 10 years	U.S. Department of Commerce, Bureau of the Census, Washington, D.C. 20233

EXHIBIT 9-3 (*continued*)

Title of Publication	SIC Industry Digit Detail[1]	Geographic Coverage	Frequency of Data or Reference Period[2]			Frequency of Publication	Issuing Agency
			Employment	Average Earnings	Aggregate Pay Roll		
County Business Patterns	2-3-4	National, States, counties	Mid-March		First quarter of the year	Annual starting with 1964 data. Prior years data were for each year 1946-51, and for 1953, 1956, 1959, and 1962.	U.S. Department of Commerce, Bureau of the Census, Washington, D.C. 20233
	2	States, and standard metropolitan statistical areas	Mid-March		First quarter of the year		
	Total industry	National, States, counties, and standard metropolitan statistical areas	Mid-March		First quarter of the year		
Employment and Earnings	2-3-4	National	Monthly (based on workweek including 12th of the month)	Weekly/hourly (representing a month)		Monthly	U.S. Department of Labor, Bureau of Labor Statistics, Washington, D.C. 20210
	1	Standard metropolitan statistical areas,	Monthly (based on workweek	Weekly/hourly (repre-			

Publication		Coverage					Source
Employment and Earnings Statistics for States and Areas	2-3 and selected 4	States, selected standard metropolitan statistical areas, and other labor market areas and other selected labor areas				Annual	U.S. Department of Labor, Bureau of Labor Statistics, Washington, D.C. 20210
Employment and Earnings Statistics for the United States	2-3-4	National	Annual average of monthly data (based on workweek including 12th of the month) Annual average and monthly	Annual average of monthly data Annual Weekly/hourly (by month and annual averages)		Annual	U.S. Department of Labor, Bureau of Labor Statistics, Washington, D.C. 20210
Employment and Wages of Workers Covered by State Unemployment Insurance Laws	1-2-3	National	Current three months		Quarterly	Quarterly	U.S. Department of Labor, Bureau of Employment Security, Washington, D.C. 20210
Unemployment Compensation for Federal Employees by Industry and State	1-2 1-2 and selected 3	Industry divisions State	Current three months Current three months		Quarterly Quarterly		
Monthly Labor Review	2-3-4	National	Monthly (based on workweek including 12th of the month)	Weekly/ hourly		Monthly (with year end supplement)	U.S. Department of Labor, Bureau of Labor Statistics, Washington, D.C. 20210
Monthly Report on the Labor Force	1 non-manufacturing and 2 manufacturing	National	Monthly (based on workweek including 12th of the month)	Weekly/ hourly (representing a month)		Monthly	U.S. Department of Labor, Bureau of Labor Statistics, Washington, D.C. 20210

EXHIBIT 9-3 (continued)

Title of Publication	SIC Industry Digit Detail[1]	Geographic Coverage	Frequency of Data or Reference Period[2]			Frequency of Publication	Issuing Agency
			Employment	Average Earnings	Aggregate Pay Roll		
State Distribution of public employment	(Not applicable)	National, State	Month of October		Month of October	Annual during inter-censal years	U.S. Department of Commerce, Bureau of the Census, Washington, D.C. 20233
Survey of Current Business[3]	1-2-3	National	Monthly and annual averages	Weekly/ hourly		Monthly	U.S. Department of Commerce, Office of Business Economics, Washington, D.C. 20230

[1] Detail of data varies by area depending on industry composition and relevance.

[2] In most instances data are given for prior periods.

[3] Reprint of figures supplied by the Bureau of Labor Statistics, U.S. Department of Labor.

[4] Government employment by functional breakdown.

EXHIBIT 9-4*
Sales Statistics from Federal Sources

Title of Publication	Kind of Data	SIC Industry Digit Detail[1]	Geographic Coverage	Reference Period	Frequency of Publication	Issuing Agency
Annual Survey of Manufacturers	Product class and product, value of shipments	2-3-4-5	National	Annual	Annual intercensal years	U.S. Department of Commerce, Bureau of the Census, Washington, D.C. 20233
	Value added by manufacture	2-3-4	National	Annual		
	Value added by manufacture	2-3	Divisions and States	Annual		
	Value added by manufacture	2	Standard metropolitan statistical areas with 40,000 or more manufacturing employees	Annual		
	Value added by manufacture	Total industry	States, standard metropolitan statistical areas and large industrial counties	Annual		
Census of Business: Retail Trade	Retail sales	2-3-4	National, regions, divisions, States, standards metropolitan statistical areas, and central business districts	Quinquennial	Every five years for years ending in "3" and "8" (Beginning 1967 and for years ending in "2" and "7")	U.S. Department of Commerce, Bureau of the Census, Washington, D.C. 20233

*Taken from Measuring Markets, A Guide to the Use of Federal and State Statistical Data, prepared by the U.S. Department of Commerce, 1966.

EXHIBIT 9-4 (continued)

Title of Publication	Kind of Data	SIC Industry Digit Detail[1]	Geographic Coverage	Reference Period	Frequency of Publication	Issuing Agency
	Retail sales	2	Counties	Quinquennial		
	Retail sales	2-3	Cities of 2,500 inhabitants or more	Quinquennial		
	Retail sales	2-3	Counties and cities with 500 establishments or more	Quinquennial		
Census of Business: Selected Services	Receipts	Total industry	National, regions, divisions, and States	Quinquennial	Every five years for years ending "3" and "8" (Beginning 1967 for years ending in "2" and "7")	U.S. Department of Commerce, Bureau of the Census, Washington, D.C. 20233
	Receipts	2	National, regions and divisions (with separate summary tables)	Quinquennial		
	Receipts	2-3-4	National, regions, divisions, States, and standard metropolitan statistical areas	Quinquennial		
	Receipts	Selected 2	Counties and cities of 2,500 or more inhabitants	Quinquennial		

Census of Business: Wholesale Trade	Receipts	2-3	Counties and cities with 200 establishments or more	Quinquennial		
	Sales	2-3-4	National, regions, divisions, States standard metropolitan statistical areas, and countless counties with 100 establishments or more	Quinquennial	Every five years for years ending in "3" and "8" (Beginning 1967 for years ending in "2" and "7")	U.S. Department of Commerce, Bureau of the Census, Washington, D.C. 20233
Census of Manufacturers	Value of shipments	2-3-4	National, regions, divisions, and States	Quinquennial	Every five years for years ending in "3" and "8" (Beginning 1967 for years ending in "2" and "7")	U.S. Department of Commerce, Bureau of the Census, Washington, D.C. 20233
	Value added by manufacture	Total industry	National, States, standard metropolitan statistical areas, counties, and cities of 10,000 or more inhabitants	Quinquennial	Every five years for years ending in "3" and "8" (Beginning 1967 for years ending in "2" and "7")	U.S. Department of Commerce, Bureau of the Census, Washington, D.C. 20233
	Value added by manufacture	2-3-4	National, regions, divisions, States and standard metropolitan statistical areas with 40,000 or more manufacturing employees	Quinquennial		

EXHIBIT 9-4 (*continued*)

Title of Publication	Kind of Data	SIC Industry Digit Detail[1]	Geographic Coverage	Reference Period	Frequency of Publication	Issuing Agency
	Value added by manufacture	2-3	Counties with industry groups with 500 or more employees	Quinquennial		
	Product class value of shipments	5-7	National	Quinquennial		
	Product class value of shipments	5	Divisions and States	Quinquennial		
Current Industrial Reports[2]	Production	5-7	National	Separate product reports vary from monthly to yearly	Frequency varies from monthly to yearly	U.S. Department of Commerce, Bureau of the Census, Washington, D.C. 20233
Current Retail Trade Reports						
Advance Monthly Retail Sales	Sales	2-3	National	Latest two months	Monthly	U.S. Department of Commerce, Bureau of the Census, Washington, D.C. 20233
Monthly Retail Trade	Sales	2-3-4	National, regions, specified divisions, large states and the five largest standard metropolitan statistical areas	Twelve months	Monthly	U.S. Department of Commerce, Bureau of the Census, Washington, D.C. 20233

Title	Data content	Code	Geographic	Period	Frequency	Source
Retail Trade Annual Report	Sales	2-3-4	National	Annual	Annual	Same as above
Weekly Retail Sales	Sales estimates	2-3	National	Current week	Weekly	Same as above
Current Wholesale Trade						
Monthly Wholesale Trade Report: Sales and Inventories	Sales	2-3-4	National, divisions	Twelve months	Monthly	U.S. Department of Commerce, Bureau of the Census, Washington, D.C. 20233
Statistics of Income Corporation Income Tax Returns	Receipts and deductions by type, profits, income tax, distributions to stockholders, assets and liabilities by industry, size of total assets, business receipts, and net income	2-3[7]	National	Annual	Annual	U.S. Treasury Department, Internal Revenue Service, Washington, D.C. 20224
Statistics of Income U.S. Business Tax Returns	Receipts, deductions by type; profits for each of the following types of busines organizations: Sole proprietorships Partnerships Corporations	2[7]	National	Annual	Annual	U.S. Treasury Department, Internal Revenue Service, Washington, D.C. 20224

EXHIBIT 9-4 (continued)

Title of Publication	Kind of Data	SIC Industry Digit Detail[1]	Geographic Coverage	Reference Period	Frequency of Publication	Issuing Agency
	Receipts, selected deductions by type; profits for each of the following: Sole proprietorships Partnerships	2-3	States	Annual	Biennial	U.S. Treasury Department, Internal Revenue Service, Washington, D.C. 20224
Survey of Current Business[3]	Retail Sales	2-4	National	Current twelve months	Monthly	U.S. Department of Commerce, Office of Business Economics, Washington, D.C. 20230
	Value of manufacturer's shipments	2-4	National	Current twelve months	Monthly	
U.S. Commodity Exports–Imports as Related to Output	Value of Shipments	2-3-4-5	National	Latest year	Annual	U.S. Department of Commerce, Bureau of the Census, Washington, D.C. 20233
U.S. Exports: Country by Commodity, Groupings, FT-410	Value of shipments	4	Country of destination	Current month and year end summary	Monthly (separate annual report)	U.S. Department of Commerce, Bureau of the Census, Washington, D.C. 20233

U.S. Exports: Country by Commodity Groupings FT-420	Value of shipments	4	Country of destination	Current month and year end summary	Monthly (separate annual report)	U.S. Department of Commerce, Bureau of the Census, Washington, D.C. 20233
U.S. Imports of Merchandise for Consumption, FT-125	Value of shipments	4	Country of origin	Current month and cumulative year to date	Monthly	U.S. Department of Commerce, Bureau of the Census, Washington, D.C. 20233
U.S. Industrial Outlook [5]	Value of shipments and selected receipts	4	National and selected States	Projections for next current year	Annual	U.S. Department of Commerce, Business and Defense Services Administration, Washington, D.C. 20230
U.S. Trade with Puerto Rico and United States Possessions, FT-800	Value of shipments	6	Trade between the United States and Puerto Rico and United States possessions	Current month and Annual	Monthly (with separate annual reports)	U.S. Department of Commerce, Bureau of the Census, Washington, D.C. 20233

[1] Detail of data varies by area depending on industry composition and relevance.

[2] Brochure listing over 100 separate reports, containing various types of data for about 2,500 products, available from issuing agency. Only some of these reports give value of production or value added by manufacturer.

[3] Reprint of figures supplied by the Bureau of Labor Statistics, U.S. Department of Labor.

[4] These data are classified in terms of the Standard International Trade Classification Revised (SITC), a structure devised by the United Nations to standardize foreign trade statistics internationally. The data in Report FT-410 are classified by Schedule B, a 7-digit expansion of the SITC: FT-410 gives data up to the 4-digit level of Schedule B; and FT-125 gives data classified by Schedule A, a 7-digit expansion of the SITC.

[5] Series covers key industries in the United States' economy; the coverage of individual industries will vary each year.

[6] Data for the United States shipments to Puerto Rico and the United States possessions classified according to Schedule Q; shipments from Puerto Rico to the United States classified according to Schedule P; data on shipments from the Virgin Islands to the United States are reported in accordance with the Classifications in Tariff Schedules of the United States Annotated.

[7] Beginning in 1963 based on Standard Enterprise system.

chapter 10

Business Research Methods, Techniques, and Tools

DISTINCTIONS BETWEEN METHODS, TECHNIQUES, AND TOOLS

The terms *methods, techniques,* and *tools* are often used carelessly and interchangeably. There are, however, useful and meaningful differences between the concepts identified by these words. The purpose of this chapter is to identify these concepts and to indicate briefly how these processes or instruments can serve the researcher. For a complete explanation at the application level, the reader should refer to books which deal extensively with the subject of interest.

Methods

A method is an orderly and systematic procedure. A scientific method is the process of selecting alternative courses of action. It is the selection of techniques which will accomplish the researcher's objective. The most general method of science has been discussed in Chapter 2. Scientific methods in business research which are specific extensions of the general method are:

1. Laboratory investigations
2. Field investigations
3. Analytic and synthetic concept investigations
4. Genetic and comparative investigations

Techniques

A technique is the manner in which an operation is performed; it is a process or course of action. A scientific technique is a way of accomplishing a task in the research process. It usually involves the application of scientific tools. There are innumerable possible techniques and the possibilities are limited only by the ingenuity of the research. A few common examples are:

1. Statistical techniques
2. Sample survey techniques
3. Projective techniques
4. Observation of customer behavior
5. Counting techniques

6. Content analysis
7. Simulation techniques
8. Mechanical measurement techniques
9. Erosion measurement techniques
10. Accretion measurement techniques

Tools

A tool is any instrument which is used to increase the efficiency of a process. In scientific investigation, a tool may be either a physical or conceptual device. A few examples of scientific tools for business research are:

1. Stopwatch
2. Electronic computer
3. Tachistiscope
4. Camera
5. Table of random numbers
6. Questionnaire
7. Sanborn maps of cities
8. Probability distribution tables

LABORATORY INVESTIGATIONS

The laboratory method of scientific research consists basically of a carefully planned process of observation carried out in a situation and environment especially designed for that purpose. It is distinguished from the field method by its greater insulation from natural environmental influences. Thus laboratory investigations are *usually* conducted in an area apart from actual business facilities and operations. In the laboratory process the investigator is able to eliminate many variables not relevant to his purpose, control other variables, and finally manipulate some variables in order to observe the effects. An examination of a variety of laboratory inquiries shows that widely varying degrees of control and precision have been accepted by necessity. Some general categories of laboratory research are:

1. Measurement of physical items or processes.
2. Measurement of performance of individuals on primarily physical tasks.
3. Effect of external environmental factors (sound, light, color, heat, noise) on individuals.
4. Measurement of physical, mental, or attitudinal attributes of a population of individuals.
5. Measurement of attributes of a sample of individuals for estimates of attributes of a population.
6. Experiments to develop or test hypotheses about behavior of people in groups.
7. Analog experiments employing animals and/or machines for the study of human behavior. (For example, the use of the electronic computer to simulate organizational behavior has become fairly common.)

In planning laboratory research to learn about organizations, the experimenter can create situations involving very simple physical processes to highly abstract mental processes. Relevant organization processes can be created in a context of no organization at one extreme through a range of situations to a completely natural organization at the other extreme.

While laboratory research solves some problems because of the control of variables, it creates other problems. The difficulty of obtaining participants, and participants with desired attributes, is common. The effect of the subjects on the experimenter's outlook as he begins to absorb the views of the subjects can distort the researcher's objective viewpoint. It may be necessary to exaggerate the input variables in order to obtain reactions strong enough to measure differences. Further, it cannot be safely assumed in advance that procedures used to manipulate variables will be successful, and hence establishing the laboratory research experiment itself may become a trial and error process. Internal and external validity are general problems at all times.[3]

There is no recipe for the research process in the laboratory. The neophyte will benefit most from first reading discussions of various techniques and experiments.[1,2] Secondly, he should then read the firsthand reports of relevant research as published in the journals. If he is next able to work with an experienced investigator, he will be fortunate. Failing this, he should start with very simple experiments involving few subjects until he gains experience with the difficulties of laboratory research.

FIELD INVESTIGATIONS

A field investigation is research conducted in the actual setting where the variables being studied occur naturally. The "field" is the real-world situation rather than one actualized by the researcher. This does not mean that the researcher cannot introduce perturbations in the field. It is usually desirable to control some variables in order to measure resulting changes. Field research may employ one or several of the following principal research strategies.

1. Surveys *of* consumers, companies, or other institutions affecting the business environment.

2. Surveys and experiments in the market place.

3. Surveys and experiments *within* the consumer's or company's environment (i.e., within the home or within the company.)

[1] See, for example, Chapter 4, "Laboratory Experiments," in Leon Festinger and Daniel Katz (eds.), *Research Methods in the Behavioral Sciences* (New York: Holt, Rinehart and Winston, 1953).

[2] See Karl E. Weick, "Organizations in the Laboratory," in Victor H. Vroom (ed.), *Methods of Organizational Research* (Pittsburgh: University of Pittsburgh Press, 1967), pp. 1–56.

[3] For an excellent discussion of internal and external validity in experimentation, see Seymour Banks, *Experimentation in Marketing* (New York: McGraw-Hill Book Company, Inc., 1965), p. 26.

4. Depth studies (primarily observation in unstructured situations in a single organization or setting to gather large amounts of relevant data not obtainable by superficial techniques).

5. Running records of activities which are maintained by the company or institution in its normal course of operation.

6. Erosion and accretion traces of activity. (This involves indirect measurement of human activities by observing the wear of items in contact with humans or the waste products left behind.)[4]

At one extreme the field researcher reacts highly with the research setting as, for example, when the researcher takes employment with the company in some operating or functional capacity. At the other extreme, data are gathered in a manner which avoids practically all reaction with the process under study.

The steps in field research generally are as follows:

1. Preliminary planning. The research problem is formulated, the strategy selected, and the variables to be controlled and manipulated are defined.

2. Preliminary field contacts are made. The researcher goes into the field to see firsthand what is involved. If research is to be conducted within firms, he will contact officials to try to obtain their cooperation. In the case of surveys, he will identify a few respondents (such as special classes of consumers, executives, or general public) and test in a preliminary way his techniques and tools to see what unexpected problems may arise. In either case, examination of the physical situation is important.

3. Reformulation and refinement of the problem.

4. Development of the complete research design.

5. Training of people who will participate in field operations.

6. Pilot run to pretest the techniques and tools.

7. Final revisions of procedures and tools.

8. Full-scale field operations.

9. Recording and classification of data.

10. Analysis of results.

11. Final report.

There is a strong relationship among all steps of the research process. They are not independent, chronologically sequenced steps but rather overlapping activities. Each step must be planned with all others in mind.

Of the above steps, particular attention should be paid to (5), the training of the field operatives. It is difficult to conceive of the many ways in which intelligent but untrained individuals can unwittingly invalidate an entire project. With even the best planning and best training, some type of interaction can weaken field research, so that all possible thought must precede the final field operations.

[4] See Eugene Webb *et al.*, *Unobtrusive Measures: Nonreactive Research in the Social Sciences* (Chicago: Rand McNally & Company, 1966).

ANALYTIC AND SYNTHETIC CONCEPT INVESTIGATIONS

Analytic concept investigations are concerned with working with available data to draw inferences directly or to develop models from which inferences can be made. Synthetic concept investigations are concerned with the synthesis of knowledge to derive general principles or models. Despite the apparent difference between these two methods of research, they have much in common, and, in fact, are usually found in combination. The general steps in these investigations for basic research are:

1. Formulate the problem.
2. Make necessary assumptions about premises and principles to be used.
3. Retrieve relevant data.
4. Derive possible solutions to the problem by analysis and/or synthesis, using premises and accepted principles.
5. Use the solution to predict.
6. Test the prediction when the future data becomes available by comparing the predicted results with the actual data.

In applied research, one very important difference in the order of the steps should be observed. This critical order is that the analysis or synthesis from which the decision rule is derived should be made *before* the input data are obtained. If the decision rule is derived *after* the data are seen by the researcher, it is almost impossible to prevent the decision rule from being influenced by the data. The analysis and decision rule will then be distorted to reflect preconceived notions since the investigator will be guided by what is "reasonable" in the light of the data.

GENETIC AND COMPARATIVE RESEARCH

Genetic research is often necessary to explain behavior of organizations in the business world which have evolved over a period of time. Thus it would be difficult to explain the behavior of unions, and particularly current changes in behavior, without studying closely the history and development of unions and their environment. A differentiating aspect of the genetic research method is the emphasis which must be placed upon identifying the principal relevant factors and on the problem of verification of data.

The comparative researcher introduces both time and space as control or bounding variables.

Ultimately, a comparative methodology professes to provide a logic whereby the general nature of a phenomenon may be specified and the conditions that give rise to its specific manifestations explained. It attempts to do this by showing that the "causes" for a phenomenon discerned in one cultural context are equally "causal" when they occur in another cultural context. If they are not the same, then the cultural

EXHIBIT 10-1
Construct for Comparative Marketing Research

Conceptions of Marketing			Aspects To Be Studied Comparatively[3] Types, amounts, and relative importance of:
Problem	Corresponding Concept	Example of Relevant Studies[2]	
"Who are the marketers?"	"Marketing is about marketers" OR Marketing as actors	E.A. Duddy and D.A. Revzan, *Marketing: An Institutional Approach*	The actors' characteristics:[4] *Physical:* number (absolute and relative), location, density *Economic:* wealth, income, borrowing power, know-how (education and training) *Political:* power (single and joint) *Social:* membership in classes, castes, ethnic groups, professions status, reputation, image *Cultural:* needs, values, attitudes, expectations, role perceptions
"What do marketers do?"	"Marketing is what marketers do" OR Marketing as a process	R.S. Vaile, E.T. Grether, and R. Cox, *Marketing in the American Economy*	The actors' activities and interactions: *Activities:* assembling, transporting, dispersing (space separation) financing, risk-managing, storing (time separation) informing, persuading (perception separation) aligning offers and bids (evaluation separation) contacting, terminating (ownership separation) *Initiatives* (Who initiates the contacts between the actors?): buyer-seller-third party *Techniques* (How do the actors use their resources in behaving towards each other?): command-manipulation-competition-cooperation
"How are marketers related to each other?"	"Marketing is about markets" OR Marketing as a structure	W. Alderson, *Marketing Behavior and Executive Action*	The actors' relationships:[5] *Membership* (Who is a marketer?): membership criteria, barriers of entry *Arena* (To whom is he related?): similar types of marketers—preceding or succeeding marketers—facilitating agencies *Scope* (Over what matters?): Geographical areas, products, activities *Nature* (In what types of relationships?): rational-traditional personal (loyalty)-impersonal egotistic-altruistic hierarchical-egalitarian
"What do marketers contribute?"	"Marketing is what marketers contribute?" OR Marketing as a function	R. Cox *et al*, *Distribution in a High-level Economy*	The actors' contributions: *Nature:* psychological, economic, political, social, cultural *Recipients:* society, lower-level organizations, ultimate consumers *Size, quality, and efficiency*
"How are marketers affected by their environment?"	"Marketing takes place within an environment" OR Marketing as system-cum-environment	R. Bartels (ed.), *Comparative Marketing*	The interdependence between environmental factors and the actors' characteristics,[6] activities, interactions, relationships, and contributions: *Physical environment* *Economic* " *Political* " *Social* " *Cultural* "

[1]Underlying marketing is the basic situation of various "separations" (in space, time, perception, evaluation and ownership) between heterogeneous needs and need-satisfying means. Thus, in the light of the concepts presented here, *marketing is marketers related in a structure and interacting in a process of activities whose function it is to bridge these separations and match these heterogeneous needs and need-satisfying means: this "bridging and matching" takes place within an environment.* This view of marketing is obviously related to Wroe Alderson's conceptions which have been analysed by Nicosia and Schwartz. A similar conception of marketing as well as the classification of marketing "separations" can be found in McInnes.

[2]Only a few books have been listed, although many other publications are relevant. Some of these books could have been listed under more than one heading.

[3]This is a partial listing of "Aspects to Be Studied Comparatively." Most of them are detailed in the Appendix ("Outline for Comparative Marketing Analysis") of Bartel's *Comparative Marketing*.

[4]*Actors* applies to whomever engages in marketing. Governmental agencies connected with marketing can be studied either under actors or under environment, depending on whether the government engages significantly in marketing activities (as in the USSR), or limits its role to the regulation, control and promotion of marketing (as in the United States).

[5]Distribution channels are part of the marketing structure. However, the flow of goods, money and information through these channels should be analyzed under process.

[6]The environment is within the marketing system to the extent that the marketing actors share the common values and institutions of their society. Nonmarketers within business organizations are also part of the marketers' environment.

Source: Abstracted from J. Boddewyn, "A Construct for Comparative Marketing Research," *Journal of Marketing Research* (May 1966), p. 151.

context is analyzed for the limiting conditions of the phenomenon in question.[5]

Comparative research may also consist of interpretation of differences and similarities of two systems in the same or different cultures at the same specified time. A comparative method for marketing research has been developed by J. Boddewyn (Exhibit 10-1). Boddewyn has developed a basic structure for comparison of either elements or relationships in marketing systems.

The steps in the comparative research method consist of:

1. Identification of elements, processes, and relationships which can be compared for two or more different systems.

2. Development of a system of classification of such elements, processes, and relationships and their characteristics.

3. Selection of a research strategy for making comparisons.

4. Measurement of similarities and differences.

5. Explanation and interpretation of similarities and differences.

FREQUENTLY USED TECHNIQUES

Statistical Estimation by Sampling

Researchers frequently wish to estimate the average or the total of some magnitude for an entire population. For example, a market researcher may wish to estimate the total number of users of Brand X or the total number of red-haired women in a city, state, or region. Similarly, he might wish to know the proportion of people who have some attribute such as the proportion who use shopping lists when shopping at local supermarkets. An unscientific method for making these estimates is simply to question a number of convenient individuals about the magnitude or attribute and then use the average for the total population being considered. The unfortunate aspect of this nonscientific technique is that no estimate of the magnitude of the error is possible.

If, however, a sample is selected so that each element in the population has a positive known chance of being selected, the size of the possible error may be stated with a specified probability. For example, a statement might be as follows:

The population mean falls within the range 76 ± 5 with a probability of 95 percent.

This means that if a large number of samples of the same size were drawn on a probability basis, in 95 percent of the cases the population mean (which is being estimated) would fall within 5 units of the sample mean. Thus, although the sample means are different for the various samples, the error remains limited

---

[5] Edward A. Suchman, "The Comparative Method in Social Research," *Rural Sociology* (June 1964), p. 126.

to 5 units in 95 percent of the samples. Such an estimate is termed an *interval estimate*, and the reliability is sometimes called the *confidence level*.

Simple random sampling is used for situations where the population elements are right at hand—as for example a list of local companies. With the aid of a table of random numbers, elements are selected with equal probability. Simple random-sampling errors are the basis for measuring the precision of other more complicated sampling designs.

Systematic sampling is the method whereby every *k*th element is selected from a list. Thus from a 1,200-page directory of corporations, every 12th page would be selected after the first page is selected at random between 1 and 12.

Stratified sampling requires the classification of data into similar groups or strata in order to estimate the mean or proportion. For example, if an estimate of the average annual per capita expenditures on vacation trips were being made, then the population might be grouped into five or six income groups, say. The samples would be drawn from each group to make up the final sample. The estimate of the mean is computed by finding the average for each stratum and then taking the weighted average of these values. The sampling error is also found by first taking a weighted average of the variance for each stratum. Stratified sampling yields a smaller sampling error when the strata observations are very homogeneous.

Cluster or area sampling is a method of sampling which is widely used today because it is an economical way of making estimates when the population elements are widely dispersed geographically. Thus on a national basis the country may be divided into "clusters" of counties and a sample of clusters selected. Observations need only be made on individuals, companies, or other desired sampling units within the selected clusters. Further, it is not necessary to list every element in the population of interest, but only those in the clusters which are finally selected from among the primary clusters. The measures of precision of the estimate is obtained by combining the variances of the data for the selected clusters. The greater the heterogeneity of elements within a cluster (and hence the less variability between clusters) the greater will be the precision of the estimate of population mean.[6,7]

Statistical Relationships and Forecasting

A common basic and applied research problem is to determine if two variables are related or at least vary together. For example, if it can be shown that sales of a glass container company increases as sales of beer and soft drinks vary, then a formula expressing this relationship may be sought. The statistical mea-

[6]For a complete treatment of sampling design, see Leslie Kish, *Survey Sampling* (New York: John Wiley & Sons, Inc., 1965) or Taro Yamane, *Elementary Sampling Theory* (Englewood Cliffs, N. J.: Prentice-Hall, Inc., 1967).

[7]U.S. Bureau of the Census, *Atlantida: A Case Study of Household Sample Surveys,* Unit IV, Sample Design Series ISPO 1, No. 1-E, 1966.

sure of the relationship among variables is the *coefficent of correlation.* Most commonly, relationships between two variables can be approximated by a linear formula or a straight-line plot. The line of best fit, called the *regression line,* is determined so that the sum of the squares of the differences between the data and the line of best fit is minimized. For this reason the line of best fit is often referred to as the *least-squares line.* With the aid of this functional relationship, if the independent variable is known, the dependent variable may be estimated, and the error of the estimate at a specified confidence level may be determined.

When a variable such as sales is correlated with time, the trend relationship may be developed. By means of other statistical techniques, seasonal variations may be computed. Under the assumption that the future will be similar to the past, such *time series analyses* are helpful in predicting the future.

Other techniques for smoothing data to determine trends are the *moving average* technique and *exponential smoothing.* Exponential smoothing is particularly valuable in short-term forecasting for production control.[8]

Statistical Decision Making by Sampling

A business may set a curtain criterion for making a decision and a corresponding decision rule. By means of sampling it is then possible to determine the course of action to be taken. For example, the company may wish to try a direct-mail advertising campaign. One thousand mailings are made. The response to the old mailings was 30 percent, so that if the response to the new mailings is *statistically significantly greater* than 30 percent, the new campaign will be adopted. By means of statistics, it is possible to determine the percentage at which the chance of difference between this percentage and 30 percent will occur only 5 percent of the time, say, due to chance alone. Hence for greater differences it may be safely assumed that the new campaign is bringing a greater response.

Another type of assertion which may be tested is that there is no difference between characteristics or attributes of two products. For example, a company wishes to determine if the life of its product is the same or different than that of its competitor. By taking a sample of each product, the hypothesis that there is no difference may be tested.

Statistical Techniques in Experimental Design to Determine Sources of Variations

It is often desired to determine which of several factors produce a specified effect. For example, which of several advertising themes produces greater sales? Does price, store, or location within the store affect sales, or do all or combinations of these affect sales? Which of several types of leadership patterns yields

---

[8]For a presentation of the computation techniques in forecasting, see Robert G. Murdick and Authur E. Schaefer, *Sales Forecasting for Lower Costs and Higher Profits,* (Englewood Cliffs, N.J.: Prentice-Hall, Inc., 1967). For a complete treatment of exponential smoothing, see Robert G. Brown, *Statistical Forecasting for Inventory Control* (New York: McGraw-Hill Book Company, Inc., 1959).

greatest productivity? Statistical techniques applied to the design of experiments permit the testing of hypotheses about the sources of variations in the independent variables.[9]

Discriminant Analysis

Managers often want to discriminate between consumers in such a way that the consumers can be divided into classes for purposes such as market segmentation. For example, it may be desirable to determine which of five socioeconomic classes a consumer falls in, or whether a consumer is a light, medium, or heavy user of some product. Credit departments may wish to determine in which of several risk classes a customer belongs. The problem is to determine the relative importance of several factors known about the consumer or customer in contributing to the prediction as to which class he belongs in.[10] In one study, for example, discriminant analysis was used to determine whether other variables than distance and mass (size) were significant factors in consumer choice of shopping centers.[11] The problem of overstatement of predictive power of discriminant analysis, procedures for estimating the overstatement, and a brief description of discriminant analysis in general has been provided by R. E. Frank and others.[12]

Quality Control Techniques

Statistical methods permit surveillance of research procedures (such as field operations of sample surveys) to detect when such procedures are being carried out properly. In addition, quality control may be a direct part of research into the quality of output of an organization or productive system.

Field Survey Techniques

The purpose of scientific sample surveys is to gather information in the environment by means of sampling in order to estimate some characteristic or attribute of a much larger group or population of elements. The design and implementation of field sample surveys is a complex undertaking which requires selections from among many techniques at each step.

In its most extensive form, the field sample survey emanates from the business or economic problem and evolves essentially by the following sequence of actions.

[9] For an exposition of experimental design techniques, see Seymour Banks, *Experimentation in Marketing* (New York: McGraw-Hill Book Company, Inc., 1965); B. J. Winer, *Statistical Principles in Experimental Design* (New York: McGraw-Hill Book Company, Inc., 1962); or George W. Snedecor, *Statistical Methods* (5th ed.; Ames, Iowa: Iowa State College Press, 1956).

[10] For a complete treatment of this technique, see Harry H. Harman, *Modern Factor Analysis* (Chicago: University of Chicago Press, 1960).

[11] Louis P. Bucklin, "The Concept of Mass in Intra-Urban Shopping," *Journal of Marketing* (October 1967), pp. 37-42.

[12] Ronald E. Frank, William F. Massy, and Donald G. Morrison, "Bias in Multiple Discriminant Analysis," *Journal of Marketing Research* (August 1965), pp. 250-257.

1. Recognize and identify problems.
2. Explore the problem selected.
   (a) Gather available information which appears pertinent to the problem area.
   (b) Define the problem area.
   (c) Define the specific problem or problems to be solved.
3. Formulate the objectives of the research.
   (a) Determine the information needed and the relative importance of each item.
   (b) Determine why the information is needed.
   (c) Evaluate how decisions will be affected by alternatives.
   (d) Specify the objectives of the research, and the decision rules in the case of applied research.
4. Estimate costs to be allocated in a trade-off with precision and reliability.
5. Define the population, the characteristics or attributes to be measured, the sampling units, and the parameters to be estimated.
6. Select the sampling design.
7. Design the questionnaire.
8. Plan the field operations.

Information which may be sought from respondents in personal interviews may relate to:

1. Perceptions
2. Recognition and recall
3. Discrimination
4. Facts
5. Opinions

Although much has been written on sampling techniques, the critical techniques in field surveys are those concerned with data collection and processing. Because the errors involved in data collection are unknown and may be large, techniques for recruiting, training, and controlling the field force require careful attention. Yet the functions of data gathering are too commonly left to the least educated, least skilled, least interested, lowest paid, and least permanent workers in the project. For detailed treatment of types of errors in interview situations and training and control of interviewers to reduce these errors, the researcher should study the literature carefully.[13-15]

[13] Harper W. Boyd, Jr., *Marketing Research, Text and Cases* (Homewood, Ill.: Richard D. Irwin, Inc., 1956), pp. 374–496.
[14] Claire Selltiz *et al.*, *Research Methods in the Social Relations* (New York: Holt, Rinehart and Winston, 1962), pp. 199–454.
[15] U.S., Bureau of the Census, *The Current Population Survey—A Report on Methodology*, Technical Paper No. 7, 1963.

Mail-Survey Techniques

The purpose of good mail-survey techniques is to obtain responses sufficient to fulfill the requirements of a probability sample. These techniques include selection of a sample, questionnaire design, follow-up techniques, and post-sampling analysis. There is much folklore surrounding mail-survey techniques, but research on the subject is increasing. For an excellent summary with an extensive bibliography on research prior to 1961 the reader is referred to Christopher Scott's article, "Research on Mail Surveys," *Journal of the Royal*

EXHIBIT 10-2

Checklist for Preparing the Cover Letter

1. Be brief.
2. Give the purpose of the study *in terms of what it will mean to the respondent.* In short, use the YOU approach because the respondent must be sold by means of the cover letter.
3. If the questionnaire is long, the due date should be stated in a diplomatic way. If the questionnaire is brief, it is best not to state the date since it is likely that the respondent will complete the questionnaire promptly or never.
4. If identification of the respondent is not necessary as is usually the case, assurance that his reply will be held confidential and appear only in summary statistical form should be clearly stated.
5. Have the letter produced by a process (Hoovenizing) which produces "original" typing. Thus automatic typewriters are best but most expensive. Offset reproduction can also be made to appear much like original typewritten material. In every case the address and salutation must be typed in matching typeface and density of black. Hectograph should never be used, and mimeograph is rarely acceptable.
6. The letter may be signed in ink to increase the impression of a personal letter. A handwritten postscript will further enhance this effect. Research on the benefits from the personal appearance is conflicting.
7. There is some question as to which of three addresses in business firms should be used to yield better results. The letter may be addressed to the individual who is most knowledgable or responsible, to the Director of Public Relations, or simply to the position (no name). Often the Director of Public Relations will maintain records of incoming questionnaires until they have been answered. He will expedite such inquiries as part of his job.
8. When consumers are being surveyed, it may be helpful to write two or more types of cover letters to different strata of respondents. If consumers are stratified on the basis of sex only, a straightforward businesslike letter may be sent to the men and friendly, chatty letter to the women.
9. If business firms are being surveyed, a postscript which asks the respondent to place a check mark if he desires a summary of results is advisable, if the cost is not too great.
10. Postage stamps rather than metering of envelopes add a personal touch and tend to increase responses. Obviously, stamps should be placed upon an enclosed return addressed envelope. Some studies have shown that airmail stamps on both outgoing and return envelopes have increased response rates. Other experiences have indicated that there is no difference or even fewer returns. (A hypothesis is that the recipient finds it more rewarding to steam off the air mail stamp and keep it.)
11. The return envelope should fit inside the outgoing envelope without folding.
12. The letterhead of the covering letter should be such that it does not arouse a bias. Companies often maintain or use marketing research organizations or titles to avoid this.
13. White paper of standard size is generally considered to be best.
14. Make sure the mailing list is up to date. People and firms move or die at a surprising rate so that costs for using old mailing lists can become excessive.

Statistical Society, Series A, Volume 124, Part 2, 1961, pp. 143-195. New journals not listed in this bibliography which carry reports of research on mail-survey techniques are the *Journal of Advertising Research* and the *Journal of Marketing Research.*

In a mail survey, a "package" is sent to each individual in the sample. The package contains at the least the second and third of the following items:

1. Background and instructional material.
2. A covering letter or letter of transmittal.
3. The questionnaire.
4. A premium.

EXHIBIT 10-3
Checklist for Preparation and Mailing of Mail Questionnaires

1. The questionnaire used in a mail survey should be brief and ask fairly simple questions.
2. The sequence of questions should be logical and interesting from the respondent's point of view.
3. The first question should be the easiest one for the respondent to answer and one which will immediately arouse interest.
4. Provide transition statements where necessary.
5. Avoid leading questions.
6. Avoid "multiple-element" (sometimes called "double-barreled" or "multi-dimensional") questions. For example, "Do you make large or small purchases when you shop in chain stores or corner stores?"
7. Attempt to use "neutral" words and avoid words which arouse emotion or bias.
8. Use language and words which are appropriate to the respondents.
9. Use "screening questions" so that numerous questions will not be asked which do not apply.
10. One researcher had a transparent colored horizontal stripe printed over a sensitive question at the end of a questionnaire in order to minimize its effect.
11. Internal check questions are sometimes advisable.
12. Be sure to include an alternative "Other" if there is any doubt as to whether all possibilities have been listed.
13. For long questionnaires, use headings to divide the questionnaire into parts.
14. When open-end questions are asked, leave plenty of room for replies.
15. Include questions for stratifying or classifying respondents if appropriate.
16. Don't ask the respondent to do anything which you can do yourself except to provide an easy lead question such as: "Is your firm a manufacturer of consumer goods, industrial goods, or both?"
17. Use lots of white space and easy-to-read typefaces.
18. Use successive requests.
    (a) First mailing.
    (b) Second mailing—"thank you and reminder" postal card about one week after the first mailing.
    (c) Third mailing—"second request" copy of the questionnaire, return envelope with accompanying letter urging and explaining the need for cooperation of nonrespondents of the first two mailings. Send this within about two weeks or so after the first mailing.
    (d) Fourth mailing—"thank you and reminder" postal card to nonrespondents of the first three mailings. Send this within a week to 10 days after the third mailing.
19. Be sure that the questionnaire is folded in such a manner that when it is refolded in the original way it will fit inside the smaller return envelope.
20. Color of the paper used for the questionnaire has been known to affect response rate.
21. Make sure each answer is identified or can easily be identified when returned by a code number and/or letter for purposes of tabulation.

Exhibits 10-2 and 10-3 provide suggestions for the preparation of the cover letter and the preparations for the mailing of the questionnaire.

Projective Techniques

Projective techniques are used in motivation research to uncover the underlying reason for people's attitudes and behavior. People do not usually give their true feelings in answer to questions on subjects about which they have anxieties. In fact, they may not be consciously aware of their true feelings. Projective techniques attempt to get individuals to attribute (or project) to other real or imaginary people their own feelings. The techniques used are:

1. Depth interviewing
2. Word association
3. Sentence completion
4. Psychodrama (acting out of roles in specified situations)
5. Cartoon completion
6. Essay writing (thematic appreception)

While projective techniques are but a few of the techniques used in research into customer behavior, the term "motivation research" has often been erroneously identified as synonomous with these.[16]

Observation of Customer Behavior

"Observation" of customer behavior may be either direct or indirect. In stores, some techniques are stationing an observer at a display section, reflecting or one-way mirrors, and hidden cameras. In the home, cameras attached to the television sets have been used with the permission of the subjects. Hidden cameras have been used on buses to determine the number of people who are exposed to advertising on the outside of the buses. Some researchers have raised questions regarding the moral or ethical issues of some forms of hidden observation.

Counting or Enumeration Techniques

Counting techniques may encompass simple counts of people passing a given store, door-to-door interviewing, mechanical or electronic systems, or searching records and documents. Ingeuity in devising a special technique in many cases will shorten the time, decrease the cost, and improve the accuracy of the count.

Content Analysis

Content analysis is a qualitative, objective, and systematic research technique for evaluation of verbal material, as for example advertising or other business communications. It may be used to detect trends in communication

---

[16]For treatments of "motivation research" to consumer and industrial buying behavior, see Ernest Dichter, *Motivation Research Handbook of Consumer Motivations* (New York: McGraw-Hill Book Co., Inc., 1964), and Industrial Advertising Research Institute, *Motives in Industrial Buying*, Report Number 9, 1959.

content, to detect and identify cultural differences in communication content, to compare media, to develop communication standards, and to analyze face-to-face interactions among people. The types of variables frequently employed in content analysis are listed in Exhibit 10-4.[17]

EXHIBIT 10-4
Variables Frequently Used in Content Analysis

A. What Is Said
1. Subject matter—what is the communication about?
2. Direction—is the treatment favorable or unfavorable toward the subject?
3. Standard—what is the basis (or grounds) on which the classification of direction is made?
4. Values—what goals are explicitly or implicitly revealed?
5. Methods—what means or actions are employed to realize goals?
6. Traits—what characteristics of persons are revealed?
7. Actor—who initiates actions?
8. Authority—in whose name are statements made?
9. Origin—what is the place of origin of the communication?
10. Target—to whom is the communication particularly directed?

B. How It Is Said
1. Form of communication—is it fiction, news, or television?
2. Form of statement—what is the grammatical or syntactical form of the unit of analysis?
3. Intensity—how much strength or excitement value does the communication have?
4. Device—what is the rhetorical or propagandistic character of the communication?

Source: Leon Festinger and Daniel Katz (eds.), *Research Methods in the Behavioral Sciences* (New York: Holt, Rinehart and Winston, 1963), pp. 456-457.

Monte Carlo Simulation

From relatively sparse data, a cumulative probability distribution may be established which provides the basis for generating statistically as much data as desired. For instance, the number of absentees per day at a new plant may be known for a period of eight months. By the Monte Carlo technique, the number of absentees per day for years in advance may be simulated in order to study the effects on production of runs of days with high absenteeism.

The Monte Carlo technique may also be used in venture analysis to calculate profits based upon a number of variables with random fluctuations. The probability distributions of the variables may be either derived empirically or deduced on the basis of management and economic theory.

[17]See Leon Festinger and Daniel Katz (eds.), *Research Methods in the Behavioral Sciences* (New York: Holt, Rinehart and Winston, 1953), pp. 421–470, and Bernard Berelson, *Content Analysis in Communication Research* (New York: Free Press, 1952).

Computer Simulations

Studies of the activities of a firm, of the behavior of people in organizations, of marketing or production systems, and of intercompany competitive activities are so comples that traditional techniques cannot cope with them. Experimental techniques and mathematical analysis must usually be restricted to small parts of the total problem. Large-scale electronic computers, however, make possible the representation of large systems in logical flow networks which include many input and output variables. Input variables and parameters may be readily changed to simulate changing conditions in the real world. In the case of management games, behavior and decision making may be studied by combining observation of people interacting with computer-simulated situations.[18]

TOOLS

A few tools were listed as examples earlier in this chapter. By far the most commonly used (and abused) tools are the personal interview questionnaire and the self-administered (mail) questionnaire. Some discussion of these will be given here to point out the need for the researcher to educate himself thoroughly in the theory of these tools before using them. Some suggestions are also provided based upon "experience" where research has not yet provided a guide. Because the personal-interview forms and self-administered forms for data collection have much in common, they will be treated together by pointing out similarities and differences. The discussion of data-collection forms is restricted to those in which respondents are involved and thus does not include enumeration or description forms.

Types of Information Obtained With Respondent Forms

Respondent forms may be used to seek the following types of information:
1. Perception
2. Recognition and recall
3. Discrimination
4. Facts
5. Attitudes
6. Opinions
7. Motivations
8. Interests
9. Intentions

Perception is the translation of sensory stimuli into the individual's own unique interpretation. If a particular model of a car is shown to a group of individuals, it may be perceived by various members as dark and dreary, black

---

[18] See Abe Shuchman (ed.), *Scientific Decision Making in Business* (New York: Holt, Rinehart and Winston, 1963), pp. 407–434, and Wroe Alderson and Stanley J. Shapiro (eds.), *Marketing and the Computer* (Englewood Cliffs, N.J.: Prentice-Hall, Inc., 1963).

and sophisticated, sporty, too small, cheap-looking, a pile of junk, or a well-built car for the money. In other words, people perceive on the basis of their experience, knowledge, and personality.

Recognition and recall are aspects of memory. Information on recognition and recall is usually obtained in measuring advertising.[19]

Factual information such as age, income, number of children in the family, brand of a product used, and shopping habits is often gathered. Attitudes are enduring beliefs and values which influence a person's reactions to stimuli. Opinions are short-term beliefs which may change with time more easily. Motivation is concerned with the "reasons why" people behave as they do, did do, or intend to do. Intentions and interests may be determined, on the other hand, without seeking knowledge of the reasons for such.

General Characteristics of the Mail Questionnaire

The mail questionnaire is used in both consumer and industrial surveys because it can be sent to a large and widely dispersed group of people at low cost. However, cost per return may be high if techniques must be used to obtain a probability sample. Industrial firms often have a public relations official who attempts to get answers to outside inquiries. In addition, mail surveys of industries permit the respondent to collect data and reply at his convenience. Both of these factors favor the mail survey technique.

In the case of consumer surveys, obtaining a probability sample may be more difficult because of the wide cross section of the population that must usually be queried. Making heavy investments in new products on the basis of a nonprobability sample may be extremely risky. Mail surveys are useful, however, in developing hypotheses.

The self-administered form may be put in the hands of the respondents in a number of ways:

1. *Direct mail.*

2. *Guarantee or register cards.* When a product is sold, the purchaser is given a short form or card to fill out and mail to the manufacturer under the guise of registering his warrantee.

3. *Newspapers or magazines.* Questionnaires printed in periodicals may, for instance, be mailed in or dropped in a box in a local store.

4. *Panel diaries.* Sheets or small booklets are supplied to respondents who agree to participate in a panel over a period of time. These forms are usually schedules or tables in which the respondent enters his observations or actions.

5. *Machines.* For example, machines have been placed at point-of-purchase positions in retail stores and customers are invited to "vote" on questions by pressing buttons.

---

[19] For an excellent treatment of measurement of many aspects of advertising, see Darrell B. Lucas and Steuart H. Britt, *Measuring Advertising Effectiveness* (New York: McGraw-Hill Book Company, Inc., 1963).

General Characteristics of Personal-Interview Forms

With personal-interview forms, the interviewer is present to hold the respondent's attention. The form may thus in some cases be fairly lengthy in some industrial situations. For interviewing the general public, a form which requires more than 15 to 20 minutes to complete tends to meet with considerable resistance. In telephone interviews, even a short form is difficult to complete if it requires over five or ten minutes, particularly since the respondent can terminate the interview with such ease. One major advantage of the personal-interview situation is that the form may be designed in conjunction with materials handed to the respondent for evaluation. Advertising material or products may be tested without loss or destruction of large quantities of these.

For either face-to-face or telephone interviews, the forms usually contain not only questions and tables to be completed, but also instructions to the interviewers. Although interviewers are well trained, the instructions serve to preserve uniformity of approach and to guide the interviewer through the interview. A good interview form will contain the exact words which the interviewer is to use to identify himself and the project he is working on. Instructions will appear following screening questions to tell the interviewer what question to skip to. Transition statements will be included to carry the respondent's thoughts along smoothly to new topics. Concluding remarks and space for entering the time, the date, and identity of the interviewer may well be a part of the form.

Developing the Mail Questionnaire

There are various types of questions on the mail questionnaire.

1. *Questions requiring unstructured answers.* These questions are framed so that the respondent answers in his own words in essay form. This form is useful in exploratory studies to develop hypotheses.

2. *Open-end questions.* These questions require the respondent to fill in a word or phrase. This form is useful for gathering factual information where many answers are possible and for motivation studies.

3. *Check-type questions.* Where the respondent checks a box, underlines a word, or circles a number.

4. *Questions requiring scaled responses.* The respondent checks along a scale designed to measure such items as preferences, opinions, attitutdes, probability of intentions, or motivation. Common forms of scaling are: (a) Semantic differential (bipolar adjectives at each end of a scale);[20] (b) Thurstone's method

---

[20]C. E. Osgood, G. J. Suci, and P. H. Tannenbaum, *The Measurement of Meaning* (Urbana, Ill.: U. of Illinois Press, 1957). For an application and validity study, see William D. Wells, "EQ, Son of EQ, and the Reaction Profile," *Journal of Marketing* (October 1964), pp. 45–52.

of equal appearing intervals; (c) Likert's summated scale; (d) Guttman undimensional scale;[21] (e) Stapel scale (single adjective and scale).[22]

Exhibit 10-3 referred to earlier includes some general guides for the development of the mail questionnaire. In addition to these, it is very desirable to take a pilot survey to test the questionnaire. A pilot run with a sample as small as 20 may uncover unsuspected ambiguities and problems and prevent complete failure of the project.[23]

Developing the Personal-Survey Questionnaire

Many of the general guidelines for the mail questionnaire apply to the personal-survey questionnaire. In the personal survey, however, the researcher needs to try to visualize the interviewing situations which are likely to occur in face-to-face contacts with a variety of respondents. Both the interviewer and the respondent will be favorably motivated by questions which are worded simply and are clear and easy to understand. The interview should be like a conversation between two people who are discussing a topic of mutual interest. The questions and transition statements should be in a sequence which maintains this conversational rapport.

The questionnaire should include at the beginning a short introduction for the interviewer to follow. In the introduction, the interviewer greets the respondent, introduces himself, identifies the agency for which he is working, gives the purpose of the survey and why it is being made, and why the person has been selected as a participant. All instructions to the interviewer which appear on the questionnaire should be set out in a different typeface than the questions themselves to reduce the likelihood that the interviewer will speak the instructions.

Screening questions should be used to skip over questions which don't apply and thus save time and goodwill. The questionnaire should clearly guide the interviewer on these. The interviewer should be free to concentrate on the conversation so that he should not be required to code answers but simply record them as given. If sensitive questions such as those about salary are asked, a set of cards may be used in conjunction with the questionnaire so that the respondent is asked which card has the information applicable to his case.

A termination statement should be included at the end of the questionnaire so that the interviewer will thank the respondent properly. At the end of the questionnaire there should also be an instruction to the interviewer to note the place, starting and ending of the interview, the date, and his name.

[21] For these first four scaling methods, see Claire Selltiz et al., Research Methods in Social Relations (New York: Holt, Rinehart and Winston, 1962), pp. 344–384.

[22] Irving Crespi, "Use of a Scaling Technique in Surveys," Journal of Marketing (July 1961), pp. 70-72.

[23] C. Scott, "Research on Mail Surveys (With Discussion)," Journal of the Royal Statistical Society, Series A (General), Vol. 124, Part 2, 1961, pp. 143-205.

Conclusion

This chapter merely provides a survey of major research methods, techniques, and tools for the novice. It also supplies a first lead to some of these topics. There are numerous books, some referenced here, which deal entirely with the subject of this chapter. In order to conduct really significant research, the reader should delve into the periodical literature to bring himself abreast of the latest work on techniques and tools.

QUESTIONS AND TOPICS FOR DISCUSSION

1. It is suggested in this chapter that there are four general methods used in business research. Compare this idea with the idea that there is a *general* scientific method, and with the idea that there is an *unlimited number* of scientific methods.

2. In thinking about the first question, do you have difficulty with the meaning of "method?"

3. In what way can comparative research contribute to the development of theory?

4. What are some general classes of business research techniques besides those listed in the text?

5. What are some additional tools used commonly in business research?

6. Find a report of a laboratory research investigation in the area of business. Identify the hypothesis tested, if any. Identify the input variables which are controlled. Identify the dependent variable. Criticize the techniques used and the validity of the results on the basis of the experimental design and techniques used.

7. Prepare a bibliography on recent scientific literature dealing with mail surveys.

8. Do you see any ethical issues involved in observing human behavior without the permission of the individuals involved?

chapter 11

Reasoning to Conclusions and Recommendations

GENERAL NATURE OF REASONING

Since research is the efficient method for developing a science or solving practical problems, it must go beyond the trial-and-error method of fact gathering alone. By means of the thought processes, the researcher adds new knowledge without the physical trials. This bridging of the gap from the known to the previously unknown is called reasoning or inferring.

In reasoning, the mind passes from one or more accepted concepts in a series of steps, each of which is subject to intellectual assent or dissent. What causes the mind to accept the conclusions from the premises must be extrinsic to both, otherwise there would be no *process*. These extrinsic factors consist of reflection and rules for connection of ideas. Often these rules are internalized, but explicit application of the methods of the science of logic should be sought wherever possible. Each step in the process of inference may thus be evolved from the rules of logic, substantiated by testing against other alternatives, tested by means of indirect proofs, or stated in terms of probability. Each step must not necessarily be indefensibly true, since otherwise no progress could be made toward solving empirical problems. The fact that all propositions in science are subject to tests at any time indicates that there are no infallible methods for reasoning to the truth. If progress is to be made, then, some stretch of the imagination is required to piece together new concepts from data and known concepts. This is expressed well in a conversation between Sherlock Holmes and Dr. Watson upon examination of an old felt hat which came into their hands.

WATSON: What can you gather from this old battered felt?

HOLMES: Here is my lens. You know my methods. What can you gather yourself as to the individuality of the man who has worn this article?

WATSON: (After examination.) I can see nothing.

HOLMES: On the contrary, Watson, you can see everything. You fail, however, to reason from what you see. You are too timid in drawing your inferences.[1]

Reasoning in research is directed toward establishing the necessary and sufficient conditions for a phenomenon. This process, called "explanation" by the philosophers of science, is the major subject of both inquiry and controversy by these philosophers. This chapter presents a practical guide to inference rather than a treatment of the fine points of philosophical difficulties.

THE TWO BASIC METHODS OF REASONING

The two basic methods of reasoning or drawing inferences are *deductive* and *inductive*. Deduction is the process of reasoning from the general to the specific. In deduction, the conclusion is drawn from principles and premises. The conclusion is embodied within the general principle and must be discovered and proved according to the laws of logic. These "laws" of logic have been developed by philosophers of science.

Induction is the process of reasoning from a set of particular cases to a general principle. Since in economics and business, it is usually necessary to work with samples of data, most research in these fields is founded upon developing conclusions on the basis of induction.

DEDUCTIVE INFERENCE

The most basic deductive argument is of the form "If general principle A is true, and premise B is true, then conclusion C must follow." An example of such a syllogism is given below.

1. Every business manager is profit-oriented.
2. Gordon is a business manager. Hence
3. Gordon is profit-oriented.

Generally, research in business depends upon drawing much more complex inferences. An example of an inference chain is:

If GNP increases, then our company sales will increase, and if our company sales increase, our company profits increases, and if company profits increase, the unions will demand higher wages. Therefore, if GNP goes up, unions will demand higher wages.

In the deductive form of reasoning, each statement should have in back of it a justification in terms of an observed fact, a clearly understood assumption, or an accepted rule of logic. In other words, the deductive process in empirical research ideally is analogous to the plane geometry proofs of high school, except that empirical facts usually form some of the premises in the former case.

[1] A. Conan Doyle, "The Adventure of the Blue Carbuncle" in *Adventures of Sherlock Holmes* (New York: Harper & Brothers, 1892), pp. 155-156. Reprinted by permission of the Estate of Sir Arthur Conan Doyle.

Deductive arguments in some areas of economics dealing with pricing come close to this ideal through the use of diagrams and mathematical reasoning. Unfortunately, much writing in the field of business research fails to define basic terms, fails to state all assumptions and premises, and leads the reader by persuasion along some path rather than by rules of logic to a necessary or likely conclusion. Value judgments are often intermixed with objective criteria in comparisons and evaluations. While value judgments may serve as assumptive criteria, for purposes of deductive reasoning, such assumptions should be clearly stated since another set of value judgments as criteria may lead to completely different conclusions.

Usually it is necessary to solve applied problems where all desired empirically based hypotheses and theoretical principles are not available. The researcher must deduce conclusions from what is and what can be made available and from outright unverified assumptions. In such cases he should examine his conclusions in the light of well-established generalizations. In a deductive system, all propositions should be consistent with each other. If a conclusion is at odds with some other accepted proposition or principle, the researcher should seek further explanation.

HOW TO REASON DEDUCTIVELY

The process of reasoning consists of developing step-by-step a chain of arguments which pass from premises to conclusions. In some cases the conclusion is envisioned by the problem solver, who hopes that he may bridge the gap by reasoning. In other cases, the conclusion evolves as the result of selecting a branch along a decision tree which appears to lead to the solution of a problem.

In order to reason from data and premises to conclusions, it is necessary to construct a series of related statements. Each statement must be connected with previous statements (including the premises as statements). The author must demonstrate or "prove" that each statement is justified. A proof is a belief which people generally would accept. Presumably each statement is such that it may be clearly accepted or rejected. Bases for acceptance of a statement may be based upon rules of logic, experience, self-evidence, or knowledge of previous research results. Lack of creditability concerning a deductive chain may arise because of (1) logical fallacies, (2) ambiguous and vague definitions, and (3) too large a gap between statements in the proof. Too large a gap between one statement and the next means that the reader must construct the intermediate steps. If he is incapable of doing so, the conclusion has not been established.

All this suggests that the most rigorous proof consists of constructing a series of steps which are closely interconnected and carry the reader along in small increments. By this means, highly technical justifications are broken into small bits, complex arguments are reduced to simple chains, and many steps will appear "self-evident" to the reader. Self evidence is the result of the reader's accumulated knowledge of reasoning processes and factual experience. While a single reader may accept an argument because of his own mistaken knowledge and beliefs, a proof rests upon general acceptance by most trained readers exposed to the argument.

There are no rules for finding each subsequent step in a proof. The researcher must make one decision after another as to what is relevant to progress toward a solution. Thus in a chain argument he must continually make a selection of data, premises, previous steps, and principles which will lead to the next conclusion. In analogical reasoning, he must select those elements which are similar and reject or explain those elements which are different among the given and proposed systems in order to reach conclusions. In comparative research he must select aspects to be studied comparatively, select frameworks or criteria for comparison, and choose from among alternatives of time, space, or cross-cultural factors as intervening variables.

There is very likely some trial and error involved in both selection of relevant data and in selection of the direction in which to proceed. The researcher may achieve some guidance by asking himself questions which, when answered, will advance him toward the solution of his problem. He may often also "intuitively" visualize major points in the reasoning progression which lead to a solution. He can then start attempting to build logical proofs to bridge one pair of major points after the other.

EVALUATING A DEDUCTIVE INTERFERENCE BY FORMAL LOGIC

Ideally, deductive arguments could be tested at every step by the formal rules of logic. However, often the mind is asked to accept some statement whose sole basis is "self-evidence." On the other hand, there are frequently chains of propositions which can be tested for internal consistency and validity of conclusions by means of formal rules of logic. A brief introduction to the nature of propositional statements, set statements, and truth statements is given here. For a complete treatment of the ramifications of these, the reader should refer to books on symbolic logic.[2]

The starting point for introducing a new topic is usually a set of definitions, and this discussion of logic is no exception.

1. A *statement* is an assertion about a subject such that the assertion is either true or false. It is not necessary that the truth or falsity be known, but only that the assertion is capable of being tested or proved true or false. For example, "The company is profitable" is a statement. Questions, exhortations, and prayers are not statements. Only declarative sentences are statements.

[2]An excellent treatment of sets and logical statements is condensed into the first three chapters of Chris A. Theodore, *Applied Mathematics: An Introduction* (Homewood, Ill.: Richard D. Irwin, Inc., 1965). A well-illustrated presentation of logic and reasoning is given in Richard B. Angell, *Reasoning and Logic* (New York: Appleton-Century-Crofts, 1964).

2. *Simple propositional statements* give a single relation between a singular subject and predicate.

Symbol	(Linguistic) Propositional Statement
P	General Electric is a diversified company.
Q	Technology is the source of American economic growth.

3. *Simple set statements* indicate a single relation between a set or group which is the subject and a predicate which may be a set or a group.

Symbol	(Linguistic) Set Statement
p	All businessmen are neat dressers.
q	Some businessmen are economists.
r	Some executives are short.
s	No executives are illiterate.

4. Simple truth functions consist of propositional variables, usually denoted by symbols as in (2) or (3) above, whose truth value depends solely on the truth values of the propositions they represent. Six basic simple truth functions are:

1. p If the statement for which p stands is true, then p is true.
2. p' This is read "not-p" and is the negation of p. It has a truth value just the opposite of p. If p is true, the opposite of p is false. If p is false, then the opposite of p is true.
3. $p \cap q$ This is read "p and q" and is true only if both p is true and q is true.
4. $p \cup q$ This is read "p or q" and is true when *either* p is true or q is true.
5. $p \rightarrow q$ This is read "if p is true, then q is true." This is not a logical relation like (1) through (4), but rather a compound statement.
6. $p \leftrightarrow q$ This is read "p is a necessary and sufficient condition for q" or "q is true if and only if p is true." This is a compound statement like (5).

Complex statements may now be tested by constructing truth tables based upon the simple logical relations above. If the table shows that the premises of an argument imply the conclusion, then the argument is said to be valid. As a simple example, consider the propositions and argument below:

p = "The stock market is a purely competitive market."
q = "A single individual cannot affect stock prices."

If ["The stock market is a purely competitive market" *implies* "a single individual cannot affect stock prices" *and* it is false that "a single individual cannot affect stock prices"], then it is false that "The stock market is a purely competitive market."

The above argument may be abbreviated with symbols as

$$[(p \longrightarrow q) \cap q'] \longrightarrow p'$$

The truth table is set up with all permutations of truth (T) or falsity (F) of the basic propositions. Each component of the argument is then tested as to whether the conclusion follows from the premise.

			Basic Premises						Chain of Argument					
	p	q		$(p \rightarrow q)$			$(p \rightarrow q)$	$\cap$	q'		$[(p \rightarrow q) \cap q']$		$\longrightarrow p'$	
	①	①		①	②	①	②	④	③		④		⑥	⑤
(a)	T	T		T	Ⓣ	T	T	Ⓕ	F		F		Ⓣ	F
(b)	T	F		T	Ⓕ	F	F	Ⓕ	T		F		Ⓣ	F
(c)	F	T		F	Ⓣ	T	T	Ⓕ	F		F		Ⓣ	T
(d)	F	F		F	Ⓣ	F	T	Ⓣ	T		T		Ⓣ	T

There are four possible permutations of T and F for p and q as shown in the table. The circled truth values refer to the logical relation expressed at the head of the column. The development of row (b) will help to explain the table. It is first assumed that p is true and q is false. If p is true and q is false, then it is false that p implies q. This is indicated by a circled F in the first column ②, which then appears again as a premise in the second column ②. Column ③ is derived by taking the opposite of q in column ①. Since q was assumed false, then q' must be true. If the premise ② is false and the premise ③ is true, the truth value of the function is false. This truth value is indicated by a circled F in column ④ which then becomes the premise for the final argument.

Column ⑥ is based on a postulate of logic which says that "The conditional of p and q is an assertion which is false if p is true and q is false; otherwise it is true." Thus in row (c), column ⑥ is T under this postulate. Note that column ⑤ is simply the contrary of column ①. Since column ⑥ gives the truth values for the complete argument, and since the argument holds for all premutations of the premises, the argument is said to be *valid*.

Logicians have developed numerous theorems which provide standardized logically valid forms. Extension of the use of Venn diagrams to set statements also has been developed to test arguments, but the truth tables touched upon above offer the most general approach to critical testing of arguments.[3]

INDUCTIVE ARGUMENTS

Basic Assumptions

Inductive argument is reasoning from incomplete data to a generalization. The generalization may be about a single entity, about a set of objects, or about

---

[3] For a good treatment of deductive logic, see Henry S. Leonard, *Principles of Right Reason* (New York: Henry Holt & Co., 1957).

causal relations and explanatory hypotheses. Arguments or reasons are developed in *support* of a conclusion in the inductive method. It is not possible to establish any purely formal test for the adequacy of an inductive explanation.

Inductive reasoning is based upon the premise that nature is orderly and uniform. Thus if one particular instance after another supports a conclusion, and no instance of essentially similar circumstances refute the conclusion, belief in the conclusion is strengthened. A simple example is the following:

1. Whenever there is an economic recession, Company A reduces its inventory.

2. Whenever there is an economic recession, Company B reduces its inventory.

3. Whenever there is an economic recession, Company C reduces its inventory.

Conclusion: Whenever there is an economic recession, all companies reduce their inventories.

The distinctive feature of an inductive argument is that there is at least one statement which, if added as a premise, will yield a false conclusion. The adequacy of an inductive argument is determined by (1) the relevancy of the reasons which support the argument, (2) the degree of support of the conclusion, (3) the degree to which alternative statements are negated and (4) the degree to which all statements which would negate the conclusion are taken into account.

General patterns which have been followed to develop inductive arguments are:

1. Simple enumeration
2. John Stuart Mill's (1806–1873) methods of
   (a) Agreement   (d) Residues
   (b) Difference   (e) Concomitant variations
   (c) Joint agreement
        and difference

Simple Enumeration

Simple enumeration is widely used in business. For example, a number of firms may be studied to determine what principles are followed in the organizing of the R&D group. The use of the mail questionnaire to determine the percent of a sample of firms which uses a certain type of product is a common example. In each case the results are extrapolated to represent a larger number of firms. Perhaps the weakest inductive argument is that based on a single case study of a firm. Yet only about a dozen case studies of firms tend to create strong beliefs in consistent patterns and apparent relationships. Some people believe that the greater the number of entities enumerated the stronger the argument. The demise of the *Literary Digest* which forecast the election of Alf Landon on the basis of a count of about 2,000,000 individuals indicates that simple enumeration without regard to selection procedures is hazardous.

Mill's Canons

Mill's methods represent an attempt to establish relevant factors and eliminate possible plausible alternatives. His method of agreement leads to the generalization that whenever A occurs, B also occurs. This is determined if it is observed that B occurs if A is among one set of factors present and still occurs when all factors except A are changed. The method of difference states that when two situations are the same except that A is present in one case and B occurs, and A is not present in the other case and B does not occur, then A and B occur together.

The joint method of agreement and difference is a combination of the first two designed to assert that B occurs if, and only if, A occurs. The method of residues is applied where it is not possible to use the other methods by changing the factors present for the occurrence of B. If the effects of some factors on B are known, then the remaining effects must be caused by the residual factors present when B occurs. Finally, the method of concomitant variation states that when two things consistently change together, one causes the other or both are caused by the same set of factors.

Some of the weaknesses of Mill's canons are:

1. Failure to classify possible relevant factors accurately.

2. Unrecognized factors as a cause of the effect.

3. Assumption that degree or amount of a factor or outcome is not a consideration so that only factors which can be considered as present or not present can be considered.

4. It is not always possible either to control the factors to be present and eliminated or measure the contribution of auxiliary factors which must be present.

5. They assume that an effect is caused by a single factor rather than by a complex of factors. At any rate, they are directed towards studying only one factor and effect at a time.

6. They assume that there is no interaction among factors.

7. They do not take into account random variations in the effect produced.[4]

Probabilistic Inference

Statements such as "We can state with a probability of .95 that between 32 and 38 percent of all housewives use Brand X" are statistical statements. Probability statements are assertions of the form, "The probability than an individual selected at random from the population of Central City has black hair is .30." Another instance of a probability conclusion is, "The probability is .15 that a new product being introduced will produce a profit of over $10,000 in the first year of sales."

[4]For a discussion with examples of Mill's methods, refer to Max Black, *Critical Thinking* (Englewood Cliffs, N.J.: Prentice-Hall, Inc., 1952), Chap. 15–16.

Such statements are probable conclusions rather than necessary conclusions. It is customary in *deductive* arguments to either accept or reject a statement as the reasoning proceeds. With a series of probability statements, this is not possible. Hence some people believe that such inductive chains of reasoning are worthless. Contrary to this somewhat unsophisticated view are two counterarguments. First, there is rarely any statement in a deductive argument that is accepted as certain beyond any shadow of doubt. Therefore, belief consists of a conviction that a statement is "highly probable." Secondly, it is possible to combine a number of probabilistic statements to obtain a conclusion with a probability attached to it. The Monte Carlo technique is one example of such a method.[5]

Probabilistic arguments are based upon the definition of probability. There are essentially three definitions of probability, of which the first two below are derived from a deductive base.

1. *Prior probability.* As an example, assume that an urn contains 10 black balls and 5 red balls. One ball is drawn in a way such that it is "equally likely" that any one of the 15 could be drawn. Then the probability of drawing a black ball is 10/15, or 2/3. This definition rests upon the basic postulates of probability.

2. *Empirical probability.* In a series of independent trials of a random experiment, the ratio of the number of successes to the number of trials approaches the probability of success on a single trial, as the number of trials becomes very large. This definition of probability as relative frequency rests upon the deductive theorem, the Law of Large Numbers.

3. *Subjective probability.* This is an intuitive and pragmatic assignment of a numerical weight to a degree of belief. Experienced men would presumably assign *approximately* the same weight (from zero to unity) to the occurrence of a future event. Such weights, or subjective probabilities, may be based to some degree upon outcomes of similar situations in the past.

Once the concept of probability has been accepted, the elaborate deductively developed tools of statistical methods offer means for estimating characteristics of a large number of elements from examination of a few elements. Hypotheses may be tested and rejected on the basis of a specified level of probability. In addition, probabilities may be combined and manipulated in various ways which are deductively justified to provide probabilistic descriptions and guides to decision making. Waiting-line or queuing problems, inventory problems, reliability problems, sales forecasting, and information costs represent just a few of the many applications of the inductive methods.

Analogy

Reasoning by analogy may be either deductive, inductive, or a combination of both. As a straightforward example of deductive analogy, the analog com-

---

[5] See, for example, David B. Hertz, "Risk analysis in Capital Investment," *Harvard Business Review* (January–February 1964), pp. 95–110.

puter is a good illustration. Electric power systems for utilities have been simulated by analog systems so that the effects of changes in design or breakdowns may be investigated by changing components in the analog system. The analog and its interpretation are based on purely deductive laws of physics.

Inductive analogies appear in several forms. In one case a prediction is made based on the hypothesis that the present situation is analogous to a previous situation. For example, it was found that offering games and prizes to customers increased sales last year, and it is concluded that offering prizes will increase sales in the coming year. Two dangers are present in this example: (1) conditions are not the same because competitors will now offer prizes, and (2) no additional potential customers are interested in games with prizes.

In a second form of reasoning by analogy, the scholar has available complete information on one system or situation. He then examines another system or situation which has many similar points or similar structure. He then reasons that the unknowns in the second system will be similar to known elements in the first system. For example, Company A and B are diversified companies with approximately the same annual sales and progressive managements. It is known that Company A has a central R&D laboratory. Therefore, it is reasoned by analogy that Company B must have such a facility. At a more sophisticated level of illustration, consider that companies test market a new product in a city which is supposed to be most analogous to the population of the country as a whole. In economic theory, use of analogies is often necessary for comparison of economic systems of countries and effects of differences.

Max Black presents the following rules for testing arguments from analogy:

1. Make sure that the analogy is being used as a basis for argument and not merely as a way of making a more vivid assertion. (Quite often the analogy is used merely as a decorative device.)

2. State explicitly the properties constituting the "basis of resemblance."

3. State explicitly some of the respects in which the objects compared do *not* resemble each other (i.e., the basis of unlikeness, or the "disanalogy' between the objects).

4. State the "linking generalization" from which the argument gets such force as it has.

5. Consider the nature of the INDEPENDENT evidence for the linking generalization. (It is especially important to check that the disanalogy between the objects compared does not upset the generalization.)[6]

Triangulation

In rudimentary sciences where it is difficult or costly to set up rigorous procedures for obtaining data which permit tightly knit reasoning to con-

[6]Max Black, *Critical Thinking* (Englewood Cliffs, N.J.: Prentice-Hall, Inc., 1952), pp. 322–323.

clusions, other means must be used to establish belief. Triangulation is the method whereby the researcher reasons from two separate sets of data and assumptions towards the truth or falsity of some concept. In some instances, the information may be so sparse that it allows the rearcher only to conclude that several hypotheses may be true. By triangulating from another base of data, it may then be possible to eliminate all but one of these.

Suppose for example that a researcher has raised the question, "Do the 500 largest industrial companies establish capital budgets on a scientific basis which takes into account such things as cost of capital, discounted returns on investment, and capital restraints?" One approach might be to talk with financial executives in a sample of the companies. Alternate conclusions might be (1) the companies take into account only a few factors, (2) the companies operate on a completely scientific basis, (3) *some* companies follow (1) or (2), or, finally, (4) financial executives exaggerate about the degree of scientific procedures used, and the budgets are based on intuition. Now an alternative approach might be possible employing only *some* of the companies in the first sample or requiring a completely different non-random sample. Such an approach would be the examination of capital budgets in recent years and an attempt to reconstruct the basis for the budget from the budgets themselves, from minutes of meetings, and from correspondence. While not very definitive conclusions may be deduced, these may modify or provide added confirmation for some of the first set of alternative conclusions. Further triangulation might be carried out by means of a mail survey in which the respondents are assured of anonymity. This method might broaden the sample and at the same time elicit less distorted information.

Triangulation requires a high degree of insight and deductive skill. It is suggestive of the reasoning process exemplified by the fictional Sherlock Holmes where bits of information from various sources must be sorted for relevancy and consistency to construct a hypothesis which is strongly supported.

RETRODICTION, PREDICTION, AND TIME

The validity of certain explanations of relationships between events may depend upon the time relationship between the events and the time at which relationship is asserted. Thus, the assertion that one event F follows an event P must be substantiated in terms of time. It also makes a considerable difference as to whether the assertion is made that P always precedes F or that F always follows P.

Exhibit 11-1 shows three possible situations for prediction and retrodiction. Prediction is the assertion that the occurrence of an event P will be followed by the occurrence of an event F. Thus P is a sufficient condition for F. Retrodiction is the assertion that if F occurs, P must have preceded it so that P is a sufficient condition for F but may not be a necessary condition. In addition, prediction and retrodiction which are successful in a case corresponding to Exhibit 11-1(c) provide no guarantee that will be successful in the future cases, Exhibit 11-1(a)

EXHIBIT 11-1
Asymmetric Situations

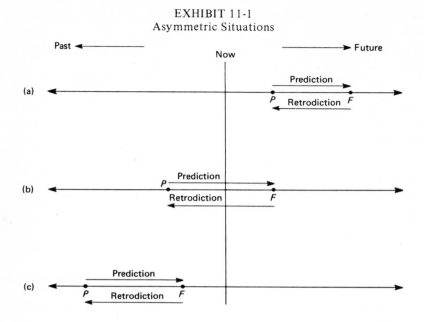

and (b). Adequate inferences relating the events must be made, and historical cases can provide only preliminary tests or special cases.[7]

CONCLUSION

It is apparent that there is no formula or procedure for reasoning from data and premises to conclusions and recommendations. Problems of definitions and semantics in the present state of the social sciences make vaugeness and ambiguity obstacles to providing proofs. Yet there are a number of methods for testing and strengthening arguments. Logical analysis, when applicable to deductive arguments, is helpful. The resort to mathematical symbols and their manipulation yields rigorous reasoning subject to the weakness of the abstract representation of the real world. Inductive techniques, analogical reasoning, and triangulation offer means for reasoning to highly likely conclusions. If progress is to be made, the business researcher must boldly use the tools at hand; refinement and revision will continue to advance the scientific aspects of business theory.

[7]For a technical treatment of this subject, see Adolph Grünbaum, "Temporally Asymmetric Principles, Parity Between Explanation and Prediction, and Mechanism Versus Teleology" in Bernard Baumrin (ed.), *Philosophy of Science, The Delaware Seminar* (New York: John Wiley & Sons, Inc., 1963), I, 1961–1962, pp. 57–133.

QUESTIONS AND TOPICS FOR DISCUSSION

1. What is meant by a *valid* inference and *invalid* inference?

2. Select a journal article and identify the connective words which tie together the author's assertions in his reasoning.

3. Select a simple argument and test it by means of a truth table.

4. Give an example illustrating each of Mill's canons and discuss the weaknesses of each "proof."

5. What kind of proof is needed to demonstrate that one event is the cause of another?

6. If the purpose of reasoning is to establish belief, why is not faith on authorities adequate evidence for a proof?

7. An "analytic statement" is one such that analysis can establish the truth or falsity of every statement having that particular form. A "synthetic statement" is one such that observation would establish the truth or falsity of the statement while analysis and inference would not. Give an example of each type of statement.

8. Find an example in the business literature of (1) reasoning by analogy, and (2) by triangulation.

9. Distinguish between inductive generalization and probabilistic inference.

10. Establish a set of rules for testing arguments employing triangulation as M. Black has done for arguments by analogy.

11. Does the study of the reasoning processes touched upon in this chapter help or hinder the business researcher?

Form and Style Guides

GENERAL

The mechanics of form and style for the various modes of business communication are generally the same, but options in format of headings and in footnotes or references are possible. Whatever options are selected, the most important consideration is consistency in using a particular option throughout.

STRUCTURE AND FORMAT FOR HEADINGS

The text of the report or paper should be divided into main sections which are indicated by the style of headings. In long documents or books, the main headings are chapters. Subheading style should be such as to indicate their lower and appropriate position in the hierarchy of the organization of topics. Any time that a heading is to be subdivided, it must have at least two subheadings, since "subdivision" into one part is obviously contradictory in concept.

A common structure for theses and dissertations is:

1. Chapter I, centered, followed below by the chapter title in capitals and centered.
2. Center heading with initial capitals for each major word or all capitals, underlined.
3. Center heading, all capitals, not underlined.
4. Side heading flush left, initial capitals for major words, underlined.
5. Side heading (flush left), not underlined.
6. Paragraph run-on headings followed by a period or dash, underlined.

An example of another logical structuring among many which could be conceived is as follows:

1. Chapter 5, centered, followed below by the chapter title in capitals and centered. (Note that Arabic instead of Roman numerals are used.)
2. Optional: Center heading, all capitals, underlined.
3. Side heading, all capitals, underlined.
4. Side heading, initial capitals for major words, underlined.
5. Indented side heading, initial capitals for major words, underlined.

REFERENCES

When material which appears in the text is quoted or the ideas are not in the general domain of the literature but are uniquely associated with one or a few individuals, reference should be made to the source. Either of two methods may accomplish this:

1. *Footnotes*

   Footnotes are usually referenced by a numerical superscript at the end of the quoted or source material. Footnotes appear at the bottom of the page and may be numbered serially on each page or throughout the text or marked with asterisks and dagger symbols on each page only. Footnotes are also used to amplify or qualify the text.

2. *Lists of References*

   In papers in scientific fields a list of references may be used. The material referenced is followed by an Arabic numeral in parentheses or square brackets on the line with the text. The reference numbers in the text run serially except to cite earlier references when necessary. At the end of the paper, the List of References is arranged in numerical order. The List of References may appear at the end of each chapter or at the end of the entire text. In the latter case, a bibliography may not be required.

SOME EXAMPLES OF FOOTNOTES AND REFERENCES

BOOKS

General format: Author or authors, Title (Place of publication: Publisher, date), page.

One Author

[1] Herbert A. Simon, Models of Man (John Wiley & Sons, Inc., 1967), p. 198.

[2] Thomas C. Schelling, The Strategy of Conflict (Cambridge, Mass.:   Harvard University Press, 1960), p. 20.

[3] Ibid., p. 199.   Referring to the same book (Schelling) without any intervening reference even though the reference may be separated by several pages.

[4] Simon, p. 202. (Refers to Simon book above—must be the same book by the same author referred to earlier in the text with intervening reference or references.)

Two Authors

[5] David W. Miller and Martin K. Starr, Executive Decisions and Operations Research (Englewood Cliffs, N.J.: Prentice-Hall, Inc., 1960), p. 5.

More Than Three Authors

[6] Ralph S. Alexander et al., Marketing (Boston: Ginn and Company, 1940), p. 120.

JOURNALS AND OTHER PERIODICALS

General format: Author, "Title of article," Name of Journal, Vol.,
No. (month and year), page.

Author Given

[7] Richard D. Crisp, "Product Planning for Future Profits," Dun's Review & Modern Industry, LXXI, No. 3 (March 1958), p. 34.

Author Not Given

[8] "Product Planning: Key to Corporate Survival," ACME Reporter, XLIX, No. 1 (January 1690), p. 31.

PROCEEDINGS AND PAPERS

[9] Albert Haring, "Product Planning & Adaptation," Business Horizons, a report on the proceedings of the First International Seminar in Marketing Management, Feb. 5–18, 1961, p. 77.

[10] M. J. Kami, "Prerequisites for Effective Long Range Planning," paper published by the Stanford Research Institute, 1960.

THESES AND DISSERTATIONS, PUBLISHED AND UNPUBLISHED

[11] Robert G. Murdick, "Product Planning—The Strategy of the Industrial Firm" (unpublished Ph.D. dissertation, University of Florida, 1962), p. 18.

BUREAU OF BUSINESS RESEARCH, NICB, AMA REPORTS

[12] Malcolm N. Smith, "Product Planner—Short Cut to Interdepartmental Team Work," in Developing a Product Strategy, American Management Association Report No. 39 (New York: American Management Association, Inc., Research and Development Division, 1959), p. 255.

GOVERNMENT PUBLICATIONS

[13] U.S. Department of Commerce, Business Cycle Developments, Series ESI No. 66–3 (Washington: Government Printing Office, March 1962), p. 39.

SPEECHES AND LETTERS

[14] Griffin Ashcroft, "Techniques of Problem Solving for Industry," speech given before Society for Advancement of Management, Hudson Valley Chapter, Albany, N.Y., Jan. 13, 1959.

ILLUSTRATIONS AND TABLES

Illustrations consist of graphs, charts showing organization of departments, plans, diagrams, maps, photographs, or other forms of artwork. An example of an illustration is shown here.

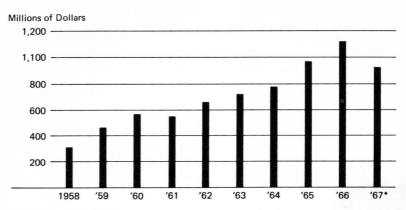

*Estimate based on anticipated capital expenditures reported by business.

Source: Office of Business Economics and Securities and Exchange Commission, from U.S. Department of Commerce, U.S. Industrial Outlook 1968 (Washington, D.C.: U.S. Government Printing Office, December 1967), p. 42.

Figure 5. New textile plant investment in 1967 reverse 5-year uptrend.

Both tables and illustrations are to be placed in the text as close as possible to the reference, written as "see Fig. 4" or "see Table 2" in the text.

In a table, numerical facts and related data are arranged in parallel columns. The use of tables helps the reader to grasp the significance of related facts.

EXAMPLE OF A TABLE

TABLE 4

TECHNICIANS, BY OCCUPATIONAL GROUP, JANUARY 1959 AND JANUARY 1960, AND PERCENT CHANGE

Occupational Group	Number		Percent Change
	January 1959	January 1960	
All groups	549,400	593,600	8.1
Draftsmen	195,200	210,000	7.6
Engineering and physical science technicians	250,300	284,600	13.7
Medical, agricultural, and biological technicians	16,100	16,100	.2
Other technicians	87,800	82,900	5.9

Source: National Science Foundation, Scientific and Technical Personnel in Industry 1960, NSF 61–75 (Washington, D.C.: Government Printing Office, 1961), p. 15.

APPENDIX

The appendix is used for material related to but not absolutely necessary to the text. In it are placed material too long or detailed to be included in the main text which may be of interest to the reader.

BIBLIOGRAPHY

Included in the bibliography are all references made in the text plus any source used which may not be quoted directly but which was substantially used to formulate ideas in preparing the paper. The bibliography should usually be classified according to types of publication such as Books, Journals and Periodicals, Reports, etc. An example of a partial bibliography is given here.

General format: Name of author in alphabetical order, last name first. (For two or three authors invert only the first author's name, as shown below in the Miller-Starr entry. For multiple authorship it is convenient to use "et al." after the first author's name.) Title. Place of publication: publisher, date of publication.

BOOKS

Alexander, Ralph S., et al. Marketing. Boston: Ginn and Company, 1940.

Miller, David W., and Martin K. Starr. Executive Decisions and Operations Research. Englewood Cliffs, N.J.: Prentice-Hall, Inc., 1960.

Simon, Herbert A. Models of Man. New York: John Wiley & Sons, Inc., 1967.

JOURNALS AND PERIODICALS

Crisp, Richard D. "Product Planning for Future Profits," Dun's Review & Modern Industry, LXXI, No. 3 (March 1958).

"Product Planning: Key to Corporate Survival," ACME Reporter, XLIX No. 1 (January 1960).

TABLE OF CONTENTS

Sample of the format of the Table of Contents is given here.

CONTENTS

Bibliography

L., *et al. Scientific Method: Optimizing Applied Research De-*
York: John Wiley & Sons, Inc., 1962.

Marketing Behavior and Executive Action. Homewood, Ill.:
·win, Inc., 1957.

and Paul E. Green. *Planning and Problem Solving in Marketing.*
Ill.: Richard D. Irwin, Inc., 1964.

and Stanley J. Shapiro (eds.). *Marketing and the Computer.*
:liffs, N. J.: Prentice-Hall, 1963.

Research and Thesis Writing. Boston: Houghton Mifflin Com-

B. *Reasoning and Logic.* New York: Appleton-Century-Crofts,

J. *Psychological Research.* 2d ed. New York: Random House,
Inc., 1965.

Backman, Jules. *Competition in the Chemical Industry.* Washington, D.C.: Manufacturing Chemists Association, 1964.

Banks, Seymour. *Experimentation in Marketing.* New York: McGraw-Hill Book
Company, 1965.

Barnette, Warren (ed.). *Readings in Psychological Tests and Measurements.*
Homewood, Ill.: Dorsey Press, 1964.

Barr, A. S., William H. Burton, and Douglas E. Scates. *The Methodology of Educational Research.* New York: Appleton-Century-Crofts, Inc., 1941.

Baumrim, B. (ed.). *Philosophy of Science.* Vol. 1. New York: John Wiley & Sons,
Inc., 1963.

Berelson, Bernard. *Content Analysis in Communication Research.* New York:
Free Press, 1952.

Black, Max. *Critical Thinking.* Englewood Cliffs, N. J.: Prentice-Hall, Inc., 1952.

Bowen, Howard R. *The Business Enterprise as a Subject for Research.* New
York: Social Science Research Council, 1955.

Boyd, Harper W., Jr. *Marketing Research, Text and Cases.* Homewood, Ill.:
Richard D. Irwin, Inc., 1956.

Braithwaite, R. B. *Scientific Explanation*. London: Cambridge University Press, 1953.

Braybrooke, David. *Philosophical Problems of the Social Sciences*. New York: The Macmillan Company, 1965.

Bridgman, P. W. *The Logic of Modern Physics*. New York: The Macmillan Company, 1927.

Brown, Robert G. *Statistical Forecasting for Inventory Control*. New York: McGraw-Hill Book Company, 1959.

Campbell, N. R. *An Account of the Principles of Measurement and Calculation*. New York: Longmans, Green and Company, 1928.

————. *What is Science?* New York: Dover Publications, Inc., 1952.

Carr, Charles R., and Charles W. Howe. *Quantitative Decision Procedures in Management and Economics*. New York: McGraw-Hill Book Company, 1964.

Churchman, C. W., and P. Ratoosh (eds.). *Measurement: Definitions and Theories*. New York: John Wiley and Sons, Inc., 1959.

Churchman, C. W., Russell L. Ackoff, and E. Leonard Arnoff. *Introduction to Operations Research*. New York: John Wiley & Sons, Inc., 1957.

Cicourel, Aaron V. *Method and Measurement in Sociology*. New York: Free Press, 1964.

Crisp, Richard D. *Marketing Research*. New York: McGraw-Hill Book Company, 1957.

Culbertson, Jack A., and Stephen P. Heneley (eds.). *Educational Research: New Perspective*. Danville, Ill.: Interstate Publishers, 1963.

Dalton, Melville. *Men Who Manage*. New York: John Wiley & Sons, Inc., 1959.

Dichter, Ernest. *Motivation Research Handbook of Consumer Motivations*. New York: McGraw-Hill Book Company, 1964.

Doyle, A. Conan. *Adventures of Sherlock Holmes*. New York: Harper & Brothers, Publishers, 1892.

Festinger, Leon, and Daniel Katz (eds.). *Research Methods in the Behavioral Sciences*. New York: Dryden Press, 1953.

Gagne, Robert M., *et al. Psychological Principles in System Development*. New York: Holt, Rinehart and Winston, Inc., 1962.

Good, Carter V., and Douglas E. Scates. *Methods of Research*. New York: Appleton-Century-Crofts, Inc., 1954.

Goode, William J., and Paul K. Hatt. *Methods in Social Research*. New York: McGraw-Hill Book Company, 1952.

Hall, Arthur D. *A Methodology for Systems Engineering*. Princeton, N.J.: D. Van Nostrand Company, Inc., 1962.

Harman, Harry H. *Modern Factor Analysis*. Chicago: University of Chicago Press, 1960.

Hayakawa, S. I. (ed.). *Language Meaning and Maturity*. New York: Harper and Row, Publishers, 1954.

Hempel, Carl G. *Aspects of Scientific Explanation and Other Essays in the Philosophy of Science*. New York: Free Press, 1965.
————. *Fundamentals of Concept Formation in Empirical Science*. Chicago: University of Chicago Press, 1952.
Hyman, Ray. *The Nature of Psychological Inquiry*. Englewood Cliffs, N.J.: Prentice-Hall, Inc., 1964.
Istvan, Donald F. *Capital-Expenditure Decisions: How They Are Made in Large Corporations*. 2d ed. Bloomington, Ind.: Indiana University, 1961.
Jennings, Eugene E. *An Anatomy of Leadership*. New York: Harper & Row, Publishers, 1960.
Johnson, Wendell. *People in Quandries*. New York: Harper & Row, Publishers, 1946.
Jones, Manley Howe. *Executive Decision Making*. Homewood, Ill.: Richard D. Irwin, Inc., 1957.
Kahn, Gilbert, and Donald J. D. Mulkerne. *The Term Paper: Step by Step*. New York: Doubleday & Company, Inc., 1964.
Kaplan, Abraham. *The Conduct of Inquiry, A Methodology for Behavioral Science*. San Francisco: Chandler Publishing Co., 1964.
Kaufman, Felix. *Methodology of the Social Sciences*. New York: Humanities Press, 1944.
Kerlinger, Fred N. *Foundations of Behavioral Research*. New York: Holt, Rinehart and Winston, Inc., 1964.
Kish, Leslie. *Survey Sampling*. New York: John Wiley & Sons, Inc., 1965.
Koefod, Paul E. *The Writing Requirements for Graduate Degrees*. Englewood Cliffs, N.J.: Prentice-Hall, Inc., 1964.
Krupp, Sherman. *Pattern in Organization Analysis*. New York: Holt, Rinehart and Winston, Inc., 1961.
Kuhn, Alfred. *The Study of Society, A Unified Approach*. Homewood, Ill.: Richard D. Irwin, Inc., 1963.
Leonard, Henry S. *Principles of Right Reason*. New York: Holt, Rinehart and Winston, Inc., 1957.
Livingston, Robert T. *The Engineering of Organization and Management*. New York: McGraw-Hill Book Company, 1949.
Lloyd, David K., and Myron Lipow. *Reliability: Management Methods and Mathematics*. Englewood Cliffs, N.J.: Prentice-Hall, Inc., 1962.
Lorie, James H., and Harry V. Roberts. *Basic Methods of Marketing Research*. New York: McGraw-Hill Book Company, 1951.
Lucas, Darrell B., and Steuart H. Britt. *Measuring Advertising Effectiveness*. New York: McGraw-Hill Book Company, 1963.
Luck, David J., Hugh G. Wales, and Donald A. Taylor. *Marketing Research*. 2d ed. Englewood Cliffs, N.J.: Prentice-Hall, Inc., 1961.
Madden, Edward (ed.). *The Structure of Scientific Thought*. Boston: Houghton Mifflin Company, 1960.

Mayer, Kurt B., and Sidney Goldstein. *The First Two Years: Problems of Small Firm Growth and Survival.* Washington, D.C.: Government Printing Office, 1961.

McDonough, Adrian M. *Information Economics and Management Systems.* New York: McGraw-Hill Book Company, 1963.

Morris, Charles. *Signs, Language, and Behavior.* New York: George Braziller, Inc., 1955.

Murdick, Robert G., and Arthur E. Schaefer. *Sales Forecasting for Lower Costs and Higher Profits.* Englewood Cliffs, N.J.: Prentice-Hall, Inc., 1967.

Nagel, Ernest. *The Structure of Science.* New York: Harcourt, Brace & World, Inc., 1961.

Nemmers, Erwin E., and John H. Myers. *Business Research, Text and Cases.* New York: McGraw-Hill Book Company, 1966.

Northrup, F. S. C. *The Logic of the Sciences and the Humanities.* New York: The Macmillan Company, 1947.

Ogden, C. K., and I. A. Richards. *The Meaning of Meaning.* New York: Harcourt, Brace & World, Inc., 1956.

O'Neill, R. F. *Theories of Knowledge.* Englewood Cliffs, N.J.: Prentice-Hall, Inc., 1959.

Osborne, Alex. *Applied Imagination.* New York: Charles Scribner's Sons, 1953.

Osgood, C. E., G. J. Suci, and P. H. Tannenbaum. *The Measurement of Meaning.* Urbana, Ill.: University of Illinois Press, 1957.

Parsons, Talcott, and Edward A. Shils (eds.). *Toward a General Theory of Action.* Cambridge, Mass.: Harvard University Press, 1951.

Peng, K. C. *The Design and Analysis of Scientific Experiments.* Cambridge, Mass.: Addison-Wesley Publishing Company, 1967.

Popper, Karl R. *The Logic of Scientific Discovery.* New York: Basic Books, Inc., 1959.

Rigby, Paul H. *Conceptual Foundations of Business Research.* New York: John Wiley & Sons, Inc., 1965.

Saaty, Thomas L. *Mathematical Methods of Operations Research.* New York: McGraw-Hill Book Company, 1959.

Scheffler, Israel. *The Anatomy of Inquiry.* New York: Alfred A. Knopf, Inc., 1963.

Selltiz, Claire, *et al. Research Methods in Social Relations.* New York: Holt, Rinehart and Winston, Inc., 1962.

Shelley, Maynard W. and Glenn L. Bryan (eds.). *Human Judgements and Optimality.* New York: John Wiley & Sons, Inc., 1964.

Shuchman, Abe (ed.). *Scientific Decision Making in Business.* New York: Holt, Rinehart and Winston, Inc., 1963.

Snedecor, George W. *Statistical Methods.* 5th ed. Ames, Iowa: Iowa State College Press, 1956.

Souther, James W. *A Guide to Technical Reporting.* Seattle: University of Washington Press, 1953

Terry, George R. *Principles of Management*. 3rd ed. Homewood, Ill.: Richard D. Irwin, Inc., 1960.

Theodore, Chris A. *Applied Mathematics: An Introduction*. Homewood, Ill.: Richard D. Irwin, Inc., 1965.

Torgerson, Warren S. *Theory and Methods of Scaling*. New York: John Wiley & Sons, Inc., 1958.

Tullock, Gordon. *The Organization of Inquiry*. Durham, N.C.: Duke University Press, 1966.

Vroom, Victor H. (ed.). *Methods of Organizational Research*. Pittsburgh: University of Pittsburgh Press, 1967.

Webb, Eugene J., *et al. Unobtrusive Measures: Nonreactive Research in the Social Sciences*. Chicago: Rand McNally and Company, 1966.

Winer, B. J. *Statistical Principles in Experimental Design*. New York: McGraw-Hill Book Company, 1962.

Yamane, Taro. *Elementary Sampling Theory*. Englewood Cliffs, N.J.: Prentice-Hall, Inc., 1967.

Zettenberg, Hans L. *On Theory and Verification in Sociology*. Totawa, N.J.: The Bidminster Press, 1963.

JOURNALS AND PERIODICALS

Ansoff, H. Igor, and Richard C. Brandenburg. "A Program of Research in Business Planning," *Management Science*, XIII, No. 6 (February 1967).

Barton, Samuel G. "A Marketing Model for Short-Term Prediction of Consumer Sales," *Journal of Marketing*, XXIX, No. 3 (July 1965).

Bass, Frank M. "Marketing Research Expenditures: A Decision Model," *The Journal of Business*, XXXVI, No. 1 (January 1963).

Bengston, Roger, and Henry Brenner. "Product Test Results Using Three Different Methodologies," *Journal of Marketing Research*, I, No. 4 (November 1964).

Boerdijk, Ir. A. H. "Step-by-Step Guide to Problem-Solving Decisions," *Product Engineering*, XXXIV, No. 3 (February 1963).

Bucklin, Louis P. "The Concept of Mass in Intra-Urban Shopping," *Journal of Marketing*, XXXI, No. 4 (October 1967).

Cohan, Avery B. "The Theory of the Firm: A View on Methodology," *Journal of Business*, XXXVI, No. 3 (July 1963).

Comrey, Andrew L. "An Operational Approach to Some Problems in Psychological Measurement," *Psychological Review*, LVII, No. 4 (July 1950).

Crespi, Irving. "Use of a Scaling Technique in Surveys," *Journal of Marketing*, XXV, No. 6 (July 1961).

Frank, Ronald E., William F. Massy, and Donald G. Morrison, "Bias in Multiple Discriminant Analysis," *Journal of Marketing Research*, II, No. 3 (August 1965).

Hertz, David B. "Risk Analysis in Capital Investment," *Harvard Business Review*, XLII, No. 1 (January–February, 1964).

Kendler, T. S. "Concept Formation," *Annual Review of Psychology*, XII (1961).

Lee, Charles E. "Measurement and the Development of Science and Marketing," *Journal of Marketing Research*, II, No. 1 (February 1965).

"Mathematical Model Becomes Marketing Tool," *Chemical and Engineering News*, XLV, No. 1 (January 1967).

Morgenbesser, S. "The Explanatory-Predictive Approach to Science," *Philosophy of Science, The Delaware Seminar*, I (1961-1962).

Nater, John and Joseph Waksberg. "Conditioning Effects from Reported Household Interviews," *Journal of Marketing*, XXVIII, No. 2 (April 1964).

Nicosia, F. M. "Marketing and Alderson's Functionalism," *The Journal of Business*, XXXV, No. 4 (October 1962).

Parsons, Talcott. "Comment" on "Preface to a Metatheoretical Framework for Sociology," *The American Journal of Sociology*, LXVII, No. 2 (September 1961).

Samuelson, Paul A. "Professor Samuelson on Theory and Realism: Reply," *American Economic Review*, LV, No. 5 (December 1965).

Schapker, Ben L. "Behavior Patterns of Supermarket Shoppers," *Journal of Marketing*, XXX, No. 4 (October 1966).

Scott, C. "Research on Mail Surveys (with Discussion)," *Journal of the Royal Statistical Society*, Series A (General), CXXIV, Part 2 (1961).

Smallter, Donald J. "Influence of Department of Defense on Corporate Planning," *Management Technology*, IV, No. 2 (December 1964).

———. "The Managerial Lag," *Chemical Engineering Progress*, LX, No. 6 (June 1964).

———. "Six Business Lessons from the Pentagon," *Harvard Business Review*, XLIV, No. 2 (March-April 1966).

Sparrow, F. T. "Mathematical Models of Growth Allowances for Public Utility Regulation—A Synthesis," *Management Science*, XIII, No. 6 (February 1967).

Suchman, Edward A. "The Comparative Method in Social Research," *Rural Sociology*, XXIX, No. 2 (June 1964).

Venkatesan, M. "Experimental Study of Consumer Behavior Conformity and Independence," *Journal of Marketing Research*, III, No. 4 (November 1966).

Vidale, M. L., and H. B. Wolfe. "An Operations Research Study of Sales Response to Advertising," *Operations Research*, IV, No. 3 (June 1957).

Vreeland, Carl. "The Jantzen Method of Short-Range Forecasting," *Journal of Marketing*, XXVII, No. 2 (April 1963).

Weinberg, Robert S. "Multiple Factor Break-even Analysis: The Application of Operations-Research Techniques to a Basic Problem of Management and Control," *Operations Research*, III, No. 2 (April 1956).

Weiss, Leonard W. "Concentration and Labor Earnings," *The American Economic Review*, LVI, No. 1 (March 1966).

Wells, William D. "EQ, Son of EQ and the Reaction Profile," *Journal of Marketing*, XXVIII, No. 4 (October 1964).

Wiest, Jerome D. "Heuristic Programs for Decision Making," *Harvard Business Review*, XLIV, No. 5 (September–October 1966).

PUBLIC DOCUMENTS

U.S. Bureau of the Census. *Atlantida: A Case Study of Household Sample Surveys*. Sample Design Series ISPO 1, No. 1-E, 1966.
————. *The Current Population Survey–A Report on Methodology*. Technical Paper No. 7, 1963.
U.S. Department of Commerce. *Survey of Current Business*. November 1964.
————. *Measuring Markets, A Guide to the Use of Federal and State Statistical Data*. 1966.
U.S. Department of Health, Education and Welfare. *A Manual for the Preparation of Proposals*. Washington: Government Printing Office, 1967.

REPORTS

Industrial Advertising Research Institute. *Motives in Industrial Buying*. Report No. 9, 1959.
Kaczka, Eugene E., and Roy V. Kirk. "A Simulation Study of Managerial Climate, Work Groups and Organizational Behavior," paper presented at the Institute of Management Sciences American Meeting, Boston, April 6, 1967.
Manpower Research and Training. Report of the Secretary of Labor. Washington: Government Printing Office, March 1965.

UNPUBLISHED MATERIAL

Sweeney, Owen C. "The Philosophies of Large Business Enterprises." Unpublished research report, State University of New York at Albany, School of Business, 1965.

OTHER SOURCES

Dutton, John M., and William H. Starbuck. *On Managers and Theories*. Reprint #86. Purdue University Graduate School, 1963.
Handy, Rollo, and Paul Kurtz. *A Current Appraisal of the Behavioral Sciences*. Massachusetts Behavioral Research Council, 1963.
"Jewel Tea Company Home Service Routes," Case Study AM 74, ICH2M83, Harvard Graduate School of Business Administration, 1957.
Martindale, Don (ed.). *Functionalism in the Social Sciences: The Strength and Limits of Functionalism in Anthropology, Economics, Political Science, and Sociology*. Monograph 5. Philadelphia: The American Academy of Political and Social Science, 1965.
Sweet, Franklyn H. *Strategic Planning: A Conceptual Study*. Research Monograph No. 26. Austin: Bureau of Business Research, University of Texas, 1964.

Indexes

NAME INDEX

SUBJECT INDEX